'Will change how you think about leadership, wellbeing and the future of work. This witty and thought-provoking book will undoubtedly keep you engaged. Packed with jaw-dropping insights that make you raise your eyebrows one moment and chuckle the next, it masterfully balances humour with hard-hitting truths. More than just ideas, it offers practical solutions for rethinking wellbeing and humanizing the workplace.'
Anetta Nova, strategic adviser

'An honest, emotional context for leadership. The book brilliantly demonstrates the reality of emotional vulnerability and its impact on teams, recognizing how social wellbeing is shown to be instrumental to a leader's success. A great read for those who want to better themselves in return for a highly functioning successful team.'
Mateen Jiwani, Executive Healthcare Leader, Essex Partnership University NHS Foundation Trust

'A good analysis of what gets in the way of wellbeing in the workplace and how we got here, and a compelling blueprint for what we can do about it.'
Matt Gitsham, Professor of Business and Sustainability, Hult International Business School

PRAISE FOR ENGAGING TEAMS

Engaging Teams

How to use social wellbeing to boost performance, retention and culture

Nick Smallman

Dan Parry

KoganPage

Publisher's note

Every possible effort has been made to ensure that the information contained in this book is accurate at the time of going to press, and the publishers and authors cannot accept responsibility for any errors or omissions, however caused. No responsibility for loss or damage occasioned to any person acting, or refraining from action, as a result of the material in this publication can be accepted by the editor, the publisher or the authors.

First published in Great Britain and the United States in 2025 by Kogan Page Limited

All rights reserved. No part of this publication may be reproduced, stored or transmitted by any means without prior written permission from Kogan Page, except as permitted under applicable copyright laws.

Kogan Page

Kogan Page Ltd, 2nd Floor, 45 Gee Street, London EC1V 3RS, United Kingdom
Kogan Page Inc, 8 W 38th Street, Suite 90, New York, NY 10018, USA
www.koganpage.com

EU Representative (GPSR)

Authorised Rep Compliance Ltd, Ground Floor, 71 Lower Baggot Street, Dublin D02 P593, Ireland
www.arccompliance.com

Kogan Page books are printed on paper from sustainable forests.

© Nick Smallman and Dan Parry, 2025

The moral rights of the authors have been asserted.

ISBNs

Hardback	978 1 3986 1979 1
Paperback	978 1 3986 1972 2
Ebook	978 1 3986 1978 4

British Library Cataloguing-in-Publication Data

A CIP record for this book is available from the British Library.

Library of Congress Control Number

2024054426

Typeset by Integra Software Services, Pondicherry
Print production managed by Jellyfish
Printed and bound by CPI Group (UK) Ltd, Croydon CR0 4YY

To those companies who put their people first
Nick

For my Mum, Liz Parry, 1944–2023
Dan

CONTENTS

ABOUT THE AUTHORS

Nick Smallman

Founder and CEO of Working Voices, Nick Smallman has been advising blue-chip clients on engagement, leadership and communication for 27 years. During that time, he has built an international reputation for thought leadership, delivering acclaimed talks for multinationals on a range of leadership and communication issues.

Working Voices began in 1998 with an ad in a shop window offering help with communication skills. Nick quickly developed the business, giving talks on every continent, expanding the UK team and opening offices in New York and Hong Kong. Today, Working Voices is a leading professional skills consultancy operating across Europe, the US and Asia.

Nick's personal philosophy, rooted in authentic, meaningful communication, shapes the Working Voices USP. Nick explains that 'we are "people people" who are committed to maintaining an empathetic relationship with clients, earning their loyalty through a deep understanding of the human psyche in the workplace'.

Engaging Teams is Nick's first book. Developed with Dan Parry, it is based on analytical research and Nick's years of practical, in-the-room experience with clients. It closely follows themes described in a series of talks delivered by Nick at multinationals in Europe and the US during 2023-24. Nick lives in London and is delivering a new venture called The Sustainable Human.

Dan Parry

With nearly 30 years' experience in the media, Dan Parry has a track record in journalism and documentaries and is a published author. Dan started out at BBC News, becoming a senior broadcast journalist before switching to documentaries. Throughout his career, Dan has focused on understanding how people respond to difficult circumstances that may or may not be of their own making.

As the Head of Research at production company Dangerous Films, Dan found interviewees and plotlines for international factual dramas. Working with the BBC, Discovery, National Geographic and other major networks, he filmed interviews with 9/11 survivors, D-Day veterans, astronauts Neil Armstrong and Buzz Aldrin, space shuttle crew members and political leaders including President George H W Bush.

Later, in a freelance role, Dan worked with SAS veterans, survivors of the wars in the former Yugoslavia and refugees stranded in camps in France and Germany. Dan's career has been about understanding people's experiences of difficult circumstances and discovering what they do to get by.

Dan has written three books: *D-Day* (BBC Books), *Blackbeard* (National Maritime Museum) and *Moonshot* – the inside story of Apollo 11 (Ebury). Dan is the Head of Communications at Working Voices and has been working with Nick since 2019. He lives in Hertfordshire where he struggles to keep his garden under control.

ACKNOWLEDGEMENTS

We are grateful to all at Kogan Page, especially Lucy Carter and Joe Ferner-Reeves for their foresight, encouragement and support.

While this book represents the collective achievements of everyone at Working Voices, we are particularly indebted to our immensely talented trainers, who come from all over the world and whose experiences, advice and humanity make our company what it is.

Though they are too many to name here, we remain in awe of their creative flair and their skill in researching and developing the courses that have informed this book from its inception. They have greatly enriched our understanding of our subject.

We would also like to thank the Working Voices support staff who heroically hold the whole business together with good humour, gold-plated flexibility and unfailing professionalism. And we particularly want to thank our clients, whose partnership, challenges, solutions and recommendations have been as enormously valuable as their unstinting loyalty over many years.

In the timeless words of Paul Zak: 'There are no human resources, just human beings'. People are the backbone of business. We are especially grateful to the many inspirational individuals who reassured us that putting people first is a principle that's universally valued, among them Working Voices employees and clients, academics and writers unfamiliar to us beyond their work, and fellow business people pushing ever forward.

Of course, we the authors remain solely responsible for errors and omissions in the text. We have credited the work of others where we can and remain vigilant and ready to address any oversight.

Introduction: Knowing your people

At the heart of every business are creative, complicated, contradictory, coffee-spilling, fun-loving, slightly worried and impressively talented people. If an outsider were to see them at work, what would they make of them? At first glance, engagement, motivation and productivity may appear to be ticking over as usual. Behind the scenes, however, things might not be as sustainable as they seem.

In 2022, Gallup's annual global survey found that 60 per cent of employees were emotionally detached at work.[1] A year later, Gallup found that 77 per cent were either not engaged or actively disengaged.[2] This figure remained consistent in Gallup's 2024 survey which noted that low employee engagement costs the global economy $8.9 trillion or 9 per cent of global GDP.[3]

Motivation is slowing down. 'Get-up-and-go' has got up and gone. Productivity is squeezed, poor retention is up and hybrid teams aren't sure if they're coming or going. Sometimes, the smooth path to progress feels like a fairground ride.

None of this is new, as we know from experience. Our company, Working Voices, is a professional skills consultancy, founded in London in 1998. Now operating globally, we're still supporting clients with the kind of engagement issues that have been around since we started. Only now, things are worse.

Wasted wellbeing initiatives

Over three years, we assessed the extent of disengagement and low productivity. We found that workforces are struggling with poor working practices, background anxiety, AI concerns, multigenerational miscommunication and challenges to critical thinking, leading to fatigue and burnout.

We also discovered that many leaders aren't sure of the causes of some of these issues or how to manage them. Consequently, well-meaning HR departments offer sticking-plaster solutions such as apps, yoga and subsidized gym memberships. New-fangled wellbeing 'solutions' come along all the time, fuelled by the internet's gargantuan appetite for ideas that are poorly researched and too good to be true.

In truth, however, we believe that many HR professionals know that disengagement is rooted in deep-seated issues that are beyond the reach of, for example, a sleep app. Rarely given the chance to properly investigate these underlying causes, they may feel powerless in the face of the business.

And so, amid a fundamental misunderstanding of disengagement, businesses are haemorrhaging millions of pounds in ineffective wellbeing programmes. Large US organizations spend about $11 million per year on wellbeing initiatives that make no discernible difference.[4]

Take-up is usually sporadic. Wellbeing programmes are often ignored by all but a minority of interested individuals. Only around a third of employees are happy to participate in such initiatives. By only reaching more proactive members of the workforce, such programmes demonstrate their questionable value whether or not they're even capable of making a difference.

Workplaces are deeply challenged by a potent and complex mix of forces. Threats to wellbeing are many and varied and success in managing them is variable at best. However, a meaningful solution is available – something that is clear, effective and supported by evidence.

The underlying causes of disengagement

As our research progressed, we identified four principal issues that cause the toxic cocktail of fatigue and disengagement:

1 **Doing more with less:** The 2007 global financial crisis plunged whole sectors of the economy into difficulty and uncertainty. The impact of this led to longer hours for some and redundancies for

others. The mantra of 'doing more with less' came to dominate company culture. This way of operating lingers on. KPIs are king. Today, many organizations exclusively focus on targets and performance, and individuals are expected to keep up. Wellbeing options are available – for those people willing to take responsibility for the impact on their physical and mental health of their employer's poor working practices. On closer inspection, responsibility for wellbeing lies with businesses too.

2 **Lack of workplace humanity:** Current workplace trends lead to a particular interpretation of efficiency that is fundamentally inefficient. We met a training participant who told us: 'I don't work here to make friends, I don't want to encourage colleagues "to be themselves". I want them to streamline their behaviour. I want meetings to be dull but effective. I just want people to get on with the job.' Jobs are more than this. By dismissing the humanity of people and ignoring human elements of work – such as personal fulfilment and team collaboration – managers risk alienating people and sidelining satisfaction. This leads to disinterest and disengagement, which are notoriously inefficient.

3 **The rise of tech:** Smartphones, laptops and similar devices erode meaningful human contact. When you're communicating with someone through a screen (via messaging or virtual calls, etc.), you're not fully interacting with them. You can deal with more people more quickly than is perhaps possible with face-to-face communication because tech allows a quicker, more transactional and less personal approach. We are social animals. Speedy, functional interaction compromises the meaningful personal connections we depend on for our mental health. Without them, we are more disconnected from others, we are more isolated. These are complex issues that can't be fixed by an app.

4 **Lack of employee autonomy:** KPIs and efficiency rely on processes that are becoming increasingly governed by AI. The keystrokes of people working from home can be monitored by spyware that assesses output during the working day. Performance is all too often constrained by processes that favour speedy, functional

delivery more than considered, creative responses. Process-heavy, tech-focused workplaces are less human than is healthy. In particular, app overload is reshaping the workplace. People who are required to use workplace apps, such as Slack, Evernote, Google Drive and Dropbox, must continuously toggle between them, including some that require hourly updates. This approach to work encourages conformity. It squeezes out water-cooler moments, breathing space and critical thinking, and replaces them with a way of working that deprives people of a nourishing sense of autonomy.

Such attitudes have been shaping the way we work since the mid-2000s. Then came the Covid-19 pandemic, when more people began to work from home. Long-term causes of disengagement continued, but suddenly the everyday cacophony of office life was suspended. Away from commuting, open-plan floors, putting on your work face and queuing for a sandwich, millions had a chance to rethink their job.

Fatigued, uncertain and wary of the future, many people asked themselves questions about what they were doing, how and who for. They were looking for meaningful answers from their employers that included a commitment to personal fulfilment, job-satisfaction and a sense of belonging.

This isn't about fancy coffee, sleep apps or other wellbeing smoke-screens that are designed to distract from poor working practices. It's about finding the wellbeing solutions that help people look forward to work and feel ready to give their best. It's about sustaining interest and engagement, it's about sustainable ways of working where well-being is an integral part of the package for everyone not a perk for the few who show an interest.

Not all organizations know how to develop and incorporate effective wellbeing. Many are not sure what undermines it in the first place. When disengagement and fatigue become too prominent to ignore, clients often ask us for resilience training, though sometimes what they're really hoping for is help with managing stress. When we ask them 'Resilience to what?', we're met with a variety of reactions that include:

- blank expression, 'tumbleweed' from ear to ear
- spluttering sentences that don't really lead to anything meaningful

- comments about 'kids not being as tough today as we were when we started'
- 'don't shoot the messenger'

On rare occasions, someone will admit: 'Our people can't cope because our environment doesn't support them'. Often however, we hear thoughts about 'younger generations needing stronger resilience'; comments that miss significant truths.

Anyone born after 2000 grew up in a very different communication environment compared with the experiences of their older managers. The perceived 'lack of resilience' of younger generations is misunderstood, which is perhaps why their stress is overlooked.

For some leaders stress can be a dirty word, perhaps because it's caused by issues they aren't keen to admit to, such as doing more with less. Rather than tackle its causes, some hide from stress, glancing at it through fingers over their eyes... which is when they start talking to us about resilience training.

Dealing with ~~stress~~ resilience

At the height of the global financial crisis, we were invited to see an MD at a major investment bank. It was a sinister moment. We found people were filling cardboard boxes, revolving doors were spinning... investor confidence was a smoking ruin.

When the MD came into the room, she showed us to a giant oak table that could almost have filled a car park. She sat at one end, we were invited to sit all the way down at the other. We felt like we were about to be taken out and dumped off a pier.

'We understand you need some help with your analysts,' we suggested tentatively.

'Not anymore,' she coolly explained. 'They were fired yesterday.'

'All of them?'

'Well,' she began, 'Yes. Their projects are now being done by the associates.' In a mental image floating through the conversation, her associates were semi-consciously dribbling into a 3am pizza. 'We need them to be resilient,' she continued. 'We want to give them some stress management training.' And a defibrillator, perhaps?

This being our first foray into wellbeing, we consulted a clinical psychologist, whose background in serial killers gave him a good grasp of the financial services industry. Together we developed a course. However – and this set alarm bells ringing – the client wouldn't let us call it stress management.

Having caused stress to their people, the client was pretending something else was happening. It was as if they were making money in a storm by selling roof tiles, except the tiles came from their own roof and their team below were getting wet. The company could do things differently – to continue the analogy, they could source tiles from somewhere else. Instead, living in denial, they were simply asking us for raincoats.

So, a month later, we ran the course. Sitting at the back of the room, a woman was scribbling away. Later, she explained she was from Occupational Health. 'That's interesting,' we said. 'You must be busy.' 'Yes,' she replied, 'I have 120 active cases!' We were slightly taken aback. 'So you're taking notes for your team,' we asked. 'No,' she replied, 'it's just me. And I'm part-time.'

A concept of sustainable wellbeing

The key causes of disengagement, years in the making, are unlikely to be cured by an afternoon of resilience training. People are feeling alienated from fulfilment at work and disconnected from each other.

In looking for an effective solution, we set out to develop a concept of wellbeing that benefitted everyone, not just a handful of eager individuals. We found that the best way to approach this was via company culture. By focusing on the organization as a whole, leaders can develop a form of wellbeing that includes the entire workforce, from the boardroom to the interns.

What should such a culture look like? Evidence for this was consistent. We noticed that many published papers in this space (e.g. Baumeister and Leary, 1995;[5] Edmondson, 1999;[6] Turner, Barling and Zacharatos, 2002;[7] Woolley et al, 2010;[8] Duhigg, 2016;[9] Zak and Nowack, 2017)[10] shared over-arching similarities that are easily overlooked.

We recognized that a common thread tied them together, inspiring us to develop a concept we came to call 'social wellbeing'. The bedrock of a people-focused culture, social wellbeing offers a way of working that successfully tackles disengagement, protects productivity and above all creates sustainable workplace practices.

Social wellbeing encourages the connectivity, trust, belonging, respect and psychological safety that together can address some of the damaging trends of recent times. For younger generations, psychological safety is especially important. Research shows that half of millennials and 75 per cent of Generation Z have left roles in the past for mental health reasons.[11]

The core feature of the workplace of the future, social wellbeing offers the direction of travel that younger generations are looking for. Leaders who ignore this and see wellbeing as an expense, rather than an investment, may settle for ineffective, half-hearted programmes that are largely ignored.

HR professionals can prevent this by making the business case for transformational and sustainable wellbeing solutions. These can include a broader view of KPIs, for example embracing assessments of how people are managed.

Ultimately, we're advocating cultural change, leading to a sustainable way of working that values connection, communication and collaboration. This is the best way of avoiding the current levels of wastage that wellbeing attracts. Given the wider problems the world faces, not least climate change, working better together is no longer just a good idea, it's the model for our future survival.

Notes

1 J Clifton et al (2022) Gallup State of the Global Workplace: 2022 Report, 2 May 2023, CCA Global, www.cca-global.com/content/latest/article/2023/05/state-of-the-global-workplace-2022-report-346/ (archived at https://perma.cc/3AKJ-DPS5)

2 J Clifton et al. Gallup State of the Global Workplace: 2023 Report, 2023, www.gallup.com/workplace/349484/state-of-the-global-workplace.aspx (archived at https://perma.cc/37H5-MYKX)

3 J Clifton et al. Gallup State of the Global Workplace: 2024 Report, 2024, www.gallup.com/workplace/349484/state-of-the-global-workplace.aspx (archived at https://perma.cc/J6F4-36FS)

4 Business Group on Health. New Research from Fidelity and Business Group on Health Finds Employers Answering the Call for Help, 31 March 2022, www.businessgrouphealth.org/newsroom/news-and-press-releases/press-releases/2022-fidelity-survey (archived at https://perma.cc/36QA-R9P6)

5 R F Baumeister and M R Leary. The need to belong: Desire for interpersonal attachments as a fundamental human motivation, *Psychological Bulletin*, 1995, **117** (3), pp. 497–529

6 A Edmondson. Psychological Safety and Learning Behavior in Work Teams, *Administrative Science Quarterly*, 1999, **44** (2), pp. 350–38

7 N Turner, J Barling and A Zacharatos. Positive psychology at work. In C R Snyder and S J Lopez (Eds.) *Handbook of Positive Psychology* (2002), Oxford University Press

8 A Woolley et al. Evidence for a Collective Intelligence Factor in the Performance of Human Groups, *Science*, 2010, **330** (6004), pp. 686–88

9 C Duhigg. What Google Learned From Its Quest to Build the Perfect Team, 25 February 2016, *The New York Times*, www.nytimes.com/2016/02/28/magazine/what-google-learned-from-its-quest-to-build-the-perfect-team.html (archived at https://perma.cc/6SS4-KD63)

10 P Zak and K Nowack. The Neuroscience in Building High Performance Trust Cultures, 9 February 2017, Chief Learning Officer.com, www.chieflearningofficer.com/2017/02/09/neuroscience-building-trust-cultures/ (archived at https://perma.cc/2763-VTVU)

11 K Greenwood, V Bapat and M Maughan. People Want Their Employers to Talk About Mental Health, 7 October 2019, *Harvard Business Review*, hbr.org/2019/10/research-people-want-their-employers-to-talk-about-mental-health (archived at https://perma.cc/8H4R-A7LD)

PART ONE

PART ONE

1

For the love of work

For many of us, our connection with work is the story of a relationship shaped by all the things that work does for us – and to us. For some, it can mean riches and opportunity. For others, work is simply a four-letter word.

Precisely what individuals get from their relationship with work depends on what they put into it. However, sometimes what work does to them in return is, to put it bluntly, unacceptable. Many employers knowingly allow their people to be drained by stressful work practices, long hours or a toxic atmosphere. For some, the relationship with work leads to fatigue and disengagement, and at times might even be described as abusive.

Researchers have identified 10 common workplace practices that can lead to ill health and even death. These include long working hours, job insecurity, low job control and high job demands. Estimating the impact of these factors on US workers, the team found that more than 120,000 deaths per year are associated with, and may be attributable to, how US companies manage their workforces.[1]

Other research shows evidence for a link between workplace stress and an increased risk of stroke – the leading cause of long-term disability among adults and the second most common cause of death globally.[2] Stroke is particularly associated with long working hours, and/or shift work. Elevated stress hormones lead to over-activation of the 'fight or flight' response, disrupting sleep, increasing muscle tension, impairing metabolic function and leading to negative effects on many of the body's organs.

Stress has been linked to high blood pressure, high cholesterol, heart disease, obesity, cancer and autoimmune diseases.[3] It can also have a damaging impact on mental health, for example leading to challenges with depression and anxiety.

In 2022, the American Psychological Association (APA) found that America's mental health is in crisis. The APA noted that employees with high levels of stress are more likely to miss work or to show lower engagement and commitment while at work, which can negatively affect an organization's bottom line. The APA suggested that business leaders are 'well-positioned' to influence a positive culture shift and normalize mental health in the workplace.[4]

Meanwhile, advice from the US surgeon general cited evidence that 76 per cent of US workers reported at least one symptom of a mental health condition, and that 84 per cent of respondents said their workplace conditions had contributed to at least one mental health challenge.[5]

It's a similar story in the UK. In 2024, *The Burnout Report* from Mental Health UK said that the combination of many factors – such as working longer hours, and societal changes caused by the pandemic – mean Britain risks becoming a 'burned-out' nation.[6] A report on the mental health of UK workers, from the Business in the Community campaign group, called for employers to stop 'harming the mental health of their employees' through poor business practices and culture.[7]

Company culture is a critical factor in workplace mental health, as we shall discover. How is culture best developed so that working practices become sustainable, businesses remain productive, leaders find inspiration and their people remain sane, successful and employed?

In offering a coherent reappraisal of company culture, we want to give business leaders a glimpse of some of the key challenges, threats and opportunities that await them over the next 10 years and beyond. And we want to explain how these will affect the performance of their people. The intention is to give leaders time to prepare by creating an environment that encourages maximum retention and results.

We also want to give employees food for thought about the type of employer they might favour. We want to show possible answers to questions such as: 'What kind of company should I be looking for? What kind of working relationships do I aspire to? What should I expect from workplace wellbeing?'

The changing relationship with work

Six days a week

In looking at the future of our relationship with work, let's begin by taking a glance over our shoulder to see how we got to where we are today. In looking back over the long and often brutal history of work, we can see how much progress we – humanity – have made.

In our distant past, for leech collectors (who used their bodies as bait), rat catchers, executioners and those who collected the dead during a plague, work could be challenging. Few of these people were protected by health and safety regulations. There were plenty of regulations in medieval England; it's just that health and safety applied to towns, not to individuals.

To protect the town from beggars, miscreants and the expense of looking after them all, social misfits could be forced to work for the monarch, regardless of their interest in doing so. When it came to royal prerogative, there were no ifs or buts. A man could be dragged into service in the navy under laws which, in Britain at least, have never been fully repealed.

In the 1680s, Italian physician Bernardino Ramazzini visited people at work and assessed their medical problems. He noted that workers in more than 50 occupations suffered illnesses that appeared to be caused by violent and irregular motions and prolonged postures.[8] Ramazzini compiled a list of common injuries and illnesses which he published in 1700 as *De Morbis Artificum Diatriba* [*Diseases of Workers*], earning him a place in history as the father of occupational medicine.

It took a while before Ramazzini's ideas caught on. During the height of the Industrial Revolution, most employers prioritized maximum profits, global reach, contented shareholders, ruthless exploitation and Christian values. The profits came six days a week, the values just on Sundays.

However, occasional leaders realized that productivity could be improved through better ways of working. Healthier practices accepted that people weren't machines but were subject to human realities and vulnerabilities.

In 1810, Welsh textile manufacturer and social reformer Robert Owen introduced a 10-hour day, later advocating 'eight hours labour, eight hours recreation, eight hours rest'. In the 1850s, Sir Titus Salt built the village of Saltaire for his millworkers, plucking them from the slums of Bradford and giving them neat stone homes with wash-houses complete with tap water. There was also a hospital, a school and an institute for recreation and education that had a library, a reading room, a concert hall, billiard room, science laboratory and a gymnasium.

Wealth and safety

By this point, Britain had become the world's sweatshop, importing raw materials from across the empire, manufacturing them and sending finished goods to markets around the globe. Anyone who could work was pressed into service, including the young, the elderly and the infirm.

The Protestant work ethic, the profits expected by powerful shareholders and the glow that some leaders got from (others') hard work overlooked brutal conditions that were accepted as standard. Rules regulating safety at work were few and far between; all too readily Britannia waived the rules in the pursuit of expansion. The consequences were as predictable as they were inevitable.

Victorian society was horrified to discover that boys and girls as young as five were working in coal mines, usually operating doors in ventilation shafts. Scandalous accidents shocked the nation and led to the Mines Act of 1842, prohibiting women and girls from working underground, along with boys under 10. Over the following decades, however, boys and girls of all ages continued to work above ground, operating machinery in factories in unsafe conditions.

Cornelia (history doesn't record her last name) was 13 when she started a new job in New York. As an orphan she had no choice but to begin eight-hour shifts in a factory, as was normal in 1852. Packing matches on Norfolk Street, Cordelia found that the fumes from the phosphorous used in matches at the time made her teeth ache. A tooth was removed, but by then the fumes had contaminated her lower jawbone, which also had to be removed.[9]

Similar health problems affected women working in match factories in Britain. In the 1880s, Sarah Chapman, 26, worked at the Bryant & May site in London's East End, an area marked by slums and deprivation. Like Cordelia, many of Sarah's friends also had 'phossy jaw', which killed 20 per cent of its victims. If a Bryant & May worker complained of toothache, they were told to have the tooth removed or be sacked.

Bryant & May employed nearly 5,000 workers, most of them women and girls who worked 10-hour shifts in return for barely enough to live on. They had to stand all day, toilet breaks were deducted from their wages, so too were fines for dropping matches, talking and even for dirty feet – which was hard to avoid given that few could afford shoes. Meanwhile, their employer paid whopping dividends to shareholders of up to 38 per cent.

By June 1888, the fumes, the illness, the poverty and the violent foremen who could hire and fire at will had been noticed by social campaigner Annie Besant, who wrote:

> A typical case is that of a girl of 16; she earns 4s. a week... Out of the earnings 2s. is paid for the rent of one room; the child lives on only bread-and-butter and tea... The splendid salary of 4s. is subject to deductions in the shape of fines... One girl was fined 1s. for letting the web twist round a machine in the endeavour to save her fingers from being cut, and was sharply told to take care of the machine, 'never mind your fingers'. Another, who carried out the instructions and lost a finger thereby, was left unsupported while she was helpless.[10]

Bryant & May insisted these were vile and spurious allegations and urged the women to write a letter praising their employer's moral rectitude, just as soon as they could get time off without being fined. Meanwhile, the 16-year-old girl suspected of being Besant's main informant was hunted down and fired.

Declining to write the pack of lies that was being asked of them, the women refused to comply. And when their friend was sacked, 1,400 went on strike. Sarah Chapman, one of the leaders of the strike committee, organized meetings with Besant that led to contact with the press, politicians and ultimately Bryant and May themselves. In the end, all the strikers' demands were met and Sarah went on to play a wider role in the union movement.

The Bryant & May Matchgirls' Strike in July 1888 has since gone down in history as a pivotal moment in the shift away from oppressive working conditions. This was the first time in London that a union of unskilled workers succeeded in striking for better pay and conditions. Chapman and others have since been recognized as 'pioneers of gender equality and fairness at work who... left a lasting legacy on the trade union movement'.[11]

Seeking social justice

Accidents, disasters and strikes highlighted the horror of 19th century working conditions, and led campaigners like Anthony Ashley Cooper and Annie Besant, and employers like Robert Owen and Sir Titus Salt, to recognize the need for change. In the early Victorian era, reform was slow. But by the first years of the 20th century, politicians in the UK and US were ready to regulate working hours, minimum ages, pay, conditions, sanitation and the right to protest.

These measures gave rise to a sense of social justice. Working people, becoming politically aware, were waking up to the idea that they were no longer simply the powerless citizens of a town that was better protected than they were. They'd become participants in the economy, central players on the stage. Protection was now available for them too.

Once again, occasional industrialists supported the wellbeing of their people. Beginning in the 1890s, the Pullman Company created an athletic association for employees in its company town of Pullman, Illinois.

Meanwhile, the National Cash Register Company offered benefits such as meal facilities, medical care, recreational programmes and educational opportunities. Company president John Henry Patterson, whose ideas revolutionized management practices, has been described as the father of industrial welfare.[12] In 1906, Milton S. Hershey created a leisure park for employees of the Hershey Chocolate Company, complete with merry-go-rounds and rollercoasters.

In 1914, social justice was nailed into US law by the Clayton Act, which confirmed that 'the labor of a human being is not a commodity or article of commerce'.[13] From now on, work was less about cold exploitation and more about recognition.

Five years later, social justice was recognized in the Treaty of Versailles. Healing the wounds of the First World War, the treaty acknowledged that 'universal and lasting peace can be established only if it is based upon social justice'. Suddenly employers were placed in the forefront of perceptions of a better future.[14]

Over time, work had shifted from leech collecting to a relationship shaped by give and take. People gave their time, they took money and security from their employers, and each needed the will of the other in a flimsy form of partnership that, much like the cars of the day, was embryonic, rickety and prone to breakdown. But it was a partnership all the same – more so certainly than was possible in Moscow, where Bolshevism demonstrated what could happen when partnership broke down.

One-sided power – whether in the guise of ruthless Victorian industrialists or revolutionary Russian workers – left little room for balance. And without balance, justice crumbles away, along with the values of a progressive society.

Social justice is a pretty broad concept, applying to society as a whole. We're going to focus on one part of it, the social contract – the balance in power between employers and employees.

During the First World War when labour and resources were marshalled on a scale never seen before, industrial leaders and army chiefs shared similar challenges about leading large numbers of people. How do you get the most from them? What should you invest, in terms of time and care, to encourage efficient performance? How do you maintain morale, incentive and purpose? These questions shaped labour relations for the rest of the 20th century.

Shifts in the social contract

How do you lead hundreds of thousands of people? It depends on what you want to get out of them. If you want every inch of their soul and then some, maybe open a Victorian coal mine. For a productive, healthy workforce who will keep you ahead of your competition, who have shoes and a life expectancy of more than 37, then best to try something different.

Scientific Management

Trying something different, better known as management theory, can look like throwing random ideas against a wall to see which one sticks. Popular options are sometimes said to be based on a vague interpretation of science. The first of these theories, known as Scientific Management, was developed between the 1890s and the 1920s by Dr Frederick W Taylor.

Taylor, a machine shop foreman at the Midvale Steel Company of Philadelphia, oversaw teams of men making different products. They were paid by item and smaller objects could be produced more quickly. Taylor needed bigger items; however, the men were reluctant to oblige and he wondered how he could win them round.

All in all, Taylor spent 26 years wondering. He focused on the need to control – but rather than applying this to the *effort* expected of his men, he concentrated on the *manner* in which they worked; in other words, more carrot, less stick. He provided standardized tools, instruction cards and training; he introduced a pay system which offered varying rates (more money for successful work, less for failure) and he encouraged organizational change.

In 1918, Horace B Drury, a California academic, wrote that Taylor's system produced, '…a complete revolution in the mental attitude of workingmen [sic] and management, the one towards the other… the two groups are said to enter into friendly cooperation and mutual help'.[15]

Scientific Management wasn't the first move towards economic efficiency. But in emphasizing concepts like structured rest breaks, its influence stretched far beyond the US. Lenin described it as 'the most widely discussed topic today in Europe, and to some extent in Russia'.[16]

In 1926, Taylor's research inspired Henry Ford to introduce a 40-hour week with five working days after he found that a 48-hour week brought only a small increase in productivity. Other manufacturers followed suit, improving the wellbeing of workers (even if doing so mainly for the benefit of employers).

During this period, production lines and industrialization were compromised by alcohol, though employers tried to keep drinking on the job down to an acceptable level. By the late 1930s, initiatives tackling alcoholism had evolved into employee assistance programmes

(EAPs) which supported people in 'recovery' who would then share their experiences with others. Enabling the rehabilitation of workers and the rise of productivity, EAPs were encouraged by employers.

Meanwhile, following the example set by Pullman and others, employee recreation programmes were becoming popular, and in 1941 four industrialists founded the National Employee Services and Recreation Association. NESRA helped organizations create services and programmes, with the intention of curbing absenteeism. These however were more about maintaining productivity than about protecting the wellbeing of individuals. In a 1984 interview, NESRA accepted that such employee programmes 'must be shown to benefit the company'.[17]

Maslow and motivation

During the First World War, the US army introduced merit rating systems. Designed to identify and dismiss poor performers, these brought more stick than carrot. In the army, who needs carrot when the stick is held by a drill instructor? Motivation comes easy when the alternative is 500 press-ups resting on your thumbs.

After the war, civilian employers, unable to threaten press-ups, turned to motivational ideas developed by academics like Abraham Maslow, a psychologist – to whom carrot was king. For Maslow, it was important to understand the things that motivated people.

In a paper published in 1943 and still influential today, Maslow believed (though failed to prove) that human behaviour was influenced by what he described as a 'hierarchy of needs'.[18] He believed that people need to satisfy their basic physiological requirements for food, water and sleep before they can pursue anything else. His next three sets of needs focused on safety, belonging and esteem.

Having satisfied their more fundamental requirements, Maslow believed that people then progress towards fulfilling their potential – the fifth and highest need that drives us towards self-expression and the realization of our ambition. 'A musician must make music, an artist must paint, a poet must write, if he is to be ultimately happy,' wrote Maslow. 'What a man can be, he must be.'[19]

By the 1960s, bosses realized that employees' hopes, feelings and needs had an impact on performance. US companies began to use appraisals in allocating rewards and encouraging motivation. Even today, Maslow's work serves as a template for the way that employers manage motivation strategies.

Maximizing potential

However, Maslow never put his theories to the test. His proposals were elegant and they made his name, but he left it to others to see if they were accurate. Researchers who tested them in the 1970s found the actual structure of motivation doesn't fit the theory.[20]

Maslow's ideas were developed by his student Douglas McGregor, who was less preoccupied with motivation and excellence and more with workshy layabouts. He developed Theory X and Theory Y, two contrasting interpretations of behaviour. Theory X assumes workers need to be managed, prodded along and monitored. It's a hands-on approach to management, geared towards people who are (or are thought to be) not particularly motivated.

By contrast, Theory Y envisages self-starters who engage with work for the satisfaction it offers them. They can be managed without supervision. Whereas Theory X might be better suited to large groups of people employed in unrewarding manual labour, Theory Y might apply to smaller groups of skilled staff. While there is room for both, only Theory Y offers a sense of partnership, a more favourable way to work than the 'them and us' framework that Theory X can lead to.

For both Maslow and McGregor, people are motivated by something they aspire to but have not yet attained, be it fulfilment of needs, recognition at work or higher pay and a better job. In other words, people aspire to improvement. This thought led to ideas connecting aspiration and fulfilment with motivation, pay and rewards. With this, the relationship between employers and employees was once again evolving.

By the 1950s, managers were beginning to recognize people as valuable assets to the company rather than as parts of the production process. For the first time, health initiatives focused on an individual's personal fitness and improvement and not just on the organization's productivity. The Pepsi Corporation led the way with an employee fitness programme in the late 1950s, later followed by Rockwell, Xerox and others in the 1960s.

At this point, physical fitness at work came to be associated with ideas developed by Dr Halbert L Dunn. Dunn drew a distinction between good health – 'freedom from illness' – and what he called 'high-level wellness', which he defined in 1959 as 'a condition of change in which the individual moves forward, climbing toward a higher potential of functioning'.[21]

The thing that caught the eye of employers (eventually) was that, according to Dunn, high-level wellness for the individual is 'orientated towards maximizing the potential of which the individual is capable, within the environment where he is functioning'.[22] Wellness wasn't just about being able to turn up at work on time; it was about being more productive once you got there.

Fundamentally, for Dunn, high-level wellness didn't focus on 'particular body parts… but rather involves the total individual, as a personality and in all of his uniqueness'. Wellness was no longer restricted to physical health. From now on, it was OK to at least think about mental health too – even if openly discussing it was still some way off.

Early concepts of wellbeing

Employee assistance programmes

By the 1970s, EAPs were becoming increasingly popular. In the US, the National Council on Alcoholism helped to spread EAP concepts through conferences and seminars sponsored by multinationals. By the end of the decade, EAP companies were operating in the UK in response to the demand for counselling and psychological services.[23]

EAPs were branching out of their original focus on alcoholism and beginning to cover other mental and physical health issues too. Employees were beginning to reassess what it meant to be well. So were their employers.

In 1972, healthcare costs at Johnson & Johnson amounted to $80.3 billion. By 1978, that number had risen to $162 billion, prompting chairman Jim Burke to encourage employees to adopt healthier lifestyles.

In 1979, Burke's concern led to Johnson & Johnson's Live for Life programme, which helped employees manage issues such as smoking, over-eating, alcohol abuse and unsafe driving. It also helped them protect their mental health.[24] That year, *60 Minutes* anchor Dan Rather declared: 'Wellness. There's a word you don't hear every day... it's a movement that is catching on all over the country.'[25]

Over the next four years, Johnson & Johnson companies that had signed up to Live for Life found that their hospital costs had dropped to a third of the rate paid by companies that hadn't committed to the programme, with absenteeism decreasing by 18 per cent. They also reported higher morale, job satisfaction and engagement.

Johnson & Johnson later said, 'Given enough time and effort, others can mimic or duplicate our products or design around our patents. We believe it is far more difficult to duplicate our organizational strength and the potential of our healthy employees.'[26]

Ranking and yanking

The 1980s brought Reagan and Thatcher, unforgiving shoulder pads and hard-nosed data. The shoulder pads came from fictional soaps like *Dynasty*; the data – from appraisals – was all too real. 'Rank and yank' policies adopted by Jack Welch, CEO at General Electric, smacked of the cold ruthlessness of the Victorian period. Only now, workers could be blamed for their own fate – as determined by the appraisal system.

Rank and yank policies were administered by managers who were tasked with firing a certain number of people each year. For every hot star in the workforce, managers were expected to identify lukewarm hangers-on whose days were numbered. This practice relied on an inflexible and unpopular approach to appraisals that looked back on past performance rather than forward to future improvement.

By his own admission, between 1981 and 1985 Welch slashed 112,000 people from his workforce, the kind of numbers which in 1980s America conjured up images of nuclear destruction.[27] 'Neutron Jack', as he was dubbed, fired the bottom 10 per cent of his managers every year because, for whatever reason, they'd fallen into the wrong category. Meanwhile, those in the top 20 per cent were rewarded with bonuses, stock options and security in a company that over successive years substantially increased its market capitalization.

The trouble with this kind of thinking is that it boxes people into categories and treats them as something less than human – something without personal commitments and responsibilities. It doesn't matter if a person has done well in their job for 10 years but a family trauma is now affecting their concentration. The personal part of the story can be disregarded. All that matters is which category they currently fit into.

Investigating these categories, documentary-maker Jacques Peretti interviewed McKinsey consultant Helen Handfield-Jones, co-author of *The War for Talent* (more on this in a moment).[28] Peretti suggested that Handfield-Jones and her colleagues categorized employees as A, B or C, inspired by the policies adopted at General Electric. He described those in the A category as 'super-talented', B as 'kind of coasting along' and C as 'people that you sack'.

When Handfield-Jones replied that this was 'mischaracterized', Peretti pushed back by asking: 'So, you didn't say that a C person should just be sacked?' To which Handfield-Jones responded, with some exasperation: 'It's not a person, it's a performer'. At that point, seemingly close to spontaneous human combustion, Peretti threw his hands into the air and insisted: 'It is a person'.[29]

Handfield-Jones tried to clarify, explaining she meant that people are assessed by their performance rather than their talent. While this may be true, it's a comment that's less redeeming than she appeared to believe. People may have been assessed on performance, but how far did this include the wider context of what else they might be experiencing?

In corporate America, being accountable for past performance mattered more than talent and personal development. Some estimates suggest that by the early 2000s as many as a third of US corporations – and 60 per cent of the Fortune 500 – had adopted a forced-ranking system.[30]

But the tide was turning. After Welch left GE in 2001, the company quietly began to drop forced ranking, fearing that it fuelled unhealthy levels of internal competition and undermined collaboration. Better instead to think about people's talent and potential.

The war for talent

Discovering someone's potential tapped into a new concept that took hold in the US in the 1970s. What if work wasn't simply about partnership after all? What if it wasn't confined to a rather dry and functional relationship that ran from 9 to 5, in which people kept one eye on performance and the other on the clock?

What if instead work was about love, involving a deeper sense of fulfilment and a spark of excitement inspired by fun, fortune and opportunity? What if work gave someone the chance to shine, to truly be themselves? Who would give that up at 5pm and slink out the door? People instead would be more likely to work longer hours, to give their heart and soul, to do what is always done in a loving relationship – and commit.

Work could offer a rewarding sense of achievement, shared with colleagues with whom you could build a meaningful connection. For many people, the emotional bonds within a team created a shared sense of belonging that was partly why they went to work in the first place.

On top of that, there was a feeling of working for the common good. It was nice to know that your organization was playing a beneficial role in society, and therefore so were you. In committing to their employer in whom they believed, people would be committing to their future. By the 2000s, work was becoming a beautiful thing.

Before we get too misty-eyed and start writing poems to each other, let's cool off with a bit of reality. People tend only to commit to an employer who they feel commits to them. Employees need to believe in the company they work for, and they expect the company to believe in them. It's a trade-off. The hours will be long but your talent will be recognized. In this kind of relationship, work is no longer about what you do or how you do it, it's about who you are.

In America, these ideas took hold in the 1970s, a time when the US car industry was slowing down while Japanese imports were speeding ahead. These brought with them the Japanese philosophy of work, which featured a level of commitment that few in the West had seen.

This was described in 1981 by Richard Pascale and Anthony Athos in their book *The Art of Japanese Management: Applications for*

American executives. Similar ideas were further developed by Tom Peters in his 1982 bestseller *In Search of Excellence.* Both valued the over-arching sense of purpose that Japanese companies managed to encourage within their people. A higher meaning of work was here to stay.

By the 1990s, identity, talent, commitment and potential were actively encouraged, partly in reaction to changing demographics. For many years, the post-Second World War baby boomer generation had given employers as many people as they needed. In the '80s and '90s, declining birth-rates meant there were fewer talented people to choose from. This led firms to compete in what Steven Hankin at McKinsey described as the 'war for talent'.[31]

In the 1990s, nearly 90 per cent of US companies were relying on appraisals, assessing past performance in settling pay and rewards. However, *comparing* people's performance was becoming less valuable to employers than *encouraging* it and nurturing it. In practice, this meant finding talented people and committing to them, in the expectation they will commit to you. The social contract was now evolving into a meaningful affair of the heart.

In 1986, the occupational safety and health movement started an initiative to highlight work-related mental health disorders, mainly related to stress. This was followed in 1991 by a project launched by the National Institute of Mental Health, called Managing Depression in the Workplace. On mental health, however, corporate wellbeing programmes were slow to keep up.[32]

Inspired by Johnson & Johnson's Live for Life initiative, and keen to keep their own eye-watering healthcare costs down, other large companies introduced similar programmes. These usually consigned wellbeing to a cost-cutting exercise in physical health, rather than considering it as an opportunity to rethink the unhealthy working practices and poor company culture that might have a damaging impact on mental health. Work may lead to stress, fatigue and burnout, but at least employees had a worksite clinic that could pick up the pieces, if you got there in time.

Love, devotion and bees

By the 2000s, work-related stress in the UK was contributing to 100,000 strokes a year, the fourth-leading cause of death. Similar figures exist in other Western economies. In Japan, 'karoshi' – literally, 'overwork death' – describes those who give their heart and soul to the point of exhaustion, with some dying at their desk.

In this period, businesses were presenting themselves as a 'family', where people used first names instead of a cold Mr or Mrs. There was a family sense of belonging (company culture), a shared sense of purpose (mission statements) and even shared days out (bonding sessions). The relationship with work was becoming wrapped in a superficial sense of cosiness. However, this masked cloying, one-sided expectation.

It was not enough just to turn up on time. Work was becoming more demanding than that. Now, you were expected to wholeheartedly commit to work, freely giving longer hours and perhaps giving up on something of yourself. Work and personal identity were merging, mixing into a hazy fug of belief and commitment – as if you'd discovered the promised land up on the 5th floor of a building that rented office space.

It was more than just milk and honey. The milk was made from almonds and the honey came from hives on the roof. Even the bees were happy. We started to go to work not to do a better job but to make the world a better place. New hires could have been forgiven for feeling that they'd joined a cult.

However, the cute, cosiness of an office that feels like home isn't always what it seems. Nor is the kindly, family spirit that some companies display. This too is carefully manufactured. The thing about families is that they're always there for you. Which means you're always there for them, 24/7, always available, always on.

In 2010, the US Chamber of Commerce, together with health campaigners Partnership for Prevention, jointly released a report entitled *Healthy Workforce 2010 and Beyond*. It made clear that organizations need to view employee health in terms of productivity rather than as an exercise in healthcare cost management. The report argued that workplace health programmes should be viewed and managed as a 'strategic investment to be maximized rather than an expense to be minimized'.[33]

The report found that the emerging discipline of health and productivity management has shown that health and productivity are 'inextricably linked' and that a healthy workforce leads to a healthy bottom line.[34] This emphatic conclusion clearly connects workplace wellbeing with company culture. Corporate studies have come to similar conclusions. In 2020, Deloitte described organizational culture as 'the top concern for employees and leadership'.[35]

Pascale, Athos, Peters and Hankin promoted the idea of devotion to work. But how devoted is work to us? This is a question that has been asked with increasing volume and vigour since the Covid pandemic. In demanding our heart and soul, what do employers give in return? Such questions had been posed for years, but after the pandemic many people found that the answer was 'not enough' – as we shall discover in the next chapter.

A new approach to wellbeing

In the 2020s, we are entering the next stage in the evolutionary process that has been shaping and reshaping employees' relationship with work since the Industrial Revolution. Where will we go next?

At the root of this are questions about company culture, workplace wellbeing, authenticity and purpose. In the current relationship with work, how will employers and employees each develop their side of the relationship so that it leads to mutual gain and healthy productivity?

If employees are happier at work than has been the case in the past, they will be more productive, and their employer will be more competitive. In turn, this means employees will be better rewarded and more able to support their family at home and contribute to society at large. All of which firmly places employers in the position of social leadership, as we shall see in subsequent chapters.

This book is intended to offer a concept of what can be achieved through a radical rethinking of wellbeing. After forensically examining data and research from a range of sources, we developed a coherent theory of workplace wellbeing that safeguards employees while simultaneously supporting organizations by enabling higher engagement, productivity and retention. In our next chapter, we'll discover why such a rethink is urgently needed.

Notes

1 J Goh et al (2015) The Relationship Between Workplace Stressors and Mortality and Health Costs in the United States, *Management Science*, **62** (2)

2 M Yang et al (2023) Occupational Risk Factors for Stroke: A Comprehensive Review, *Journal of Stroke*, **25** (3), pp. 327–37

3 American Psychological Association. How stress affects your health, 31 October 2022, www.apa.org/topics/stress/health (archived at https://perma.cc/Q2A6-6H6Y)

4 American Psychological Association. Striving for mental health excellence in the workplace, March 2023, www.apa.org/topics/healthy-workplaces/mental-health (archived at https://perma.cc/8V79-97C8)

5 Office of the Surgeon General. Workplace Mental Health and Well-Being, www.hhs.gov/surgeongeneral/priorities/workplace-well-being/index.html (archived at https://perma.cc/BJP3-F2YV)

6 B Dow et al. *The Burnout Report*, January 2024, Mental Health UK, euc7zxtct58.exactdn.com/wp-content/uploads/2024/01/19145241/Mental-Health-UK_The-Burnout-Report-2024.pdf (archived at https://perma.cc/3CQA-QX67)

7 L Aston et al. Time to take ownership, Mental Health at work 2019 report, September 2019, Business in the Community, bitc.org.uk/wp-content/uploads/2019/10/bitc-wellbeing-report-mhawmentalhealthworkfullreport2019-sept2019-2.pdf (archived at https://perma.cc/QH3N-NH8U)

8 G Franco and F Franco. Bernardino Ramazzini: The Father of Occupational Medicine, *American Journal of Public Health*, **91** (9), p. 1382

9 S Isaac. "Phossy jaw" and the matchgirls: a nineteenth-century industrial disease, 28 September 2018, Royal College of Surgeons, rcseng.ac.uk/library-and-publications/library/blog/phossy-jaw-and-the-matchgirls/ (archived at https://perma.cc/5AL7-PF5C)

10 A Besant. White slavery in London, 23 June 1888, The Link, www.mernick.org.uk/thhol/thelink.html (archived at https://perma.cc/YPZ7-9HLS)

11 A Begum et al (2020) Sarah Chapman's grave, 22 July 2020, UK Parliament, edm.parliament.uk/early-day-motion/57324/sarah-chapmans-grave (archived at https://perma.cc/JQQ4-4SR8)

12 G E Biles (1993) John Henry Patterson's contributions to industrial welfare, *International Journal of Public Administration*, **16** (5), pp. 627–47

13 GovInfo.gov. 15 U.S.C. 17 – Antitrust laws not applicable to labor organizations, www.govinfo.gov/app/details/USCODE-2011-title15/USCODE-2011-title15-chap1-sec17 (archived at https://perma.cc/C4U8-JZZV)

14 International Labour Office, Official Bulletin, April 1919-August 1920, ilo.org/wcmsp5/groups/public/---dgreports/---jur/documents/genericdocument/wcms_441862.pdf (archived at https://perma.cc/UNF4-65QD)

15 H B Drury (1918) *Scientific Management: A history and criticism*, Cornell University Library

16 V I Lenin (1913) A "Scientific" System of Sweating, Pravda 60, www.marxists. org/archive/lenin/works/1913/mar/13.htm (archived at https://perma.cc/ K3TG-ZB9J)

17 Visions Editors (1984) National Employee Service and Recreation Association (NESRA), *Visions in Leisure and Business*, **3** (3)

18 A H Maslow (1943) A theory of human motivation, *Psychological Review*, 50 (4), pp. 370–96

19 A H Maslow (1954) *Motivation and Personality*, Harper & Brothers

20 W Kremer and C Hammond. Abraham Maslow and the pyramid that beguiled business, 1 September 2013, BBC News, www.bbc.co.uk/news/ magazine-23902918 (archived at https://perma.cc/8NDX-Y7BH)

21 H L Dunn (1959) What High-Level Wellness Means, *Canadian Journal of Public Health*, 50 (11), pp. 447–57

22 H L Dunn (1959) What High-Level Wellness Means, *Canadian Journal of Public Health*, 50 (11), pp. 447–57

23 EAP Association. History of EAPs, www.eapa.org.uk/organisational-background/ (archived at https://perma.cc/VAC8-YRXR)

24 F Isaac and P Flynn (2001) Johnson & Johnson Live for Life program: Now and then, *American Journal of Health Promotion*, **15** (5), pp. 365–67

25 D Blei. The False Promises of Wellness Culture, 4 January 2017, Daily from JSTOR, daily.jstor.org/the-false-promises-of-wellness-culture/ (archived at https://perma.cc/A6AH-2RYF)

26 D Blei. The False Promises of Wellness Culture, 4 January 2017, Daily from JSTOR, daily.jstor.org/the-false-promises-of-wellness-culture/ (archived at https://perma.cc/6BY9-XAHU)

27 J Welch (2001) *Straight from the Gut*, Warner

28 B Axelrod et al (2001) *The War For Talent*, Harvard Business Review Press

29 J Peretti (2017) *Billion Dollar Deals and How They Changed Your World: Work* (episode 3), Pulse Films for BBC

30 P Cappelli and A Tavis (2016) The Performance Management Revolution, *Harvard Business Review*, hbr.org/2016/10/the-performance-management-revolution (archived at https://perma.cc/XSA8-H88B)

31 S Keller. Attracting and retaining the right talent, 24 November 2017, McKinsey, www.mckinsey.com/capabilities/people-and-organizational-performance/our-insights/attracting-and-retaining-the-right-talent (archived at https://perma.cc/69U9-RYVQ)

32 M Rucker. The Interesting History of Workplace Wellness, 20 May 2016, michaelrucker.com, michaelrucker.com/well-being/the-history-of-workplace-wellness/ (archived at https://perma.cc/QXE4-JGHF)

33 Partnership for Prevention and US Chamber of Commerce. *Healthy Workforce 2010 and Beyond*, 2009, www.uschamber.com/assets/archived/images/documents/files/HealthyWorkforce2010FINALElectronicVersion111709.pdf (archived at https://perma.cc/M7DS-Y6XQ)

34 Partnership for Prevention and US Chamber of Commerce. *Healthy Workforce 2010 and Beyond*, 2009, www.uschamber.com/assets/archived/images/documents/files/HealthyWorkforce2010FINALElectronicVersion111709.pdf (archived at https://perma.cc/W45T-VSJG)

35 J Radin and C Korba. COVID-19 as catalyst: The future of work and the workplace in health care, 12 November 2020, Deloitte, www2.deloitte.com/us/en/insights/industry/health-care/health-care-workforce-trends.html (archived at https://perma.cc/27Q3-PT9J)

2

Wellbeing strategies that aren't fit for purpose

In the 2020s, there is a chronic need for effective workplace wellbeing. In the US, unplanned absences were estimated (in 2022) to cost the economy $47.6 billion in lost productivity.[1] A year later, sickness absence in the UK reached its highest level in 15 years, according to the Chartered Institute of Personnel and Development (CIPD). The CIPD also found that more than three-quarters of survey respondents (76 per cent) reported stress-related absence.[2]

Employees feel stressed at work, because of work. Yet, reluctant to acknowledge this, many employers persist with stressful work practices – hoping that wellbeing apps and perks will compensate, or at least indicate that wellbeing isn't ignored.

In 2022, large employers were spending an average of $11 million per year on corporate wellbeing.[3] By 2026, the global workplace wellbeing market is set to reach $94.6 billion – up from $61.2 billion in 2021.[4]

Research suggests 93 per cent of employees believe their wellbeing at work is as important as their salary.[5] Deloitte's 2023 Well-Being at Work survey found that, for 74 per cent of respondents, improving their wellbeing is more important than advancing their career.[6]

None of this will come as a surprise to HR officers – the hard-pressed, overlooked and under-valued matchmakers who fit people to roles and help them sustain their relationship with work. Keeping the flame alive isn't easy. It involves company culture, continuous learning and development and managing retention and progression.

It also involves tight budgets, competing business priorities and C-suite personalities who may be reluctant to abandon the 'way we do things'. Any of these factors can disrupt HR's attempts to improve poor workplace practices. Consequently, employees find that the relationship with work has its up and downs. For many, effective wellbeing is a pipe dream.

Meaningful wellbeing may well require a shake-up of working practices. However, as we saw at the beginning of Chapter 1, leaders aren't always happy to go that far. For various reasons, they choose stopgap actions instead, which HR officers are obliged to adopt – with varying results.

Organizations offer wellbeing options that are supposedly about protecting people. However, HR officers all too often find themselves giving employees wellbeing initiatives chosen by employers that prioritize the business, for example cost-effective apps that are largely ineffective for people. Initiatives such as these are usually counter-productive.

For evidence of how organizations like to manage wellbeing, let's ask a simple question: are corporate wellbeing policies effective? Or are they at best patchy, and at worst peppered with options that on closer inspection are the highest order of hornswoggle that even pigeons can recognize as hokum from way up on the roof?

'Need to be seen to be doing something'

Defining wellbeing

To assess the effectiveness of the typical programmes on offer, let's be clear about what we mean by wellbeing. Workplace wellbeing can refer to two things: the sense of wellness that employees feel at work and initiatives aimed at supporting this.

Because businesses rely on a healthy workforce, many invest in optional programmes intended to support their employees' physical and/or mental health. In the US, wellness – as opposed to well-being – often refers to workplace programmes that are not optional but which employees are required to sign up to, at risk of financial penalties.

Obligatory wellness requires employees to participate in work-place programmes. This is a consequence of the so-called 'Safeway Amendment' to the 2010 Affordable Care Act that allows employers to make 30 per cent of non-smokers' total healthcare premiums – and

50 per cent of smokers' premiums – contingent on their adopting healthy behaviours.[7]

Employees who refuse to submit to healthcare services at their employer's request risk facing a fine, forfeiting tax breaks or even losing health benefits. This allows employers to withhold or reclaim large sums of money from such employees. Companies peddling wellness programmes to organizations often describe these financial penalties as 'savings' for employers.

Al Lewis, author of best-selling book *Why Nobody Believes the Numbers*, suggests that such vendors 'routinely disregard clinical guidelines that are designed to avoid overtreatment, inappropriate doctor visits, and increasingly ubiquitous crash-dieting contests'.[8]

Optional wellbeing

Leaving aside the questionable ethics of the obligatory schemes, for now we're only focusing on optional wellbeing programmes. These share a common feature in that they assign responsibility to the individual. Employees choose what to participate in and for how long. In this way, wellbeing is delegated to individuals, who are expected to assume responsibility for managing the physical and psychological fallout of their employer's working practices.

Organizations that find it easier or more comfortable to ignore the impact of their workplace practices may offer their people superficial distractions such as ineffective apps and perks. 'Employers want to be seen as doing something, but they don't want to look closely and change the way work is organized,' according to Tony D LaMontagne, a professor of work, health and wellbeing at Deakin University in Melbourne, Australia.[9]

Consequently, individuals are offered choices that may reflect budget, trends and ease of delivery rather than anything based on detailed analysis of healthier ways of working. These can include in-person sessions in mindfulness, yoga or physical fitness; virtual therapies – delivered by apps focusing on sleep, nutrition or exercise; perks like free eye tests, gym discounts or cycle to work schemes; and environmental factors such as fruit bowls, fresh coffee and ergonomic chairs.

Larger organizations sometimes have in-house mental health specialists. However, to access them an employee might first need to reveal their darkest moments to their line manager, leading to concerns about breaches of confidentiality. Outreach charity Business in the Community found that in small or mid-sized organizations, 88 per cent of employees with work-related poor mental health did not disclose these problems to either their line manager or HR.[10]

Other organizations offer therapy apps, where employees can access a virtual therapist, whose training, qualifications (if any) or even identity can't be verified. Worse, some apps connect to AI chat-bots that, dispensing with an actual human, offer multi-choice answers to your harrowing psychological challenges.

The so-called 'Uberization' of mental health care brings with it a Candyland regard to therapy. Rather than breakthroughs and progress, this approach offers routine 'checking-in' and 'levelling up' through apps that dish out 'you can do it' statements more usually associated with sportswear.

These are the sorts of wellbeing options that organizations tend to offer. So, do they work?

Is workplace wellbeing working?

No, for two reasons:

1 **Too few people use workplace wellbeing initiatives.** Deloitte found that 68 per cent of workers surveyed said they did not use the full value of the wellbeing resources offered by their organization.[11] This figure chimes with similar research suggesting that only a third of US workers regularly participate in workplace wellbeing programmes.[12] However, a survey for insurer Vitality found that only 25 per cent of 4,000 respondents said they used wellbeing initiatives offered by their employer.[13]

2 **Such programmes do nothing about deep-seated underlying problems,** issues that challenge wellbeing in the first place. Oxford University researcher Dr William Fleming analysed survey responses from 46,336 employees.[14] He found that those who took part in programmes such as mindfulness sessions, coaching, apps or relaxation classes were no better off than colleagues who did not.

After considering the outcomes of 90 different interventions, Fleming found that almost none had any significant impact on workplace wellbeing or job satisfaction. Training sessions on resilience and stress management even seemed to have a negative effect.

Only charity or volunteer work seemed to have improved wellbeing. This is work that notably enables people to build meaningful connections with others, replacing the competitive nature of work with something more satisfactory. Connecting with people brings a sense of reward that serves as an antidote to isolating workplace practices. Pursuing this line of thought, in Chapter 5 we'll explore connectivity as a key component of successful workplace wellbeing.

In the past, wellbeing programmes were hard to dispute. They implied good intentions and no-one could say for sure that they weren't effective. Now that rigorous study has held them to the light, it's easier to see them for what they are.

Fleming's research isn't the only study to cast doubt on typical workplace wellbeing programmes. His results echoed similar findings in a US poll of nearly 33,000 people who were working for a large warehousing company and whose verdict on wellbeing was similarly lukewarm.[15]

These studies do not conclude that actions like mindfulness or yoga are without value at all. Both are known to be of great support to individuals, psychologically and physically, whether practised at work or elsewhere. But neither offer a comprehensive strategy capable of alleviating the long-term causes of disengagement, such as poor working practices. Nor are they universally popular across the workforce. Nor are apps, gym discounts or fruit bowls.

Analysis of popular initiatives points to the need for a hard-headed reassessment of the way that organizations are operating. Fleming said, 'If employees want access to mindfulness apps and sleep programmes and wellbeing apps, there is not anything wrong with that, but if you're seriously trying to drive employees' wellbeing, then it has to be about working practices.'[16] The authors of Deloitte's 2023 report *The well-being imperative* suggested that, instead of putting the burden of action on employees, 'organizations need to take a hard look at the structure of work'.[17]

How can organizations develop better, more effective ways of working? The best place to start is by breaking this down into two further questions:

1 **What are the key challenges** to engagement that a successful wellbeing strategy must tackle effectively?

2 **How can a successful strategy support the whole workforce,** not just the minority who are happy to participate?

Denial and masking

To be effective, workplace wellbeing must identify the underlying causes of stress, fatigue and disengagement. These must be neutralized if leaders are to break the cycle of poor workplace practices that repeatedly undermine mental and physical health.

Poor workplace wellbeing stems from a complex tangle of factors. Unpicking them, however, is sometimes blurred by two common tactics. The first involves denial and disconnect.

Employers could create a less stressful atmosphere by changing the way they do things. But this would be to admit that their current practices are unacceptably stressful – which, in our experience, the vast majority deny. While 70 per cent of employers believe they provide good access to health and wellness support, only 23 per cent of employees agree.[18]

Deloitte's survey of 2,000 C-suite leaders from the US, UK, Canada and Australia 'found that more than three out of four executives inaccurately believe that their workforce's wellbeing improved [over the previous 12 months], illustrating that leaders don't have a firm grasp on how their teams are really doing'.[19]

When outright denial is difficult, the second tactic favoured by organizations when confronted with an uncomfortable truth involves masking the issue. When asking themselves about managing stress, businesses might, for example, respond by raising pay. But this doesn't answer the question.

In fact, an international survey found that 58 per cent of respondents in the US and 54 per cent in the UK said they have previously taken a pay cut to accept a job that made them happier.[20] These figures 'should serve as a wakeup call for employers,' said business psychologist Portia Hickey. 'If your staff aren't happy, they will consider going elsewhere, no matter how much you pay them.'[21]

Alternatively, businesses may try masking their toxic cocktail of fatigue and disengagement behind suggestions about the lingering effects of Covid. The pandemic, however, was not responsible for long-term difficulties that were years in the making.

It is true that Covid provoked new interest in wellbeing, in all its forms. The impact of simultaneous change, loss and uncertainty inspired new demand for better ways of working. And those who didn't find them in their current job were prepared to quit and look elsewhere.

Understanding disengagement

Rethinking a sense of purpose

The impact of Covid on the international workforce was sudden, multi-faceted and largely inescapable. Nothing like it had been seen in a century. Overnight, millions of people were told to work from home, often in difficult circumstances.

It was initially assumed that after the pandemic, employees would go back to the way things had been. But as the virus persisted, and the old ways receded into the past, a new reality emerged. It became clear that changes in the workplace brought on by the pandemic were wide-ranging and permanent, among them revised perceptions of purpose.

Away from the office, many people recognized that some things were more important to them than they had previously realized. Less commuting meant more personal time. There was less need for formal clothes and less contact with tricky colleagues. More personal space led many to reassess their personal values and objectives.

Consultants McKinsey surveyed more than a thousand US employees, publishing their findings in April 2021 in a report entitled *Help your employees find purpose – or watch them leave*. Nearly two-thirds of respondents said the pandemic caused them to reflect on their life's purpose, including the things that are most important to them and are worth prioritizing.[22]

Nearly half those surveyed said that, because of the pandemic, they were reconsidering the kind of work they do. Millennials were three times more likely than others to say that they were re-evaluating work. When asked if they were living their purpose in their day-to-day work, only 15 per cent of frontline managers and frontline employees agreed.

What do people prioritize as 'purpose'? It's evident that many no longer felt they belonged – whether in their role, or at their employer, or both. McKinsey warned: 'Employees expect their jobs to bring a significant sense of purpose to their lives. Employers need to help meet this need, or be prepared to lose talent to companies that will.'[23]

After the pandemic, these thoughts gave rise to new mindsets at work. Millions of people in the US, the UK and elsewhere began to question whether they were in the right job or with the right employer. Others began looking for new opportunities that promised better personal development and more flexibility.

Throughout 2021, fatigued and unhappy employees were rethinking things. Millions felt ready to look for a new job. Others, who weren't ready to return to the past, favoured a hybrid work pattern which would allow them to spend part of the week in the office, part at home. Employees looked for stronger commitments to flexibility and clearer focus on personal development.

The Great Resignation

In October 2021, research consultancy Gartner surveyed 3,500 employees around the world and found that 65 per cent agreed that during the pandemic they had 'shifted their attitude toward the value of aspects outside work'. The same percentage agreed that Covid 'made me rethink the place that work should have in my life'.[24]

In re-evaluating their lives, people were going back to basics, looking at the fundamentals of what made them happy or unhappy at work. The pandemic induced what Gartner called a period of 'great reflection'. Many people were no longer content with the way things had been before the pandemic.

By December 2021, 47.8 million US workers had quit their jobs over the course of the year, in a trend that became known as the Great Resignation.[25] In the UK and Ireland, poor retention cost organizations £16.9 billion.[26]

This unprecedented level of change prompted research (e.g. Deloitte, 2022; World Economic Forum, 2022), into the long-term motivation and intention of employees.[27] Many people reported disturbing levels of disengagement and unhappiness in their jobs.

As well as finding that 60 per cent of people felt emotionally detached at work, research by Gallup (in 2022) indicated that 19 per cent felt miserable.[28] Employees in Europe and South Asia said their sense of wellbeing was five percentage points lower than in 2021. Workers in these regions not only felt that life was worse than it had been, their hope for the future had also dropped.[29]

At the same time, 50 per cent of US workers reported feeling stressed in their jobs on a daily basis, 41 per cent described themselves as being worried, 22 per cent as sad and 18 per cent angry. Working women in the US and Canada were among the most stressed employees globally.[30]

The pandemic gave people an opportunity to re-examine things. In seeking greater happiness, many noticed their own discontent. Long-standing concerns about how organizations were run broke through to the surface. There was clear evidence of this in the high number of resignations. Despite offering a window on wellbeing, Covid was not the underlying cause of deep-seated disengagement. There's nothing new in stress.

Today, the 'new normal', that was much heralded during the pandemic, looks strikingly familiar to the way that things were done before. Only by identifying and accepting the long-term causes of disengagement will organizations succeed in breaking the cycle of poor workplace wellbeing.

So, what are the leading causes of stress and poor wellbeing?

Keeping up with company culture

Stress and disengagement can't be dismissed as the difficulties of a few individuals. These issues are global, entrenched and touch all generations within the workforce. They imply over-arching short-comings in company culture that are common across Europe, Asia and the Americas. What might these involve?

Over the last 30 years, fundamental developments in society, politics, technology and in the way we spend our free time have had an inevitable impact on company culture. Some of these factors will have been more influential than others. Together, their combined force has been impossible to escape.

During this period, smartphones arrived. Social media changed the way we lived. So did the climate emergency. The global financial crisis changed the way we worked, the rise of populism affected the way we voted, and the development of AI is changing everything. Organizations were battered by Covid, by the impact of geopolitical tensions and by widespread economic uncertainty. To stay in business and stay ahead of competitors, businesses had to adapt.

These developments merged into forceful change, catapulting Western economies into the 2020s with such force that our clunky analogue past was flung back into the mists of time with bewildering speed. We, humanity, have had a hard time keeping up with this pace of change.

Physiologically, we are no different to early humans – the neolithic hunters whose main interests were chasing big animals and banging the rocks together. Since then, the world might have evolved at a rate of knots but we as a species have not.

Covid gave employees a chance to catch their breath. It was an opportunity to reset and think about personal identity. Millions discovered that they had been struggling to keep up with the pace of change at work. Consequently, organizations encountered a new consciousness among employees, rooted in new perceptions of personal values and identity.

These discoveries in personal identity led many people to quit their job. Others stayed on but zoned out in a fug of fatigue and quiet quitting – presenting itself as disengagement, which is prevalent in the mid-2020s.

Together, these developments – along with flexibility and hybrid working – began to erode traditional company culture. Leaders could no longer rely on the unifying gravitational forces that had held things together in the past, such as a uniform commitment to working 9–5, Monday to Friday, in the office. With more people working on a hybrid basis, being 'at work' has come to mean different things on different days. In many organizations, the office has been down-sized or even sold.

No surprise then, that given everything, leaders have struggled to maintain morale and motivation. They are understandably concerned about company culture, communication challenges and change and uncertainty in the years ahead.

Throughout the 2020s and into the 2030s, disinterest and disen-gagement will continue to be exacerbated by many factors – inside and outside work – including:

- **digital processes** – fuelling fast and demoralizing ways of working
- **hybrid working** – disrupting teams, weakening company culture
- **development of AI** – contributing to anxiety and job insecurity
- **short-term contracts** – gig economy concerns about employers' commitment
- **battle for attention** – chronic distraction and attention deficit due to social media
- **improbable aspirations** – influencers promoting 'instant' wealth, fame and success

These issues lead to or exacerbate problems such as:

- **fatigue** – weariness and anxiety due to 'always-on' availability
- **loneliness** – deepened (and masked) by isolation at work
- **lack of meaning at work** – disenchantment due to disconnection and alienation
- **presenteeism** – being there, but disengaged and not finding any value
- **job insecurity** – short-term, half-hearted commitment undermines trust
- **erosion of trust** – sharpening perceptions of selfishness and exclusion

In their efforts to compete and maintain growth, leaders may over-look factors that weaken organizational resilience. Where there is disregard for people's needs or opinions, individuals can feel frozen out. Finding it hard to present a fair version of themselves, they may struggle to fulfil their potential.

Elon Musk, who said he lived in his Tesla factories for 'three years straight', sleeping on the floor to encourage his team, demonstrated an approach to efficiency that when played out to its full extreme doesn't always motivate people.[31] When Musk gave Twitter employees an ultimatum to either sign up for 'long hours at high intensity' or leave, hundreds quit.[32] Such suggestions imply that work is a dehumanized, functional process. How many people from Generation Z are queuing up for that?

Managers advocating this kind of efficiency may find that their days are numbered. Not just because such outdated attitudes will be dismantled by future trends towards something healthier. But because dehumanized working practices, and the people advocating them, may well be replaced by AI.

Seeing the bigger picture

How have these seismic developments in company culture affected people's personal experience of work?

Since 1998, Working Voices has trained upwards of 100,000 people, the vast majority through in-person work with our trainers. Many also benefitted from our one-to-one coaching programmes. During these sessions, people often explained their own personal circumstances. Their stories frequently shared similar details. Successes such as recognition and promotion were commonly sought after; challenges like poor company culture and feeling overlooked were also frequently felt.

Over time, we found that common needs and difficulties built into a coherent picture of work that would have been familiar to most people, whether they chose to share their own story with us or not. By looking at people's experiences – including management practices, teamwork, the impact of technology and opportunities to succeed – we could assess how these had changed over the quarter of a century that we'd been in business.

By tracking these changes in personal interpretations of work, we could then map them against the major changes in company culture that have occurred since 2000. By looking for overlaps between the two, we could see how personal experience has been influenced by major social change.

At that point, our picture of work could be seen in a clearer light. Long-term trends began to emerge, common workplace concerns and choices were easier to understand. By bringing everything together, we were able to explain shifts in workplace practices and understand fundamental challenges to the way that people preferred to work. In other words, we could identify the long-term causes of disengagement. The first two that we found were as follows.

CAUSE 1: DOING MORE WITH LESS

The financial crash that began in 2007 led to the collapse of banks and other businesses. Redundancies and tighter budgets culminated in tough working practices, such as longer hours, that continued through the years that followed. People were expected to do more with less. Many still are, leading to fatigue and burnout.

Over time, being asked to do more with less in the interests of efficiency becomes incrementally more difficult. Where do you draw the line? In the metaphor of the frog in a pan of tepid water, it notices too late that the heat is gradually getting higher and that it's slowly being boiled to death.

Employers who are slowly boiling their workforce might do well to think about the tragedy of the commons: imagine a wheat field, and a village dependent on bread. Grain is taken from the field, bread is made, people eat, everyone's happy. However, the village can't go on taking wheat indefinitely. Sooner or later, they must work in the field, sow grain and nurture it – by watering it and protecting it from birds. After they harvest the grain, they must sow it again and so on. Only give and take lets people live sustainably.

Some organizations do more taking than giving. The asset they depend on most, their workforce, is continually asked to give more. The organization continues day after day as if all is well, exhausting its field of human talent, depleting the life-force on which it depends, seemingly unaware of the dangers of famine. This situation, the depletion of essential resources, is described by economists as the tragedy of the commons.

Unrelenting demands at work, including longer hours and steeper targets, take an ever-deepening toll on people's physical and mental health. In these conditions, employees grow ever more fatigued and can struggle to get by.

In 2022, a survey by the CIPD found that 67 per cent of respondents have seen 'leaveism' at work – taking holiday to catch up on your work backlog – in the past year.[33] It's hard to think of a more unsustainable statistic than that.

Corporate commitments to efficiency and processes sometimes fail to accommodate human needs and sustainable ways of working. Many organizations, however, have been slow to acknowledge this. This is because efficiency and processes can be measured, shown in a chart and geared towards targets that need to be met. People, however, are more complicated than this.

People don't always fit neatly into efficiencies, processes and targets. Consequently, if their wellbeing is overlooked in favour of long hours, little flexibility, low levels of trust and poor work–life balance, then stress and fatigue are inevitable.

Worse, stress can be contagious, spreading across the workplace. As it creeps from one person to the next, spread by tension and tiredness, it creates a toxic environment, an atmosphere of excessive internal competition and mistrust, where 'lunch is for wimps', according to Gordon Gekko – the villainous character portrayed by Michael Douglas in the 1987 film *Wall Street*.

A toxic environment is marked by behaviours that are disrespectful, non-inclusive, unethical, cut-throat or abusive. Research suggests that a toxic corporate culture is '10.4 times more powerful than compensation in predicting a company's attrition rate compared with its industry'.[34]

CAUSE 2: LACK OF WORKPLACE HUMANITY

Humans are social animals. Without the fangs and claws to go it alone, we've always been tribal. We depend on each other; we always have done. Evidence for this lies in our ancient need for belonging and our capacity for language.

Social contact may partly explain why we, modern humans, developed big brains and long childhoods – long enough to learn social cues. It's also the reason, researchers suggest, that humans are unique among primates in having highly visible white sclerae – the 'whites of our eyes' – that enhance the 'gaze signal'. We like to be sure of eye contact, even at distance.[35]

Tension arises when our social nature is dismissed by leaders who ignore fundamental rules governing how humans work. Such people might have a clear business model in mind, a model that doesn't always include the need for social contact. Their simple need to get things done leads to a functional attitude towards others, an attitude that they may well encourage in their managers.

Here's an example. As mentioned in the introduction, a manager told us, 'I don't work here to make friends, I don't want to encourage colleagues "to be themselves". I want them to streamline their behaviour. I want meetings to be dull but effective. I just want people to get on with the job.'

This approach is counter-productive. The manager wanted streamlined efficiency. He also wanted his people to put aside individualism. These two positions, however, are incompatible. This form of efficiency is dehumanizing and demoralizing. It leads to disengagement, which is notoriously inefficient. How many quiet-quitters did he have in his team?

Leadership experts Christine Porath and Christine Pearson asked thousands of employees about how they were treated at work. They found: 'Employees are less creative when they feel disrespected, and many get fed up and leave. About half deliberately decrease their effort or lower the quality of their work.'[36]

Disengagement has many causes, not all of which are easy to identify – especially since organizations aren't always keen to try. Aware of rising levels of fatigue, they may offer wellbeing programmes but do so without always seeking to understand the underlying causes of disengagement. This is perhaps because some of these causes are associated with poor workplace practices that organizations are reluctant to admit to.

Instead, companies place their faith in wellbeing perks and initiatives. These, however, are largely ineffective, according to the research from Oxford University researcher Dr William Fleming. And so people continue to struggle with workplace practices. When the pandemic gave a little perspective on things, many quit their employer during the Great Resignation.

What would a better way of working look like? To answer this, it's important to begin with an honest assessment of the underlying causes of disengagement. We've noted two already and in our next chapter we shall discover two more. Once we see what we're up against, we'll be able to construct an appropriate response, one that will take a more effective approach to workplace wellbeing.

Notes

1 D Witters and S Agrawal. The Economic Cost of Poor Employee Mental Health, 3 November 2022, Gallup, www.gallup.com/workplace/404174/economic-cost-poor-employee-mental-health.aspx (archived at https://perma.cc/V784-D2P6)
2 Chartered Institute of Personnel and Development. Health and wellbeing at work 2023, September 2023, www.cipd.org/globalassets/media/knowledge/knowledge-hub/reports/2023-pdfs/8436-health-and-wellbeing-report-2023.pdf (archived at https://perma.cc/PT37-7CXZ)
3 Business Group on Health. New Research from Fidelity and Business Group on Health Finds Employers Answering the Call for Help, 31 March 2022, www.businessgrouphealth.org/newsroom/news-and-press-releases/press-releases/2022-fidelity-survey (archived at https://perma.cc/XZ22-UBDL)
4 MarketsandMarkets. Corporate Wellness Solutions Market worth $94.6 billion by 2026, 21 June 2021, PR Newswire, www.prnewswire.com/news-releases/corporate-wellness-solutions-market-worth-94-6-billion-by-2026--exclusive-report-by-marketsandmarkets-301316218.html (archived at https://perma.cc/9FX6-BB9V)
5 T Walker. Gympass research finds 93 per cent of people saying wellbeing at work is as important as salary, 19 October 2023, Health Club Management, www.healthclubmanagement.co.uk/health-club-management-news/87-per-cent-of-people-would-consider-leaving-workplace-that-doesnt-focus-on-employee-wellbeing/351997 (archived at https://perma.cc/2B9S-7QJF)
6 J Fisher et al. As workforce well-being dips, leaders ask: What will it take to move the needle? 20 June 2023, Deloitte, www2.deloitte.com/uk/en/insights/topics/talent/workplace-well-being-research.html (archived at https://perma.cc/TG9A-V7HH)

7   A Lewis (2017) The Outcomes, Economics, and Ethics of the Workplace Wellness Industry, *Health Matrix*, 27 (1)

8   A Lewis (2017) The Outcomes, Economics, and Ethics of the Workplace Wellness Industry, *Health Matrix*, 27 (1)

9   E Barry. Workplace Wellness Programs Have Little Benefit, Study Finds, 15 January 2024, *New York Times*, www.nytimes.com/2024/01/15/health/employee-wellness-benefits.html (archived at https://perma.cc/8T96-UC89)

10 L Aston et al. Time to take ownership, Mental Health at work 2019 report, September 2019, Business in the Community, bitc.org.uk/wp-content/uploads/2019/10/bitc-wellbeing-report-mhawmentalhealthworkfullreport2019-sept2019-2.pdf (archived at https://perma.cc/QV65-2Y8Z)

11 J Bhatt, C Bordeaux and J Fisher. The workforce well-being imperative, 13 March 2023, Deloitte Insights, www2.deloitte.com/uk/en/insights/topics/talent/employee-wellbeing.html (archived at https://perma.cc/2XZG-3HKU)

12 American Psychological Association. Workplace Well-being Linked to Senior Leadership Support, New Survey Finds, June 2016, www.apa.org/news/press/releases/2016/06/workplace-well-being (archived at https://perma.cc/9SG4-2M8G)

13 Vitality. Poor Health at Work is Responsible for £138bn Loss to UK Economy Each Year, 23 January 2024, www.vitality.co.uk/media/poor-health-at-work-is-responsible-for-138bn-loss-to-uk-economy-each-year/ (archived at https://perma.cc/3SE9-6LD8)

14 W Fleming (2024) Employee well-being outcomes from individual-level mental health interventions: Cross-sectional evidence from the United Kingdom, *Industrial Relations Journal*, 55 (2), pp. 162–82

15 Z Song and K Baicker. Effect of a Workplace Wellness Program on Employee Health and Economic Outcomes, 16 April 2019, JAMA Network, jamanetwork.com/journals/jama/fullarticle/2730614?resultClick=1 (archived at https://perma.cc/V8E7-WF93)

16 E Barry. Workplace Wellness Programs Have Little Benefit, Study Finds, 15 January 2024, *New York Times*, www.nytimes.com/2024/01/15/health/employee-wellness-benefits.html (archived at https://perma.cc/8T96-UC89)

17 T Ott. Why corporate well-being initiatives aren't doing so well—and what companies can do about it, 15 February 2023, Deloitte Insights, www2.deloitte.com/us/en/insights/multimedia/podcasts/the-problem-with-employee-wellness-programs.html (archived at https://perma.cc/A9E9-3G6U)

18 S Miller et al. Business of Health 2020: Tackling polarised perceptions in corporate health and wellness, 2020, Aetna, aetnainternational.com/content/dam/aetna/pdfs/aetna-international/Explorer/Business-of-Health-2020-Tackling-Polarised-Perceptions.pdf (archived at https://perma.cc/84TK-5TSA)

19 J Fisher et al. As workforce well-being dips, leaders ask: What will it take to move the needle? 20 June 2023, Deloitte, www2.deloitte.com/uk/en/insights/topics/talent/workplace-well-being-research.html (archived at https://perma.cc/3CZU-Y6MH)

20 Wrike. From Positivity to Productivity: Exposing the Truth Behind Workplace Happiness, www.wrike.com/ebook-happiness-survey-report/ (archived at https://perma.cc/29LV-A5XR)

21 Employer News. Over 50 Percent Of UK Employees Choose Job Happiness Over Pay Cheque Size, 8 May 2019, employernews.co.uk/hr-news/over-50-percent-of-uk-employees-choose-job-happiness-over-pay-cheque-size/ (archived at https://perma.cc/S56B-NJLZ)

22 N Dhingra et al. Help your employees find purpose—or watch them leave, 5 April 2021, McKinsey, www.mckinsey.com/capabilities/people-and-organizational-performance/our-insights/help-your-employees-find-purpose-or-watch-them-leave (archived at https://perma.cc/6USG-AATB)

23 N Dhingra et al. Help your employees find purpose—or watch them leave, 5 April 2021, McKinsey, www.mckinsey.com/capabilities/people-and-organizational-performance/our-insights/help-your-employees-find-purpose-or-watch-them-leave (archived at https://perma.cc/6USG-AATB)

24 J Wiles. Employees Seek Personal Value and Purpose at Work. Be Prepared to Deliver, 29 March 2023, Gartner, www.gartner.com/en/articles/employees-seek-personal-value-and-purpose-at-work-be-prepared-to-deliver (archived at https://perma.cc/9CYU-BZ6Z)

25 J Fuller and W Kerr. The Great Resignation Didn't Start with the Pandemic, 23 March 2022, *Harvard Business Review*, hbr.org/2022/03/the-great-resignation-didnt-start-with-the-pandemic (archived at https://perma.cc/68LN-EWXW)

26 D Rowland and P Pivcevic. Leading change post pandemic: belonging, 8 April 2022, London School of Economics, blogs.lse.ac.uk/businessreview/2022/04/08/leading-change-post-pandemic/ (archived at https://perma.cc/TL3V-8RR2)

27 S Hatfield. New Deloitte report calls on global business to hit reset amid the Great Resignation, 11 May 2022, Deloitte, deloitte.com/ke/en/about/press-room/new-deloitte-report-calls-on-global-business-to-hit-reset-amid-the-great-resignation.html (archived at https://perma.cc/2S6B-XDRJ); S Ellerbeck. The Great Resignation is not over: A fifth of workers plan to quit in 2022, 24 June 2022, World Economic Forum, www.weforum.org/agenda/2022/06/the-great-resignation-is-not-over/ (archived at https://perma.cc/J9QJ-ZTWW)

28 J Clifton et al. Gallup State of the Global Workplace: 2022 Report, 2 May 2022, Gallup, www.cca-global.com/content/latest/article/2023/05/state-of-the-global-workplace-2022-report-346/ (archived at https://perma.cc/7SBS-5DMY)

29 J Clifton et al. Gallup State of the Global Workplace: 2022 Report, 2 May 2022, Gallup, www.cca-global.com/content/latest/article/2023/05/state-of-the-global-workplace-2022-report-346/ (archived at https://perma.cc/929S-F58P)

30 J Clifton et al. Gallup State of the Global Workplace: 2022 Report, 2 May 2022, Gallup, www.cca-global.com/content/latest/article/2023/05/state-of-the-global-workplace-2022-report-346/ (archived at https://perma.cc/JE9H-LA7L)

31 Buzz Staff. When Elon Musk Slept On Factory's Floor To Set Example For Employees, 28 February 2024, News18, www.news18.com/viral/when-elon-musk-slept-on-factorys-floor-to-set-example-for-employees-8796642.html# (archived at https://perma.cc/Y3KJ-2XU8)

32 J Taylor and D Milmo. Twitter 'closes offices' after Elon Musk's loyalty oath sparks wave of resignations, 17 November 2022, *The Guardian*, www.theguardian.com/technology/2022/nov/17/elon-musk-twitter-closes-offices-loyalty-oath-resignations (archived at https://perma.cc/G64C-E49D)

33 R Suff et al. Health and wellbeing at work 2022, April 2022, Chartered Institute of Personnel and Development, www.cipd.org/globalassets/media/comms/news/ahealth-wellbeing-work-report-2022_tcm18-108440.pdf (archived at https://perma.cc/A597-2HVP)

34 D Sull, C Sull and B Zweig et al. Toxic culture is driving the Great Resignation, 11 January 2022, MIT Sloan Management Review, sloanreview.mit.edu/article/toxic-culture-is-driving-the-great-resignation/ (archived at https://perma.cc/P8HB-GMKA)

35 H Kobayashi and S Kohshim. Unique morphology of the human eye and its adaptive meaning: comparative studies on external morphology of the primate eye, *Journal of Human Evolution*, **40** (5), pp. 419–35

36 C Porath and C Pearson. The Price of Incivility, January-February 2013, Harvard Business Review, hbr.org/2013/01/the-price-of-incivility (archived at https://perma.cc/TWZ4-CHT4)

3

Managing our relationship
with technology

One night in early April 2020, a phone mast in Birmingham caught fire. The 70-foot tower had been deliberately set alight, blazing into the night sky like a medieval beacon. Those behind the attack believed the mast had been providing 5G services and that these were linked to the spread of Covid, rampaging across the UK at the time.

In fact, the mast had simply been relaying non-5G phone signals to thousands of local people, including staff at a nearby hospital. Undaunted by science, the risk to life and the fact that 5G has nothing to do with Covid, arsonists across the UK burned more than 70 phone masts or related equipment and attacked engineers sent to repair them.

Similar incidents, in Italy, Ireland, Belgium, the Netherlands and Cyprus, were encouraged by conspiracy theories across social media falsely suggesting that '5G radio waves' caused small changes to people's bodies which made them succumb to the virus.

Analysis by the *New York Times* in April 2020 found '487 Facebook communities, 84 Instagram accounts, 52 Twitter accounts, and dozens of other posts and videos pushing the conspiracy. The Facebook communities added nearly half a million new followers over the past two weeks. On Instagram, a network of 40 accounts nearly doubled its audience this month to 58,800 followers'.[1]

Despite lacklustre efforts by social media platforms to limit its exposure, the conspiracy theory emerged in more than 30 countries, from Switzerland to Japan. In Britain, people who were perfectly rational in other aspects of life were prepared to believe knee-wobbling claims that there was a 5G tower on the (then) new £20 note – which, rather than a sinister coded message, turned out to be the Margate lighthouse.

There's nothing new in reactions like this. Humanity's desire to destroy new developments with our oldest (fire) is a familiar story. Most recently it was 5G masts. In times gone by, we were burning manifestations of the devil.

When a dog mysteriously died in the Norfolk town of King's Lynn in 1590, a shadow of suspicion fell on one Margaret Read. Things got worse for Margaret when a villager who had been spurned in love came to her for help, so the story goes. Soon after this visit, the villager's former lover developed chest pains and was struck dead three days later. Margaret was seized by the authorities and after trial by ducking she was burned at the stake in the town's marketplace.

Between 1400 and 1782, more than 40,000 people, mainly women, were executed across Europe for witchcraft, amid destabilizing fear associated with changes in religious practices. Nearly 250 years on, we have better teeth but not much else has changed. The desire to restore order by ridding ourselves of things we don't understand is persistent and potentially destructive.

Recognizing human vulnerabilities

In this and the next chapter, we'll look at reactions to a changing future, including the fear and anxiety that are stirred up when we slip into uncertainty.

Keeping a grip on fear

In the 2020s, uncertainty has been fuelled by many factors in a short space of time, from Covid to geopolitical tensions to economic instability. Such issues have the potential to loosen our grip on a comfortable sense of control. Together, uncertainty, fear and anxiety can leave people feeling overwhelmed, which is a key component of fatigue.

Fatigue isn't feeling a bit weary at the end of the day, it's a numbness that prevents you absorbing new experiences and taking them in your stride. Fatigue, in which your psychological 'stride' becomes more of a shuffle, is associated with difficulties in processing, making it hard to keep up with things.

It's not simply high workloads that induce fatigue. How can you keep up with work when you feel obstructed by overwhelming uncertainty and fear, emotions that aren't easily sidestepped? Uncertainty and fear can slow you down, or even stop you in your tracks. They can feel too much to manage, they can sap you of confidence and leave you feeling fatigued and too numb to continue. This leads to disengagement, which at its worst becomes burnout.

Of the common causes of workplace uncertainty, unfamiliar technology can be especially daunting. At a superficial level, tech can trigger concern about using a new bit of software or getting the best from AI. However, as we saw with 5G masts, technology can also provoke much deeper fears. These relate to perceived threats to our own personal safety which we imagine may be compromised by something that's coming our way some day soon, sooner than we would like.

If we believe that a pandemic, or job insecurity or a changing way of working are heading our way, we might worry about our future. This worry, this deep apprehensive fear for what's coming, leads us to vigilantly monitor our immediate surroundings, like a radar sweeping for signals of an approaching threat.

Our sense of security, alert and alarmed, pings like a blip on a radar screen when we come across something potentially threatening. From steam-powered looms destroyed in the early 19th century to 5G masts targeted in our own times, many people initially regard new developments as the beginning of something sinister. Such objects become proxies for fear. The threat comes not just from what they are, but what they represent, in particular the loss of safe routine and familiarity.

To feel that we're about to be dragged out of our comfort zone and dumped into a situation beyond our control is fearful, unbearable even. By rejecting or even attacking this threat, via proxies, we can protect ourselves from fearful times ahead. It's as if, by destroying a scapegoat, people feel that they're bringing the future back under control.

Targeting an object that's linked (however tenuously) to potentially disruptive forces can make everything feel better again. This is why, in fearful times, 'making your country feel great again' succeeds as a mantra for populist strongmen. By targeting scapegoats, whether individuals or a certain segment of society, they exploit voters' deep-seated fears about a slippery, uncertain and seemingly uncontrollable future.

New developments in technology are a guaranteed feature of the future. And they're coming faster than we might feel comfortable with. We can't gauge the extent of their impact, we just know we need to get ready for sweeping, wholesale change.

None of this is easy. In the mid-twentieth century, tech was heralded as the great liberator. At home and at work, tech seemed like the light at the end of the tunnel. There were excited promises about all the things it would do for us, so many in fact that we'd have bags of free time. Back then however, we felt in control of tech. Now, not so much. In the 2020s, many people feel daunted by tech, these days the light at the tunnel sometimes feels like an oncoming train.

The need to belong

Organizations are looking at how tech can change the way they operate. Just as important, however, are questions about how tech has been changing their people. Slowly but surely, social developments imposed upon us by tech have been burrowing into our lives. It's important to assess these processes so that we can better understand them and monitor their impact on us.

Within a period of just 30 years, tech's all-embracing reach radically upended everything. The internet in the 1990s, smartphone technology in the 2000s and social media in the 2010s each came at such a rate that questions about their value quickly became meaningless. Today, we can't imagine how we lived without them.

To explain more, let's start with some numbers:

- In 2023, almost 98 per cent of UK adults aged 16-54 owned a smartphone.[2]
- In the UK, 71 per cent of all measured time spent online was on smartphones.[3]
- Americans check their phones 96 times a day; for 18–24-year-olds the rate is higher.[4]

Millions of people are wedded to a device they regard almost as a physical extension of their identity. What impact does an overwhelming commitment to smartphones, and social media platforms, have on employees? How does our online life affect our mental health, the capacity to think, our ability to build relationships with others and our workplace performance? What impact does it have on someone who leaders might regard as an ideal employee, someone who is:

- confident in themselves
- switched on, engaged and efficient
- resilient and resourceful
- a team player and socially mindful of colleagues
- capable of sustained concentration and focus
- capable of carefully resolving problems
- capable of thinking critically and creatively
- capable of explaining ideas, concepts and challenges
- committed 9–5, five days a week

An employer who hires people with these qualities will be unlikely to know about their medical histories that may or may not include challenges to mental health. New employees are expected to fit in quickly; however, not everyone finds this easy.

In fact, many common difficulties are exacerbated by our unhealthy relationship with tech. These problems begin when tech disrupts fundamental elements of what it is to be human – for example our need to be social.

In 1995, social psychologists Roy Baumeister and Mark Leary showed that the desire to belong is a deeply rooted human motivation.[5] Stemming from our ancestral origins, belonging is a fundamental need that permeates our thoughts, feelings and behaviours. Baumeister and Leary's work was later developed by Matthew Lieberman, a cognitive neuroscientist at UCLA. Lieberman explained that the human need to belong and feel valued is as fundamental as food and water.[6]

Individuals feel a need to belong. However, this need is being exploited by tech manufacturers, the social media platforms they support and the algorithms these rely on. This has been happening since the arrival of smartphones in the mid-2000s.

Phones and social media platforms are deliberately designed to capture our attention. They represent the frontline in a sustained and manipulative campaign in which the odds are heavily stacked against users.

The 'secret' truth of smartphones

People who use smartphones and social media find it all too easy to imagine that they are the customer – despite the fact they don't pay for social media. In truth, users are a commodity whose attention is sold to the actual customers of big tech – the organizations who buy advertising rights. They do this is in the form of 'ad auctions', where advertisers bid for the opportunity to put their ad in front of a specific audience, for example, female Generation Z sports fans in North America.

In a lightning-fast, automated auction, powerful algorithms determine variables such as which of the competing advertisers is likely to hold users' attention based on the performance of past ads. Selected advertisers who win coveted space can expect their ad to be shown to their favoured group of users among the billions online in that moment.

We the users don't get much of a say in any of this. On one side of this fight, powerful tech companies have huge budgets and thousands of employees. On our side of the fight, we have the capacity to think for ourselves. We can choose what we give our attention to, or at least we think we can.

In truth, smartphones and social media are chipping away at what it is to be human. They do this by exploiting a specific psychological process, initially described by Nobel laureate Daniel Kahneman in his 2011 book *Thinking, Fast and Slow*.

For Kahneman, our mental processes include two speeds of thought. **'Fast thinking'** leads to quick and impulsive responses, the kind of automatic reactions (known as heuristics) that carry us through mundane moments such as driving, making a sandwich or replying to a simple request.

The brain saves time and energy by simply repeating previous actions, this limits the need to think much about them. In busy moments, we automatically say or do what we did before. It's how we can drive home without thinking about it.

In contrast, in moments of **'slow thinking'** we stand back and look at the bigger picture, actively considering the nuances and deeper issues that may otherwise be overlooked. Examples include managing conflict, negotiating a deal or developing a new course of action.

We get through the day with a healthy mix of fast and slow thinking, toggling back and forth between the two – except when we're on social media, which pesters us for a snap reaction, the kind of thing that fast thinking excels at. Pushing aside slow and careful thoughts, fast thinking is rife with simple (and often flawed) assumptions – sometimes about groups of people we don't trust.

Slow thinking would normally serve as a filter, helping us check things from a rational, clear-thinking perspective. We might even put the phone down and take time to think. But in the battle for our attention, putting the phone down is a blow against the advertisers. For them, instant purchases are more likely in a fast-paced world of instant, unthinking posts, comments, likes and responses.

This is why our phone continually demands our attention. It beeps, pings, vibrates and nags until we come back to it and send a fast reply. And we love coming back to it in the hope of finding new updates, new likes and new followers.

Neuroscientists have shown that social interactions are processed in the brain's reward system where they stimulate the neurotransmitter dopamine.[7] Each time we're notified of a message, we want to give it our attention; doing so is neurologically rewarding.

Amid all this urgency, there's not much room for 'slow thinking'. We're getting used to doing without it. We're becoming less than our potential, less balanced in our thinking, less capable and less of who we are. In skipping deeper thought processes, we float in a fast-paced, febrile atmosphere where conspiracy theories are more likely to lead to real-world consequences, for example the destruction of things that represent a fearful future.

Technology in business

Fast thinking in business practices

Organizations sometimes exacerbate the problems associated with fast thinking. Businesses are in competition, urgently seeking an edge over their rivals, which they can get from fast tech and immediate reactions. In recent decades, tech has enabled businesses to work faster and faster. Speed has become a feature of company culture.

But this can be counterproductive. For example, organizations frequently use apps to speed up processes, to the point that the quantity of workplace apps is overpowering their value. People who are required to use many apps, such as Slack, Evernote, Google Drive and Dropbox, must continuously flip between them, including some that require hourly updates. Research suggests that workers can lose up to 32 days a year navigating between the very apps intended to speed up workplace productivity.[8]

In their demand for urgency, leaders may set deadlines more from habit than from need, sometimes at the expense of the deeper and slower thinking that a) might lead to a better outcome and b) allows the range of thoughts that is central to mental health. For some leaders, slow and considered thought is helpful in business as long as you can do it quickly.

However, fast thinking can lead to poor thinking. Figures often quoted from an article by writer David Grossman suggest that 400 large companies cited an average loss per business of $62.4 million per year because of inadequate communication with and between employees.[9]

The pace of life sped up in 2002 with the release of the BlackBerry which enabled emails on the go. BlackBerry users appeared to be addicted, almost; the devices were nicknamed 'crackberries'. They were a mark of status, everyone wanted one. To be given one by an employer was the equivalent of stripes on your arm, evidence of your rank and relevance. Yet this was the moment when employers first hooked people into an 'always-on culture', where they could be emailed 24/7.

Since then, we've become adept at blanking out the real world with ease, staring at screens, hungering for whatever the 'digiverse' can feed us next. We clamour to be fed, like chicks in a nest.

More urgency, more anxiety, less time

Over the last 20 years, we've seen our clients' anxiety go up and attention levels go down. Relationship-building lunches have become replaced by half-hour virtual calls. Distracted by their phones, people tune out of meetings. These days, instant human interaction such as a phone call has to be arranged in advance. Unannounced personal contact feels more intrusive than it used to.

Even when contact is prearranged, it can feel unfulfilling and isolating when – in a virtual call – people keep their camera switched off. When body language is absent, we are deprived of perhaps our most primitive, most ingrained aid to communication.

Sometimes, people remain on mute too. In a meeting or a virtual training session, some participants appear as nothing more than a name on a black screen, as if you're just broadcasting at them from a TV studio. Without seeing or hearing them, it's hard to develop rapport. How do you know they are not actually in the kitchen making a cup of tea?

Relationship-building has become all the harder. There used to be more time for relaxed moments at work, hanging out in the kitchen, going for a drink after work or chatting over the watercooler between meetings. These moments of incidental communication were of intrinsic value. In the 2020s, reduced face-to-face contact and less chance to rest are factors that induce fatigue, provoke disengagement and reduce rather than increase efficiency.

Now that many people have a hybrid work pattern, we are more dependent on remote contact such as virtual calls. Back-to-back virtual calls are worn by some as a badge of honour. More than one client has posted an out-of-office reply declaring that 'I'm in back-to-back meetings so I may not be able to get back to you'. Such virtue signalling does little to challenge a company culture that champions fast thinking at the expense of a broader approach to mental health.

In the past, there was no need for organizations to worry about their fast company culture. People reacted fast at work and then relaxed at home. Now, fatigued employees seeking escape may look for it, ironically, online – further delaying the need to switch off.

The dehumanizing impact of surveillance

At the heart of tech, artificial intelligence (AI) – the unseen ghost in the machine – has been with us since the advent of smartphones. In the beginning, AI offered us predictor text and optimized battery life. Over time, it also gave us voice recognition, language translation, travel advice and personalized content.

At work, AI facilitates speedier processes that increase business efficiencies. From the automation of routine tasks to the analysis of complex data sets, AI is a key component of the digital transformation of the workplace. However, AI has also allowed managers to watch over people's shoulders, especially individuals working from home. This is another factor that contributes to fatigue and disengagement.

During the pandemic, more people began working from home and this led to an increase in spyware. A UK survey found that 60 per cent of workers reported surveillance and monitoring in 2021, compared with 53 per cent in 2020, prompting concerns from union leaders about 'a huge lack of transparency over the use of AI at work'.[10]

Organizations that use AI to monitor keystrokes, take snapshots of content on a computer screen, or activate webcams and audio recording, are drifting towards micromanaging and a lack of trust – strategies that were recognized as counter-productive decades before digitization. Blanket mistrust is hardly inspiring.

Spyware doesn't just disrupt employees, it also implies that managers are incapable of identifying individuals who aren't pulling their weight. Smart managers will know that better solutions are available, such as building a team they trust and setting clear deliverables for individuals they're concerned about.

Monitoring 'activity scores' by using AI to assess keystrokes and mouse movements is too primitive to be meaningful. How highly do such systems rate someone who's sitting motionless in a virtual meeting? One employee reported dry eyes and a sore head at the end of the working day, as 'tracking doesn't allow for thinking time or stepping away and coming back to work – it's very intense'.[11]

Automated tracking devices may log the number of hours worked at the end of the day, though useful calls, meetings and moments of creative deliberation might not appear in the stats. This may push an employee into working longer hours just to keep an automated system happy so it doesn't give misleading information to a manager. Feedback – that previously might have focused on meaningful performance – now risks descending into a chat about mouse movements and toilet breaks.

This over-reliance on automation removes an element of humanity from the workplace. At best, this practice leads to inaccurate assessments of people; at worse it's degrading and dehumanizing and contributes to anxiety. This way of working is not motivating and it undermines engagement. Much like the manager who 'doesn't work here to make friends', some attitudes to efficiency are notably inefficient.

AI is infiltrating our lives and re-coding them in its own image, such that younger generations are now 'digital natives'. We communicate digitally, favour online onboarding and engage in e-business through virtual calls with team members around the world, while managers are able to monitor our every move. In the future, things are likely to get even more complicated. Soon, we could be committing to forms of AI from which there will be no going back.

Is AI out of control?

Whether we're ready for AI or not is an empty question. Unsettling change is already washing across us. With an ice cream and a smile, we are children on a beach naively looking at how the sea is gently retreating, unaware that today's AI is the first sign of an all-consuming tsunami that's about to hit us with a force we can barely imagine.

Let's take our cue from the pioneers of AI, the very people behind it – who themselves are a little jittery. 'Mitigating the risk of extinction from AI', they wrote in a joint statement in May 2023, 'should be a global priority alongside other societal-scale risks such as pandemics and nuclear war'.[12] Come again? Extinction?! The biggest threat from tech used to be dropping your phone in liquid.

To summarize, developers who recklessly took the reins off risk are now warning that their horse has bolted, the stable door is flapping in the wind and the rest of us should, you know, probably do something about it. If only we could have seen it coming.

Perhaps the chief executives of Google's DeepMind, the ChatGPT developer OpenAI, the AI startup Anthropic and the hundreds of executives and academics who signed the 2023 statement, did see it coming but pursued their work nonetheless. Frontiers will always be explored. But along with their work in developing AI, there was nothing to stop these people simultaneously exploring their commitments to ethics, responsibility, copyright and a cautious approach to delivery.

In reality, of course they had no choice but to release their AI when they did. AI projects in development are many, varied and inevitable. They stem from the same competitive impulse to be first that has driven successful endeavours since the dawn of humanity. Progress in AI can no more be slowed than it can in anything else. Artificial intelligence is not a controllable, one-off novelty, the shiny brainchild of an intern in Silicon Valley. It's the next chapter in our history.

We could have done a better job in mitigating the risks, but we are human, and we have a tendency to react after the event. Meanwhile, throughout the second half of the 2020s, AI developers will be working on artificial general intelligence (AGI). More than a disembodied voice in a box that plays music at your request, AGI is the real deal, the stuff of Hal in *2001: A Space Odyssey* and Mother in *Alien*.

AGI promises a future where we may each have our own personally tailored AI assistant that's skilled and experienced in managing our online self. Manifesting itself through your phone, streaming devices, car, fridge, wardrobe, television, doctor and workplace, your HMLI (high-level machine intelligence) assistant will respond to your voice, know your online tastes and be trusted in all things from managing your finances to booking a holiday.

At work, in some respects AGI will exceed the capabilities of people, particularly in areas that rely on difficult judgements (metal fatigue in aircraft for example) or that rely on consistently accurate interpretations of complex regulation (such as tax laws across Europe). In fact, a defining feature of AGI is that it would be capable of surpassing our own intelligence.

The potential ability to perform jobs currently carried out by people is something that contributes to the fear and uncertainty surrounding AI. This has always been the way with tech. From the spinning jenny to chatbots, tech is consistent, flawless and never gets tired.

So, when can we expect fully developed AGI? Predictions vary between a few years and a century, if we achieve it at all. A detailed survey of industry experts estimated a 50 per cent chance of high-level machine intelligence arriving by 2060 and a 10 per cent chance by 2029.[13] The future isn't trapped in a galaxy far, far away, it's coming our way sooner than we might imagine.

For many people, the development of AI implies change, uncertainty and fear for the future. In the workplace, fear like this doesn't take the form of a sudden response – it's different to the feelings we have when facing a dangerous dog or a speeding driver. Instead, fear at work simmers underneath, unseen but shaping attitudes, steadily contributing to anxiety, fatigue and disengagement.

To manage these challenges, the lesson we've learned already from AI is that it's better to prepare in advance, before the full onslaught of change takes hold. Bearing this in mind, how should employers and employees prepare for the future?

Determining the impact of AI

In the past, new tech tended to affect routine tasks. AI has the potential to automate non-routine tasks that were once considered exclusive to humans. This exposes large swathes of the workforce to potential disruption.

For example, in healthcare AI can be used to automate the tasks of sorting through medical images to diagnose conditions. In manufacturing, AI can be used to automate the tasks of quality control and inspection. By automating these tasks, AI has the potential to free up workers' time so that they can focus on higher-level tasks. In addition, AI has the potential to improve the accuracy of these tasks, as well as to identify tasks that are most suitable for automation.

The jobs that AI can do also include writing books. The previous paragraph (…and only the previous paragraph!) was written by GPT-3, the AI engine from OpenAI. While we were enjoying a coffee with our feet up, it was responding to the prompt: 'write a paragraph describing how AI can benefit the workforce'.[14] It's bland but it does the job. Will it do yours?

In 2017, McKinsey found that between 400 million and 800 million individuals around the world could be displaced by automation by 2030 and would need to find new jobs.[15] In 2018, PwC's analysis of 200,000 jobs in 29 countries concluded that:

- 3 per cent of jobs are at potential risk of automation by the early 2020s
- 30 per cent of jobs are at potential risk of automation by the early 2030s
- 44 per cent of workers with low education are at risk of automation by mid-2030s[16]

In 2020, the World Economic Forum predicted that by 2025, for the first time, tasks will be equally split 50-50 between machines and humans.[17]

In 2023, Goldman Sachs reported that roughly two-thirds of all jobs in Europe and the US are exposed to some degree of AI automation. Globally, this would potentially mean that 300 million jobs could be scaled back or cut altogether as a result of AI. Roles in office admin, legal, architecture and engineering, business and financial operations, management, sales, healthcare and art and design were highlighted as being at particular risk.[18]

One widespread impact of AI will be less about particular sectors and more about its disproportionate effect on blue-collar workers across the economy. Already we've seen driverless vehicles, pay-kiosks in fast-food restaurants and DIY checkouts in shops.

In fact, sophisticated technologies have long been contributing to a divide in wealth and income equality. Declining wages among blue-collar workers since the 1980s can be explained by the rise in automation.[19] Numerically controlled machinery and industrial robots have replaced many jobs in manufacturing and clerical workers have been replaced by specialized software.

A silver lining in the 2023 Goldman Sachs report suggests that the loss of jobs to automation has historically been offset by the creation of new jobs. Though, how far this has benefitted blue-collar workers is unclear. AI may support employment growth in the long run, but this may largely benefit white-collar staff.

The World Economic Forum (WEF) believes that AI will create more jobs than it destroys. The WEF suggests that while an estimated 85 million jobs will be displaced across 26 countries by 2025, 97 million new jobs will be created.[20]

As well as boosting employment, AI may support other elements of the economy too. For Goldman Sachs, gains will come from the combination of higher productivity and savings in labour costs. PwC came to similar conclusions, predicting that AI will bring a potential boost of around $15.7 trillion to the global economy by 2030.[21]

The picture that is emerging is one of AI causing substantial change rather than widespread unemployment. This matches historical patterns. Researchers looking at how jobs have changed over the years reviewed new job titles listed in US census returns. They estimated that more than 60 per cent of US jobs listed in 2018 did not exist in 1940, among them fingernail technician, solar photovoltaic electrician and artificial intelligence specialist.[22]

Most of the reports we've just been considering were published *before* the arrival of AI chatbots in 2022/23. While these may bring a tsunami of change, individuals and organizations who learn to ride the crest of the wave will potentially thrive. What exactly will they need to learn?

New jobs will need new abilities, requiring significant investment in upskilling and reskilling. It's expected that the US labour market alone – at particular risk of disruption given the speed of automation – will be required to retrain an estimated 11.5 million people.[23] In Part 2, we'll look at the future skills they will benefit from if they are to gain the most from our changing relationship with tech.

The impact of tech on wellbeing

Understanding disruption

Our relationship with tech is complicated. The advantages of AI are undeniable. Furthering the interests of progress and efficiency are part of what it is to be human.

There's more to us than just efficiency. The creative, collaborative and kind ways of people come with a need to communicate, to reflect on the best course of action, to take scheduled screen breaks and to work free from needless causes of anxiety. AI doesn't need to pause. Does it know that we do?

Algorithms disrupt elements of what it is to be human. Tech interferes with our need for social interaction, our abilities to connect with people and our capacity for careful thought. Together, these factors have been undermining wellbeing since smartphones first enabled 24/7 availability, facilitating an environment that doesn't sleep – much like AI.

We, however, do sleep. It's not a weakness – it's simply how we are. The dichotomy between the way that AI works and the way that people do, must be understood and accepted by big tech and by businesses that buy its products. Riding roughshod over the realities of human nature will likely lead to further fatigue and disengagement.

In Chapter 2, we recognized two long-term causes of fatigue:

1 Doing more with less
Unrelenting demands at work, including longer hours and steeper targets, take an ever-deepening toll on people's physical and mental health.

2 Lack of workplace humanity
Tension arises when our social nature is dismissed by leaders who ignore fundamental rules governing how humans work.

Here in this chapter, we have identified two further causes of disengagement.

CAUSE 3: THE RISE OF TECH

Smartphones arrived in 2007, and since then we've never looked up. In the beginning, we imagined they were just fancier versions of the phones we were already using. Older models allowed us to readily reach people. Smartphones promised the same, with the added feature of hooking us up to the internet. Two separate tools, both fundamentally useful and available when we needed them.

But smartphones did something new, something that largely went unnoticed. They had the capacity to keep us hooked to the internet 24/7, where we could be reached first by emails and later by social media. We soon found that smartphones constantly nudged us, seeking our attention, feeding us likes and followers, pestering to be noticed. And deliberately so.

Smartphones and social media disrupted natural thought processes. They also opened us up to being permanently available to friends, acquaintances and our employer. Soon, our range of personal relationships with others began to merge together in a fog of 'other people' whom we could talk to or not, at will. Instead of participating in quality communication, we now needed to manage the quantity of messages – acknowledging some, ignoring others and shortening our responses to all.

At work, tech disrupts meaningful interaction, often replacing it with a functional, unfulfilling and isolating approach to communication. It facilitates flexibility, such as working from home and virtual calls, but this leads to faster working and fewer meaningful moments of connection.

Employees spend 250 per cent more time in meetings today compared with pre-pandemic days.[24] Yet our fast and functional approach to communication, through virtual calls and monosyllabic messaging, leads to isolating experiences. Through tech, we've never been more connected – and disconnected. Driving isolation and loneliness, tech contributes to individualism and the breakdown of company culture.

CAUSE 4: LACK OF EMPLOYEE AUTONOMY

The rise of workplace AI, if not carefully managed, can lead to an erosion of trust. Skills and experience used to form the basis of decisions and actions. Now, data analysis supplements basic human judgements, supporting people with essential tools and information that can make a difference between launching a new product this year or next.

However, when AI's inflexible analysis casts doubt on the work of employees, questions arise about the relationship between people and tech. In this complex partnership, which side is playing an automaton support role? Which side of the relationship is respected by leaders?

When AI systems erode trust in employees by monitoring keystrokes, assessing promotions, questioning performance and assigning disciplinary measures, people feel subservient to systems they cannot appeal to or negotiate with, and that are far from transparent. For example, AI-powered technologies are now used to analyse facial expressions, tone of voice and accents, to assess candidates' suitability for roles.[25]

AI has made room for itself in the workplace. People are no longer the only option, employees are less secure at work than they used to be. Once, they were in a 50-50 relationship with employers. Now, employees are in a three-way split. Many are less autonomous in their job than they used to be. Losing part of your autonomy at work is demotivating and erodes job fulfilment and satisfaction. This in turn contributes to fatigue and anxiety, undermining workplace wellbeing.

Deloitte found that switching tasks constantly, and not being able to make your own decisions about how you work, are 'the most detrimental aspects to wellbeing in terms of how work gets done'.[26] Lack of workplace autonomy disrupts the benefits of career experience, agile creativity and emotional intelligence – human abilities that businesses depend on and that AI cannot match.

Resetting our relationship with tech

Our current relationship with tech is destabilizing. What would Abraham Maslow have made of it? Living at a time when 'hi-tech' meant television, he might have been appalled to see how tech has disrupted our fundamental need to belong.

The tech that keeps us connected at work, wherever we're working, is valuable and necessary. But we must learn to build a better relationship with it rather than simply letting things develop in a piecemeal, unplanned approach.

Politicians can't afford to leave people behind, or allow them to feel excluded – for example, abandoning them in the wake of AI developments. In this regard, the US doesn't have a great track record. 'America's failure to pay serious attention to those left behind by technological change is arguably responsible for much of the public outrage on both right and left that erupted in the 2016 election', wrote Alice Rivlin, senior fellow at the Brookings Institution.[27]

Helping people adjust involves more than just training them in technical know-how. There is a need for a new appreciation of humanity's oldest abilities – in communication and creativity, leadership and emotional intelligence, abilities that used to be called 'soft skills'.

As is increasingly being recognized, these are the very skills that will be at the forefront of a hard-headed approach to a healthier relationship with tech, in which our innate human qualities are recognized, valued and prioritized. They will need to be. They are the skills that define who we are and will always keep us a step ahead of AI.

Training in emotional intelligence, critical thinking and in-person communication will help people restore the balance in fast and slow thinking, help them become better at decision making and objective analysis and help them to feel more present.

Above all, these human skills will help workers restore a meaningful sense of connection with each other, their managers and their company. Employees themselves recognize a need to learn new skills. A 2021 survey of 15,000 US adults found that more than half (57 per cent) were 'extremely' or 'very' interested in participating in an upskilling programme.[28]

Leaders can prepare for this shift in skills by investing in training and by developing a healthy company culture that focuses on a humancentric workplace. By protecting their people, any business's greatest asset, leaders will be laying the groundwork for the difficult years ahead. Now's the time to act. Beyond the strengthening grip of tech, other forms of change also threaten to entangle us, as we shall discover in our next chapter.

Notes

1   A Satariano and D Alba, Burning Cell Towers, Out of Baseless Fear They Spread the Virus, 4 October 2020, *New York Times*, www.nytimes.com/2020/04/10/technology/coronavirus-5g-uk.html (archived at https://perma.cc/SR7E-D73Z)

2   N Baker. UK mobile phone statistics 2024, 7 February 2024, uswitch.com, www.uswitch.com/mobiles/studies/mobile-statistics/ (archived at https://perma.cc/VWW4-J4N4)

3   Ofcom. Online Nation 2020 Report, 24 June 2020, www.ofcom.org.uk/__data/assets/pdf_file/0027/196407/online-nation-2020-report.pdf (archived at https://perma.cc/6TX7-M4W3)

4   Asurion. Americans Check Their Phones 96 Times a Day, 21 November 2019, www.asurion.com/about/press-releases/americans-check-their-phones-96-times-a-day/ (archived at https://perma.cc/FKF8-UVB6)

5   R F Baumeister and M R Leary (1995) The need to belong: Desire for interpersonal attachments as a fundamental human motivation, *Psychological Bulletin*, **117** (3), pp. 497–529

6   M Lieberman (2013) *Social: Why our brains are wired to connect*, Oxford University Press

7   S Krach et al (2010) The rewarding nature of social interactions, *Frontiers in Behavioural Neuroscience*, **4** (22)

8   RingCentral. From workplace to chaos to Zen: How app overload is reshaping the digital workplace, January 2018, netstorage.ringcentral.com/documents/connected_workplace.pdf (archived at https://perma.cc/2SXF-UXGT)

9   D Grossman. The Cost Of Poor Communications, 16 July 2011, PRovoke Media, www.provokemedia.com/latest/article/the-cost-of-poor-communications (archived at https://perma.cc/DY5P-K32R)

10 TUC. Intrusive worker surveillance tech risks "spiralling out of control" without stronger regulation, TUC warns, 28 February 2022, www.tuc.org.uk/news/intrusive-worker-surveillance-tech-risks-spiralling-out-control-without-stronger-regulation (archived at https://perma.cc/ZXZ5-QPZS)

11 C Skopeliti. 'I feel constantly watched': the employees working under surveillance, 30 May 2023, *The Guardian*, www.theguardian.com/money/2023/may/30/i-feel-constantly-watched-employees-working-under-surveillance-monitorig-software-productivity (archived at https://perma.cc/R8A8-VF7X)

12 Center for AI Safety. Statement on AI Risk, www.safe.ai/statement-on-ai-risk#open-letter (archived at https://perma.cc/FY6S-CH7N)

13 K Grace et al. 2022 Expert Survey on Progress in AI, 4 August 2022, AI Impacts, aiimpacts.org/2022-expert-survey-on-progress-in-ai/ (archived at https://perma.cc/AJE7-PERW)

14 WhiteHouse.gov. The Impact Of Artificial Intelligence On The Future Of Workforces In The European Union And The United States Of America, 12 May 2022, www.whitehouse.gov/wp-content/uploads/2022/12/TTC-EC-CEA-AI-Report-12052022-1.pdf (archived at https://perma.cc/6W98-SCTV)

15 J Manyika et al. Jobs lost, jobs gained: What the future of work will mean for jobs, skills, and wages, 28 November 2017, McKinsey Global Institute, www.mckinsey.com/featured-insights/future-of-work/jobs-lost-jobs-gained-what-the-future-of-work-will-mean-for-jobs-skills-and-wages (archived at https://perma.cc/CZ9Q-WPGX)

16 J Hawksworth, R Berriman and E Cameron. Will robots really steal our jobs? February 2018, PwC, www.pwc.co.uk/economic-services/assets/international-impact-of-automation-feb-2018.pdf (archived at https://perma.cc/2CN5-NFXG)

17 K Schwab et al. The Future of Jobs Report 2020, 20 October 2020, World Economic Forum, www.weforum.org/reports/the-future-of-jobs-report-2020 (archived at https://perma.cc/8VQS-ABQN)

18 J Hatzius et al. The Potentially Large Effects of Artificial Intelligence on Economic Growth, 26 March 2023, Key4Biz, www.key4biz.it/wp-content/uploads/2023/03/Global-Economics-Analyst_-The-Potentially-Large-Effects-of-Artificial-Intelligence-on-Economic-Growth-Briggs_Kodnani.pdf (archived at https://perma.cc/SXL9-926N)

19 D Acemoglu and P Restrepo. Tasks, Automation, and the Rise in US Wage Inequality, June 2021, National Bureau of Economic Research, www.nber.org/papers/w28920 (archived at https://perma.cc/7GWE-N8PE)

20 K Schwab et al. The Future of Jobs Report 2020, 20 October 2020, World Economic Forum, www.weforum.org/reports/the-future-of-jobs-report-2020 (archived at https://perma.cc/8VQS-ABQN)

21 A Rao et al. Sizing the prize – Global Artificial Intelligence Study: Exploiting the AI Revolution, 2017, PwC, www.pwc.com/gx/en/issues/data-and-analytics/publications/artificial-intelligence-study.html (archived at https://perma.cc/L2LB-HS55)

22 D Autor et al. New Frontiers: The Origins And Content Of New Work, 1940–2018, August 2022, National Bureau Economic Research, www.nber.org/system/files/working_papers/w30389/w30389.pdf (archived at https://perma.cc/WGU2-NEUN)

23 J Kelly. U.S. Lost Over 60 Million Jobs – Now Robots, Tech And Artificial Intelligence Will Take Millions More, 27 October 2020, *Forbes*, www.forbes.com/sites/jackkelly/2020/10/27/us-lost-over-60-million-jobs-now-robots-tech-and-artificial-intelligence-will-take-millions-more/?sh=412a3ec91a52 (archived at https://perma.cc/E4TX-CAZN)

24 D Thompson. This is what happens when there are too many meetings, 4 April 2022, *The Atlantic*, www.theatlantic.com/newsletters/archive/2022/04/triple-peak-day-work-from-home/629457/ (archived at https://perma.cc/5PX7-T3XD)

25 TUC. Intrusive worker surveillance tech risks 'spiralling out of control' without stronger regulation, TUC warns, 28 February 2022, www.tuc.org.uk/news/intrusive-worker-surveillance-tech-risks-spiralling-out-control-without-stronger-regulation (archived at https://perma.cc/ZXZ5-QPZS)

26 J Bhatt, C Bordeaux and J Fisher. The workforce well-being imperative, 13 March 2023, Deloitte Insights, www2.deloitte.com/uk/en/insights/topics/talent/employee-wellbeing.html (archived at https://perma.cc/FGR8-GRWU)

27 R Wartzman. The First Time America Freaked Out Over Automation, 30 May 2017, *Politico Magazine*, www.politico.com/magazine/story/2017/05/30/rick-wartzman-book-excerpt-automation-donald-trump-215207/ (archived at https://perma.cc/R3T3-HRG2)

28 J Rothwell. The American Upskilling Study shows workers want skills training, 9 September 2021, About Amazon, www.aboutamazon.com/news/workplace/the-american-upskilling-study-shows-workers-want-skills-training (archived at https://perma.cc/BEC7-458V)

4

The impact of global threats

In February 2024, a branch of UK retailer Sainsbury's displayed the following notice: 'We are experiencing supply issues affecting the nationwide supply of black tea. We apologise for any inconvenience and hope to be back in full supply soon.'[1]

At the same time, Tetley Tea, the UK's second biggest tea brand, said supplies were 'much tighter' than it would like.[2] Meanwhile market leader Yorkshire Tea confirmed it was 'monitoring the situation closely'.[3]

In the UK, 100 million cups of tea are drunk daily.[4] Britain and tea go hand in hand like strawberries and cream or leather on willow. Disruption to sales was bound to raise an eyebrow, though the famous British stiff upper lip would surely prevail.

'Oh my God, life is over,' wailed one social media user. 'What are we going to do?' cried a second.[5] Similar sentiments had rung out in the spring of 2020 when Covid first held the nation in its grip. Shoppers reacted by panic-buying toilet paper in preparation for an illness that conspicuously had nothing to do with sudden dashes to the bathroom. The less than edifying lunge for loo-roll represented an attempt to reclaim control over a fearful future.

In the past, rather than a rush to wipe our sorrows away, in the UK we used to face down turmoil with a fortifying blast of Blitz spirit. Now, we worry about loo-breaks and tea supplies. This softening in attitudes came with the gradual shift from wartime hardships towards plentiful supply and an easier way of life.

Today, our lifestyle is facilitated by complex international supply chains that enable continuous just-in-time distribution and reduced storage costs and capacity. Producers, processors, auctions, wholesalers, packers, distributors and retailers operate in a global network that allows the ready supply of products to be taken for granted on the basis that the system runs like clockwork.

When things go wrong, however, our reduced capacity for storage quickly leads to knock-on effects, especially in retail. For example, in the first two months of 2024, shipping through the Suez Canal dropped by 50 per cent from a year earlier amid geopolitical tension in the Red Sea – gateway to the Suez Canal which is the shortest maritime route between Asia and Europe.[6]

Major shipping companies diverted around the southern tip of Africa, a journey that can take up to three weeks longer, adding to insurance bills, raising costs and leading to delays in supplies of, among other things, tea.[7]

In a survey of companies by the British Chambers of Commerce, more than a third said they had been affected. That figure rose to more than half among exporters.[8] At the same time, on the other side of the world, a severe drought at the Panama Canal led to tight restrictions, substantially reducing the number of daily journeys between the Pacific and Atlantic oceans.

The steady supply of imports and exports relies on a stable geopolitical environment. The more finely interwoven distribution networks become, the more vulnerable they are to the global shocks that in recent years have become increasingly common. The tension in the Red Sea was the latest in a sequence of events that include the 2011 tsunami off the coast of Japan, Brexit, the pandemic, post-pandemic supply shortages, US trade sanctions on China and the war in Ukraine.

Developing organizational resilience

In the 2020s, businesses find themselves at the centre of a maelstrom whipped up by a multitude of stormy forces. Given the complexity of international logistics, instability in one part of the world can soon disrupt supermarkets in another. Consumers across Europe – even in post-Brexit Britain – cannot escape the fact that nations and industries are tightly bound together. Wellbeing and resilience aren't just matters for individuals.

The business case for wellbeing

We've seen the case for effective wellbeing from the perspective of employees. Having identified (in Chapters 2 and 3) four key issues that contribute to disengagement, it's clear that people are struggling.

According to global analysis by Gallup, in 2022 59 per cent of people were not engaged at work, while a further 18 per cent were actively disengaged.[9] Only 23 per cent reported feeling engaged – a rate only slightly higher than the previous year (21 per cent) when the world was engulfed by Covid.[10] In 2023, these figures remained roughly similar.[11]

Disengagement at this level is not just an HR issue. Employees who are not engaged cost the world $8.9 trillion in lost productivity, equal to 9 per cent of global GDP a year.[12] Meanwhile, organizations with engaged workers report 23 per cent higher profit. This is significant at a time when margins are vulnerable to international instability.[13]

Businesses are struggling with disengagement and disruption. While the former is within their control, the latter is not. To develop the organizational resilience that survives disruption, it's important to safeguard assets that are within leaders' control, beginning with protecting an experienced and engaged workforce.

In other words, in the turmoil of the 2020s, business wellbeing and resilience begins with healthy, productive people. This means protecting them from the primary causes of disengagement. Doing so will also address secondary factors, like loneliness, that contribute to anxiety, fatigue and burnout.

The $154 billion epidemic that's not Covid

Paradoxically, in the 21st century, despite our better digital connections millions of people feel isolated. Twenty per cent of the world's employees experience daily loneliness.[14]

Loneliness is a silent epidemic, costing US employers more than $154 billion per year in stress-related absenteeism.[15] In the UK, a conservative estimate suggests that more than a million workers experience loneliness, leading to a cost estimated at £2.5 billion per year.[16] This is primarily owing to:

- **poor health** of employees and associated sickness absence
- **loneliness** affecting the health of people who are cared for by friends or relatives in work
- **lower productivity** related to poor wellbeing
- **increased staff turnover** reflecting underlying tensions

Research by health insurance multinational Cigna found that 62 per cent of US workers could be regarded as lonely – that's 97 million people.[17] That's a huge number; let's just take that in for a second. Cigna's findings, based on a survey of nearly 6,000 US employees, found that lonely workers demonstrate higher rates of stress-related absenteeism, missing more than five additional work days per year than those who did not identify as lonely.

That was before the pandemic. Covid condemned millions to long periods of isolation, leading to disturbing consequences. In the 12 months to June 2021, 47 per cent of Americans lost touch with friends. By that point, nearly half of Americans (49 per cent) reported having three or fewer close friends, nearly a twofold increase on the percentage noted in 1990.[18]

Workplace loneliness can stem from poor communication, low morale, failure to connect with colleagues, insufficient team cohesion, lack of work–life balance, a new job or a change in circumstances. While it can affect people in different ways, typically employees don't reveal their loneliness or its impact on their physical and mental well-being.

A fundamental part of wellbeing includes feeling part of the team. In the workplace, people value the trust, respect and psychological safety that together lead to a secure sense of belonging. Without this, they are vulnerable to loneliness. Consequently, people value employers who encourage cohesion by:

- offering fair recognition and reward
- supporting professional development
- advocating sustainable work practices

In short, by encouraging the belonging and cohesion that support wellbeing, employers are better able to protect their workforce and thereby strengthen their organization's resilience. As a practical example of this, training opportunities help people feel that they belong to an organization that supports their professional development.

In the 2020s, businesses have been tested far more than long-term projections had anticipated. By building motivation and engagement, progressive companies are better able to rely on their people the next time international markets are shaken by unexpected disruption.

Ignoring the need for resilience is risky. Future challenges threaten to change not only the way we work, but even the way we live. In particular, the climate emergency is likely to destabilize the wellbeing of organizations and their people.

Code-red for humanity

Earth has been warm – in other words ice-free everywhere – for about 85 per cent of its history. The other 15 per cent was dominated by five major ice ages, with cool or cold phases that came and went over time. In fact, with ice still at both poles today we're technically in an ice age right now.

The fact that the Earth is getting warmer only partly explains the widespread concern among scientists. More worrying is the fact that never before has the climate changed so rapidly. This is down to the actions of people, in the past and today, the consequences of which will touch us all in one way or another.

Most of what the UN knows about the climate emergency comes from the IPCC, its panel of 270 experts.[19] Results published by the IPCC in 2021 were summarized by the Yale School of the Environment as predicting 'a hellish northern summer laced with deadly heat waves, perilous floods and massive wildfires'.[20] Dr Friederike Otto, one of the authors of the IPCC report, said: 'We will also see an increase in heavy rainfall events on a global scale, and increases in some types of droughts.'[21]

The report was described in the press as the 'starkest warning yet' of 'major inevitable and irreversible climate changes'.[22] Subsequent updates didn't make easier reading. IPCC analysis published in February 2022 found that the impact to China will be particularly damaging, including food insecurity, water scarcity and flooding especially in coastal areas – where most of the population lives – due to rising sea levels.[23] Overall, the IPCC's 2022 update identified 127 threats associated with climate change worldwide, some of them irreversible.[24]

Damage to food-producing regions, homelessness and migration, decreasing availability of natural resources, interruptions in the supply of international commodities and economic turmoil including inflation will come together in a perfect storm. For clues on how the knock-on effects will touch organizations downstream, we can look at the Colorado and Rio Grande river systems, the most controlled and litigated in the world.[25]

The two river systems supply many US states, among them Nevada, Arizona and California. Amid bitter arguments about who gets how much water in these regions, the climate crisis has left America's two biggest reservoirs dangerously depleted, threatening 15 per cent of the country's farmland and compromising supplies for 40 million people in cities from Denver to Los Angeles.[26]

How will climate change affect organizations in these states? Many in America's West are already finding out; for example, insecurity in sectors such as farming undermines jobs. Many people will leave these states and head elsewhere. Imagine what it's going to be like when these problems are played out on a global scale. The mass movement of people – nationally and internationally – will place greater strain on local resources, which in turn may provoke greater risk of conflict.

This then is a ripple effect that organizations will struggle to avoid. Commenting on the impact of the climate emergency, UN Secretary-General António Guterres warned that the IPCC's 2021 report should be taken as a 'code-red for humanity'.[27] The global rise in temperatures will affect lives, homes and food supplies in a way that will make recent supermarket shortages seem like a storm in a teacup.

Managing the impact of climate change

Not surprisingly, the expected consequences of the climate emergency resonate most with those who will inherit them. A survey by the Pew Research Center found that Generation Z and millennials – i.e. current graduates and analysts – are talking more than older adults about the need for action on climate change.[28]

They notice climate change content online more than older generations and they are doing more to get involved through volunteering and attending protests.[29] Young people are particularly likely to express anxiety about the future. The Pew survey found that:

- among social media users, nearly 69 per cent of Generation Z said they felt anxious about the future when they last saw content on climate change
- 59 per cent of millennial social media users felt anxious the last time they saw climate change content
- fewer than half of Generation X (46 per cent) and older (41 per cent) social media users said the same

In a 2021 survey, the largest of its kind, researchers spoke to 10,000 young people in 10 countries, 60 per cent of whom were very or extremely worried about government responses to the crisis.[30] On being asked to describe their emotions on climate change, they replied:

- sad   68%
- afraid   68%
- anxious   63%
- angry   58%
- powerless   57%
- guilty   51%
- optimistic   32%
- indifferent   30%

Imperial College London similarly found that young people were concerned about the consequences for their future. While many associated the pandemic with feelings of isolation, loss and grief, they associated climate change with anger, disgust, guilt and shame.[31]

How will leaders manage the impact of the climate emergency on their business and their people?

There are two parts to this. Firstly, this is a question that comes back to resilience and the ability to rely on an engaged workforce who are committed to their employer.

This in turn requires leaders to recognize people's need for job satisfaction including a sense of fulfilment and belonging. Professional development opportunities, flexible working and a healthy approach to AI demonstrate awareness of the personal values that have changed the landscape since Covid, as we noted in Chapter 2 when we looked at the Great Resignation.

Secondly, personal values reflect more than a person's job. People are conscious of the need to conserve energy, water and natural resources. Employers who are slow to prioritize environmental concerns might struggle to recruit the skilled people they'll rely on when climate change batters markets, disrupts supply chains and weakens infrastructure.

Individuals expect their employer to be aware of environmental issues. For leaders, this means being sincerely committed to working for a greener future. Opportunity awaits organizations with in-depth resilience, an appetite for growth and long-term environmental values.

Meeting ESG requirements

Tightening the rules on disclosure

Responding to the pace of change in the 2020s, organizations – like their people – may choose to embrace new self-awareness. In practical terms, this could mean expanding their commitments to corporate social responsibility (CSR). Introduced in the 1970s and gaining widespread prominence by the early 2000s, CSR includes business support for local people, teams and projects.

More recently, CSR has shifted towards environmental, social and governance (ESG) strategies. Introducing measuring and transparency, ESG objectives hold companies to account over their sustainability claims, and help stakeholders (among them shareholders) evaluate performance. ESG has become an increasingly important reflection of a company's values, goals, leadership and reputation.[32]

Historically, ESG issues in the US were subject to no more than voluntary disclosures. However, following an order from President Biden in 2021, the Securities and Exchange Commission (SEC) created an ESG task force to encourage disclosures on issues such as energy consumption and employee turnover. The initial focus of the task force is to identify material gaps or misstatements in companies' disclosure of climate risks.[33]

In 2022, the task force announced several enforcement actions relating to disclosures on ESG matters. In May 2023, Vale S.A., one of the world's largest iron ore producers, agreed a $56 million settlement after being charged by the SEC in relation to claims about the safety of its dams prior to the collapse of its Brumadinho dam in Brazil in January 2019.[34]

In Europe too, ESG governance has been tightened up in the mid-2020s. Companies are expected to comply with the European Union's ESG rules such as the Corporate Sustainability Reporting Directive (CSRD) and the Sustainable Finance Disclosure Regulation (SFDR). These are aligned with the UN's sustainable development goals on issues such as gender equality and climate action.[35]

By 2026, under the CSRD, any company operating in the EU and meeting two of the three following criteria will be required to track and collect ESG data:[36]

- 250 employees
- €50 million in revenues
- €25 million in balance sheet

Under the CSRD, ESG data covers issues such as carbon emissions, waste management, diversity and inclusion, employee rights and governance factors, and will be overseen by the International Sustainability Standards Board and frameworks like the Global Reporting Initiative.

The SFDR requires companies in financial markets to disclose information about the ESG risks and opportunities of their investment products. Overseen by the European Commission and enforced by national regulatory authorities in EU member states, the SFDR is an attempt to reduce greenwashing.

According to the UN, 'greenwashing manifests itself in several ways – some more obvious than others. Tactics include:

- **Claiming to be on track** to reduce a company's polluting emissions to net zero when no credible plan is actually in place.
- **Being purposely vague** or non-specific about a company's operations or materials used.

- **Applying intentionally misleading labels** such as 'green' or 'eco-friendly,' which do not have standard definitions and can be easily misinterpreted.

- **Implying that a minor improvement has a major impact** or promoting a product that meets the minimum regulatory requirements as if it is significantly better than the standard.

- **Emphasizing a single environmental attribute** while ignoring other impacts.

- **Claiming to avoid illegal or non-standard practices** that are irrelevant to a product.

- **Communicating the sustainability attributes of a product in isolation of brand activities** (and vice versa) – e.g. a garment made from recycled materials that is produced in a high-emitting factory that pollutes the air and nearby waterways.[37]

In the UK, ESG requirements are regulated by the Financial Conduct Authority (FCA). It's been suggested that UK companies are taking a more proactive approach on ESG than US organizations, though this may simply reflect the differing regulatory regimes.[38] In 2023, in an open letter to CEOs, the FCA warned it might take enforcement action over issues including:

- ESG benchmark administrators not fully implementing disclosure requirements

- administrators not implementing their ESG methodologies correctly (for instance using outdated data and ratings, or failing to apply ESG exclusion criteria)

- not ensuring underlying methodologies are accessible, clearly presented and explained to users

- not including enough detail on the ESG factors within these methodologies[39]

Unlike ESG, CSR specifically includes a reference to corporate responsibility, as demonstrated by multinationals on many occasions. In the 1990s, a Swedish TV documentary highlighted child labour in Pakistan's rug industry, where thousands of children were engaged in hazardous work.[40] Many of the rugs were supplied to IKEA, at the time the world's largest furniture retailer.

Contracts in Pakistan were reviewed and IKEA managers paid closer attention to rug production in Nepal, Bangladesh and India. Area manager Marianne Barner went on surprise raids at rug factories, and later recalled: 'We saw child labour with our own eyes and were sometimes literally thrown out.'[41]

Realizing there was an opportunity to influence and help change things, IKEA met charity Save the Children and UN bodies like UNICEF. Developing codes of conduct to tackle child labour and debt slavery, since 2001 IKEA has donated millions of dollars to projects that support healthier environments for children.[42]

Other leading multinationals have similarly been involved in campaigns for social change. In 2018, a 19-year-old killed 17 students and staff at a high school in Parkland, Florida, the deadliest mass shooting at a high school in the US. Soon after, Citigroup published an article that began: 'For too many years, in too many places, our country has seen acts of gun violence.'[43]

The article went on to say: 'We have waited to see our...nation adopt common-sense measures that would help prevent firearms from getting into the wrong hands. That action has sadly never come.'[44] Announcing the bank's own US firearms policy, the blog explained that new retail clients would need to commit to 'best practices' when selling guns or ammunition.

Citi's bold decision was not taken lightly, nor in isolation. The article added: 'We would like to convene those in the financial services industry and other stakeholders to tackle these challenges together.' Common-sense measures can bring businesses together, taking a lead when politicians fall short.

The coming together of businesses in support of a common cause is advocated by Chief Executives for Corporate Purpose (CECP), a coalition of CEOs that helps many of the world's biggest companies support communities on social and political issues. 'Companies realize that to increase profits over time, they need to be good citizens of the world,' according to CECP CEO Daryl Brewster.[45]

The idea of companies acting as 'citizens of the world' isn't just a dream for the future. ESG commitments are already nudging organizations in this direction. A Thomson Reuters poll on risk and compliance found 'ESG compliance has become so in-grained into the fabric of corporate governance that two-thirds of survey respondents agreed that their organization has a duty to both stakeholders and society to address ESG-related issues'.[46]

Organizations as global citizens

Taking a lead on social challenges

Old-school, profits-focused capitalism is losing ground with consumers and customers. The 2024 Edelman Trust Barometer, a survey of 32,000 people in 28 countries, found that 57 per cent believe that 'capitalism as it exists today does more harm than good in the world', a figure 17 percentage points up on 2023.[47]

Kantar, a global analytics company, found that '80 per cent of global consumers like it when companies make it clear what they stand for and stay true to their values'.[48] Kantar also found that 64 per cent of global consumers say it is business's responsibility to solve climate and environmental issues.[49]

Generation Z in particular want brands to take a lead on social challenges and demonstrate a commitment to community issues. A 2023 survey of 2,000 US consumers found that 88 per cent of Generation Z 'agree that companies have a role to play in addressing the major challenges facing society'.[50] A 2024 survey of 2,000 UK consumers found that 75 per cent of Generation Z are more likely to buy from brands that give a portion of their sales to charity.[51]

In a new approach to capitalism, companies acting as 'citizens of the world' may work more closely together on advocating change in areas where there is a deficit of political leadership. A good example of this came after the US Supreme Court's 2022 decision to overturn the landmark 1973 Roe v. Wade ruling giving women the constitutional right to abortion. The decision meant individual states could ban the procedure.

In response, Amazon said it would pay up to $4,000 in travel expenses each year for treatment that wasn't available nearby. Disney, JP Morgan, Meta, Microsoft, Starbucks and review website Yelp said they too would cover travel expenses for abortions, as did six other major companies.[52]

'Business leaders must speak out,' Yelp chief executive Jeremy Stoppelman said on Twitter.[53] Yelp's chief diversity officer Miriam Warren explained: 'We recognize that our employees, our consumers and our customers were looking for us to be vocal on this issue.'[54]

People want organizations to speak out on issues that are important to them, and few are more important than the climate emergency. However, in many countries politicians have treated the issue like a bar of soap, flipping it back and forth and frequently dropping it while washing their hands of meaningful responsibility.

Given that complex trade networks connect cities, countries and companies around the world, the impact of national energy policies, water management and food strategies is not restricted to any one country in isolation. Ignoring this will lead to multipolar traps – where each nation acts in its best short-term interests, leading to collective behaviour that is in everyone's worst interests in the long-term, thereby deepening the worst effects of climate change.

Young people in particular want a more meaningful response to the climate emergency. An organization's younger rising stars and graduate trainees expect their employer to recognize that international challenges touch us all and that solutions require transnational communication that rises above national interests.

Operating around the world, multinationals can play a leading role in building collective strategies that offer escape from multipolar traps. Working together as global citizens, organizations can encourage progressive thinking on climate change, just as they can help to defend markets; promote education, communication and democratic values; and lead on labour reform and support communities.

Long-term corporate social responsibility at this level goes beyond short-term focus on keeping shareholders happy. CSR's long-term dividends include deep-seated organizational resilience that comes from investing in people. Businesses committed to external communities are more likely to support their own people internally. This in turn strengthens the core components of business resilience including belonging, engagement and retention. There is however one caveat to this way of working.

The authenticity caveat

People generally and Generation Z in particular can smell inauthenticity a mile away. Already, we've seen evidence of this in our assessment of ineffective corporate wellbeing strategies. Companies that ask people to do more with less, in a workplace with less humanity than is healthy, while favouring tech over employees and eroding autonomy, struggle to attract people to corporate wellbeing offerings.

Wellbeing perks that are demonstrably unconnected to the reasons why people need help with wellbeing in the first place are a false economy. Employees readily see how ineffective they are, which is why so few sign up to them. Expecting people to regularly work beyond their hours, and then trying to placate them with fresh coffee and a yoga mat, feels disingenuous and inauthentic.

Similarly, diversity and inclusion (D&I) strategies that try to get by with an hour of unconscious bias training feel like box ticking. Half-hearted strategies in wellbeing or D&I aren't very convincing or therefore effective.

The same can be said for disingenuous stabs at CSR, for example fast fashion brands that claimed to champion women's rights – while relying on female exploitation in manufacturing.[55] 'Woke-washing' becomes counter-productive the moment it's picked up on social media.

Social enterprise, where multinationals take on a role as global citizens, only works when their message carries the support of employees and consumers. However, once the message becomes lost in an ethereal fog of fallacies and falsehoods, support drifts like smoke in the wind.

Companies that want to be seen to be doing the right thing have two choices: actually doing the right thing, or just pretending to, which is a thought that leads us to a wide selection of oil and gas companies.

'The godfathers of climate chaos'

In 2024, campaign group Oil Change International (OCI) examined the climate pledges of eight major energy giants. OCI assessed these promises against 10 criteria representing the minimum action needed to meet the objectives of the 2015 Paris Agreement, which sought to limit global heating to less than a 1.5°C rise above pre-industrial times.[56]

In response to the Paris Agreement, energy companies drafted a range of carefully-worded proposals about reducing production levels by 2030 (net reductions rather than absolute), taking action on 'climate-related risk' (referencing risk rather than reality), transitioning to 'nature-based solutions' (which could simply mean switching from oil to gas), and stopping exploration (in new countries where an operator wasn't already exploring).

Of the eight companies investigated by OCI, three (Chevron, ConocoPhillips and ExxonMobil) were found to be 'grossly insufficient' – OCI's lowest rating – on all 10 criteria. All eight companies were 'grossly insufficient' or 'insufficient' on a majority of criteria.[57]

Words are always disingenuous when divorced from sentiment. An oil giant might talk about reductions but this won't stop questions about where their true interests lie. In truth, the current oil and gas extraction plans of these eight companies are consistent with more than 2.4°C of global temperature rise, 'likely leading to global devastation', according to OCI. The campaign group found that, promises aside, 'there is evidence that [energy] companies are greenwashing, lobbying against climate action and otherwise manoeuvring to undermine the energy transition'.[58]

While OCI fears 'global devastation', perhaps more measured voices take a different view; the United Nations, for example. 'The godfathers of climate chaos – the fossil-fuel industry – rake in record profits and feast off trillions in taxpayer-funded subsidies,' UN secretary-general António Guterres said in 2024.

Warning that new data from the World Meteorological Organization shows there is an 80 per cent chance the planet will breach the 1.5°C limit in at least one of the years between 2025 and 2030, Guterres urged, 'every country to ban advertising from fossil-fuel companies. And I urge news media and tech companies to stop taking fossil-fuel advertising.'[59]

While there is a gulf between what the energy companies are saying and doing, there is nothing naïve about their actions. It is questionable whether they sincerely believe in their promises, or that they even expect others to. In today's climate of optics and reputations, they have to be seen to be saying something. Fossil fuel companies are good at smokescreens.

But that won't wash with younger generations' compulsive demand for authenticity. Authenticity is associated with a sense of honesty that you expect of yourself and of others. It therefore encompasses empathy, along with attempts to define and support the 'greater good'. Fundamentally it's about being grounded in reality. And there's the rub. The blend of empathy and reality leads to a simple conclusion: there's no point indulging in delusion – greenwashing, for example – because others will always see your dishonesty.

Authenticity penetrates the deluded claims of narcissists and bullies, cheats and conspiracy theorists, and disingenuous organizations. It supports diversity and opportunity. It offers freedom from inauthentic falsehoods, and opens the door to ambition and the freedom to be who you are. No surprise that younger generations are committed to it and demand the same from brands that market to them.

The *Gen Z Insights Report* from consultants EY found that authenticity ranks as Gen Z's most important value, with 92 per cent saying that being true to oneself was very or extremely important. This ranked ahead of being independent, changing the world and being rich or famous. EY found that Generation Z feel 'it is difficult to accomplish anything else if not first true to themselves'.[60]

With the passage of time, societies evolve towards something more than they were before. Authenticity is part of the mix of values – along with empathy, psychological safety, belonging and others – that differentiate work in the 2020s from how things were in the not too distant past.

Multinationals with international reach, a need for long-term resilience, and an interest in safeguarding their future have an opportunity to operate as global citizens and take a lead in the shape of things to come. Daryl Brewster, CEO of Chief Executives for Corporate Purpose, expects companies to speak out more on social and political issues. He believes: 'Business has an opportunity, if not to find common ground, but to find a higher ground that society can move towards.'[61]

Developing resilience through skills

From 2020 to 2024, the resilience of businesses worldwide was tested by a multitude of successive challenges. When Covid receded in 2021, demand bounced back like a jack-in-the-box, leading to supply chain delays as global as the illness that triggered them. In 2022, the IPCC released its update on climate change. In that week, Russia invaded Ukraine, sparking an economic reaction that touched the lives of people across Europe.

In the recent past, the populations of Europe or America might have found it hard to feel the impact of conflict, for example in Iraq or Afghanistan. But Russia's assault led to a spike in prices, particularly in energy and food, that contributed to an international cost of living crisis.

Organizations have had to respond to these challenges, taking into account the needs of their people, their clients and their shareholders, though not always in that order. Financial instability, new work patterns, adjusting to AI and new ethical values haven't always come easy. In the midst of everything else, businesses have also needed to become more mindful of gender issues, down to rethinking who uses which toilet.

In developing organizational resilience ahead of an uncertain future, businesses can begin by investing in skills. Some leaders may consider this a risky business. In discussing skills with a senior City banker, we talked about the value of training his graduates. 'Why would I be interested in that?', he asked blandly. 'Once I've trained them, they might quit!'

People might well quit, but let's put that into context: not training them is hardly an inducement to stay. Long-term investment in training contributes to trust and belonging, and ensures that an organization is ready to meet the future challenges that are heading their way. To prepare for these, which skills and training should organizations invest in? What form of wellbeing will be effective in supporting organizational resilience?

By taking a lead in questions such as these, organizations can better support their people and the communities they serve. In our next chapter, we'll discover some of the answers they'll rely on.

Notes

1 S Marsh. UK shoppers could face tea shortages due to trade route disruptions, 12 February 2024, *The Guardian*, www.theguardian.com/business/2024/feb/12/uk-shoppers-could-face-tea-shortages-due-to-trade-route-disruptions (archived at https://perma.cc/M9C2-T3K4). For photo of Sainsbury's sign, see J Dempsey. Tetley monitoring its supplies on a daily basis, 13 February 2024, BBC News, www.bbc.co.uk/news/business-68284391 (archived at https://perma.cc/W7CA-S9Q2)

2 J Dempsey. Tetley monitoring its supplies on a daily basis, 13 February 2024, BBC News, www.bbc.co.uk/news/business-68284391 (archived at https://perma.cc/T43V-D3N7)

3 J Dempsey. Tetley monitoring its supplies on a daily basis, 13 February 2024, BBC News, www.bbc.co.uk/news/business-68284391 (archived at https://perma.cc/RJL3-8HXZ)

4 J Dempsey. Tetley monitoring its supplies on a daily basis, 13 February 2024, BBC News, www.bbc.co.uk/news/business-68284391 (archived at https://perma.cc/8NET-YD6W)

5 O Marshall. 'Keep calm' scream shoppers as major supermarket warns of tea shortage, 13 February 2024, *The Sun*, www.thesun.co.uk/money/25899381/supermarket-warns-tea-shortage-sainsburys-red-sea/ (archived at https://perma.cc/34PA-CA2J)

6 P Kamali. Red Sea attacks disrupt global trade, 7 March 2024, International Monetary Fund, www.imf.org/en/Blogs/Articles/2024/03/07/Red-Sea-Attacks-Disrupt-Global-Trade (archived at https://perma.cc/5XRW-TRE8)

7 J Kalra. Houthi missile attacks threaten UK's tea supply, 3 March 2024, The Maritime Executive, maritime-executive.com/editorials/houthi-missile-attacks-threaten-uk-s-tea-supply (archived at https://perma.cc/RH3T-5BLR)

8 L Hooker. Red Sea attacks delaying goods and pushing up costs, firms say, 26 February 2024, BBC News, www.bbc.co.uk/news/business-68398413 (archived at https://perma.cc/QTQ2-37NV)

9 J Clifton et al. Gallup State of the Global Workplace: 2023 Report, 2023

10 J Clifton et al. Gallup State of the Global Workplace: 2023 Report, 2023

11 J Clifton et al. Gallup State of the Global Workplace: 2024 Report, 2024, www.gallup.com/workplace/349484/state-of-the-global-workplace.aspx (archived at https://perma.cc/Q4WM-53CZ)

12 J Clifton et al. Gallup State of the Global Workplace: 2024 Report, 2024, www.gallup.com/workplace/349484/state-of-the-global-workplace.aspx (archived at https://perma.cc/Q4WM-53CZ)

13 R Pendell. Employee engagement strategies: fixing the world's $8.8 trillion problem, 14 June 2022, Gallup, www.gallup.com/workplace/393497/world-trillion-workplace-problem.aspx (archived at https://perma.cc/K68U-H2J4)

14 J Clifton et al. Gallup State of the Global Workplace: 2024 Report, 2024, www.gallup.com/workplace/349484/state-of-the-global-workplace.aspx (archived at https://perma.cc/3XMB-XW4G)

15 Cigna Healthcare. The Business Case for Addressing Loneliness in the Workforce, newsroom.cigna.com/business-case-addressing-loneliness-workforce (archived at https://perma.cc/K7G9-D2RU)

16 J Michaelson, K Jeffrey and S Abdallah. The Cost of Loneliness to UK Employers: The impact of loneliness upon business across the UK, 20 February 2017, New Economics Foundation, neweconomics.org/2017/02/cost-loneliness-uk-employers (archived at https://perma.cc/BHX7-JJPM)

17 Cigna Healthcare. The Business Case for Addressing Loneliness in the Workforce, newsroom.cigna.com/business-case-addressing-loneliness-workforce (archived at https://perma.cc/Q3J4-6ZVP)

18 D A Cox. The State of American Friendship: Change, Challenges, and Loss, 8 June 2021, Survey Center on American Life, www.americansurveycenter.org/research/the-state-of-american-friendship-change-challenges-and-loss/ (archived at https://perma.cc/84ZQ-UEYG)

19 IPCC. Sixth Assessment Report, contributions from working groups I, II, and III, 20 March 2023, www.ipcc.ch/assessment-report/ar6/ (archived at https://perma.cc/2FSL-EJYE)

20 B Henson. Key takeaways from the new IPCC report, 9 August 2021, Yale Climate Connections, yaleclimateconnections.org/2021/08/key-takeaways-from-the-new-ipcc-report/ (archived at https://perma.cc/KWE7-4B6A)

21 M McGrath. Climate change: IPCC report is 'code red for humanity', 9 August 2021, BBC News, www.bbc.co.uk/news/science-environment-58130705 (archived at https://perma.cc/F6LB-SU6U)

22 F Harvey. Major climate changes inevitable and irreversible – IPCC's starkest warning yet, 9 August 2021, *The Guardian*, www.theguardian.com/science/2021/aug/09/humans-have-caused-unprecedented-and-irreversible-change-to-climate-scientists-warn (archived at https://perma.cc/9ZEM-AJGG)

23 Y Yuan. IPCC Warns China Will Be Hit Hard by Climate Change, 3 March 2022, Sixth Tone, www.sixthtone.com/news/1009809/ipcc-warns-china-will-be-hit-hard-by-climate-change (archived at https://perma.cc/JT7R-LVBP)

24 S Borenstein. UN climate report: 'Atlas of human suffering' worse, bigger, 28 February 2022, AP News, apnews.com/article/climate-science-europe-united-nations-weather-8d5e277660f7125ffdab7a833d9856a3 (archived at https://perma.cc/6BRQ-TJS6)

25 J Entsminger. The Colorado River: Sharing a Limited Resource, 9 September 2019, Southern Nevada Water Authority, watercenter.colostate.edu/wp-content/uploads/sites/91/gravity_forms/49-0fc76052b462c95d8ea8f54af155fa27/2019/10/09-09-19-CSU-Presentation-JJE_v2.pdf (archived at https://perma.cc/7SZW-7GLE)

26 Ceres. Feeding Ourselves Thirsty, 2021, feedingourselvesthirsty.ceres.org/ regional-analysis/colorado-river (archived at https://perma.cc/RB7G-93SU)

27 A Guterres. Secretary-General's statement on the IPCC Working Group 1 Report on the Physical Science Basis of the Sixth Assessment, 9 August 2021, United Nations, www.un.org/sg/en/content/secretary-generals-statement- the-ipcc-working-group-1-report-the-physical-science-basis-of-the-sixth- assessment (archived at https://perma.cc/LL4D-NMFG)

28 A Tyson et al. Gen Z, Millennials Stand Out for Climate Change Activism, Social Media Engagement With Issue, 26 May 2021, Pew Research Center, www.pewresearch.org/science/2021/05/26/gen-z-millennials-stand-out-for- climate-change-activism-social-media-engagement-with-issue/ (archived at https://perma.cc/SMU9-KVSY)

29 A Tyson et al. Gen Z, Millennials Stand Out for Climate Change Activism, Social Media Engagement With Issue, 26 May 2021, Pew Research Center, www.pewresearch.org/science/2021/05/26/gen-z-millennials-stand-out-for- climate-change-activism-social-media-engagement-with-issue/ (archived at https://perma.cc/SMU9-KVSY)

30 T Thompson. Young people's climate anxiety revealed in landmark survey, 22 September 2021, Nature.com, www.nature.com/articles/d41586-021-02582-8 (archived at https://perma.cc/2HWG-DPKU)

31 M Patel. Majority of young people distressed about climate change, even during pandemic, 7 September 2022, Imperial College London, www.imperial. ac.uk/news/239251/majority-young-people-distressed-about-climate/ (archived at https://perma.cc/PXJ5-XVJ7)

32 N Runyon. UK-based companies more proactive in implementing ESG compliance, according to new research, 1 December 2023, Thomson Reuters, www.thomsonreuters.com/en-us/posts/esg/uk-esg-compliance/ (archived at https://perma.cc/KB6G-W8G9)

33 US SEC. SEC Announces Enforcement Task Force Focused on Climate and ESG Issues, 4 March 2021, www.sec.gov/newsroom/press-releases/2021-42 (archived at https://perma.cc/U6KJ-XM3B)

34 D Silk and C Lu. Environmental, Social & Governance Law 2024, 17 January 2024, ICLG.com, iclg.com/practice-areas/environmental-social-and-governance- law/usa (archived at https://perma.cc/K7R6-D78R)

35 United Nations. Do you know all 17 SDGs? sdgs.un.org/goals (archived at https://perma.cc/B4Y5-FFH4)

36 Key ESG. Your need-to-know summary of ESG regulations and frameworks, 24 April 2024, www.keyesg.com/article/your-need-to-know-summary-of-esg- regulations-and-frameworks (archived at https://perma.cc/HSF4-C9CE)

37 United Nations. Greenwashing – the deceptive tactics behind environmental claims, www.un.org/en/climatechange/science/climate-issues/greenwashing (archived at https://perma.cc/3CWF-QY3N)

38 N Runyon. UK-based companies more proactive in implementing ESG compliance, according to new research, 1 December 2023, Thomson Reuters, www.thomsonreuters.com/en-us/posts/esg/uk-esg-compliance/ (archived at https://perma.cc/7CTH-YRHC)

39 S Hickey. FCA considers enforcement action over 'poor' ESG benchmarks, 20 March 2023, Financial Times Adviser, www.ftadviser.com/fca/2023/03/20/fca-considers-enforcement-action-over-poor-esg-benchmarks/ (archived at https://perma.cc/U6YD-QAMZ)

40 A Hansen and P D Rosell. Children Working in the Carpet industry of Pakistan: Prevalence and Conditions, May 2012, ICF International, ecommons.cornell.edu/server/api/core/bitstreams/eccfbe50-6a85-4150-8091-95873c545aa6/content (archived at https://perma.cc/M9Q6-6GQK)

41 IKEA. A new compass, ikeamuseum.com/en/explore/the-story-of-ikea/a-new-compass/ (archived at https://perma.cc/S4Q4-EUX4)

42 B Hope. Top 10: Global companies with best social impact initiatives, 5 April 2022, *Sustainability Magazine*, sustainabilitymag.com/top10/top-10-global-companies-with-best-social-impact-initiatives-esg (archived at https://perma.cc/KNW4-2PL9)

43 E Skyler. Announcing Our U.S. Commercial Firearms Policy, 22 March 2018, Citi, www.citigroup.com/global/news/perspective/2018/announcing-our-us-commercial-firearms-policy (archived at https://perma.cc/RM2E-M8SY)

44 E Skyler. Announcing Our U.S. Commercial Firearms Policy, 22 March 2018, Citi, www.citigroup.com/global/news/perspective/2018/announcing-our-us-commercial-firearms-policy (archived at https://perma.cc/RM2E-M8SY)

45 J Josephs. Why do companies get involved in social issues? 20 July 2022, BBC News, www.bbc.co.uk/news/business-62139217 (archived at https://perma.cc/36KY-4QV4)

46 N Runyon. UK-based companies more proactive in implementing ESG compliance, according to new research, 1 December 2023, Thomson Reuters, www.thomsonreuters.com/en-us/posts/esg/uk-esg-compliance/ (archived at https://perma.cc/6SAJ-5PEA)

47 T Ries et al. 2024 Edelman Trust Barometer, Global Report, Edelman Trust Institute, www.edelman.com/sites/g/files/aatuss191/files/2024-02/2024%20Edelman%20Trust%20Barometer%20Global%20Report_FINAL.pdf (archived at https://perma.cc/GAZ2-4YNN)

48 M Fisher. Investing in sustainability can be good for people, the planet and the business, 15 April 2024, Kantar, www.kantar.com/inspiration/sustainability/what-is-the-sustainability-value-case-for-brands (archived at https://perma.cc/Z8G9-FFTV)

49 M Fisher. Investing in sustainability can be good for people, the planet and the business, 15 April 2024, Kantar, www.kantar.com/inspiration/sustainability/what-is-the-sustainability-value-case-for-brands (archived at https://perma.cc/PNS9-7TF9)

50 K Sprehe and A Hay. How Can Brands Win the Hearts and Minds of Gen Z?, 6 January 2023, Apco, apcoworldwide.com/blog/how-can-brands-win-the-hearts-and-minds-of-gen-z/ (archived at https://perma.cc/7LVU-S5Z2)

51 D Truman et al. Read the Room: Pursuing Happiness 2024, 22 May 2024, Dentsu, www.dentsu.com/uk/en/our-latest-thinking (archived at https://perma.cc/P7GE-V2TU)

52 K Birch. 9 companies taking a stance on political or social issues, 26 August 2022, BusinessChief.com, businesschief.com/leadership-and-strategy/9-companies-taking-a-stance-on-political-or-social-issues (archived at https://perma.cc/4ZX5-NLA9)

53 J Stoppelman. x.com/jeremys/status/1540358219226161152 (archived at https://perma.cc/KW7P-6BZU)

54 J Josephs. Why do companies get involved in social issues? 20 July 2022, BBC News, www.bbc.co.uk/news/business-62139217 (archived at https://perma.cc/B4E9-QDE5)

55 D Paterek. A prime example of woke washing: fast fashion and International Women's Day, 2 April 2021, Impact Nottingham, impactnottingham.com/2021/04/a-prime-example-of-woke-washing-fast-fashion-and-international-womens-day/ (archived at https://perma.cc/P9NU-9Y32)

56 A Johnson-Kurts. Big Oil Reality Check: Oil and Gas Companies Failing on Climate, 21 May 2024, Oil Change International, priceofoil.org/2024/05/21/press-release-big-oil-reality-check-oil-and-gas-companies-failing-on-climate/ (archived at https://perma.cc/V83H-9JUF)

57 A Johnson-Kurts. Big Oil Reality Check: Oil and Gas Companies Failing on Climate, 21 May 2024, Oil Change International, priceofoil.org/2024/05/21/press-release-big-oil-reality-check-oil-and-gas-companies-failing-on-climate/ (archived at https://perma.cc/MEC9-7EHS)

58 A Johnson-Kurts. Big Oil Reality Check: Oil and Gas Companies Failing on Climate, 21 May 2024, Oil Change International, priceofoil.org/2024/05/21/press-release-big-oil-reality-check-oil-and-gas-companies-failing-on-climate/ (archived at https://perma.cc/TN6Z-XQQ7)

59 O Milman. 'Godfathers of climate chaos': UN chief urges global fossil-fuel advertising ban, 5 June 2024, The Guardian, www.theguardian.com/environment/article/2024/jun/05/antonio-guterres-un-chief-fossil-fuels-advertising (archived at https://perma.cc/WS4Q-9JX5)

60 M Merriman et al. Is Gen Z the spark we need to see the light?, 2021, EY, assets.ey.com/content/dam/ey-sites/ey-com/en_us/topics/consulting/ey-is-gen-z-the-spark-we-need-to-see-the-light-full-report.pdf (archived at https://perma.cc/7EGH-GG5D)

61 J Josephs. Why do companies get involved in social issues? 20 July 2022, BBC News, www.bbc.co.uk/news/business-62139217 (archived at https://perma.cc/7296-AGRK)

5

A theory of social wellbeing

In 2020, Jason Gelinas was a senior vice president in Citigroup's technology department. According to Bloomberg, he 'led an AI project and oversaw a team of software developers. He was married with kids and had a comfortable house in a New Jersey suburb'.[1] In the run up to the 2008 election, Gelinas had registered as a Democrat, but had begun to drift to the right.[2]

Gelinas became immersed in right-wing internet conspiracies that, by the time of the 2016 presidential election, were promoting scandalous claims about Hillary Clinton and other leading Democrats.[3] The allegations centred on Comet Ping Pong, a pizza restaurant in Washington DC. 'The conspiracy supposedly is run out of the restaurant's basement,' the BBC reported on 2 December.[4]

These claims had an impact on people across America. On 4 December, Edgar Maddison Welch set off from his home in North Carolina, drove to Comet Ping Pong and fired three shots from a semi-automatic rifle in an attempt to 'self-investigate' the story, as he later admitted to police.[5] 'We don't even have a basement,' the restaurant's owner James Alefantis told the BBC.[6]

The stories were picked up by the QAnon group who publicized allegations said to come from an anonymous high-level government official known as 'Q'. The reports were initially restricted to online subculture sites like 4chan. But by 2018, QAnon had made it on to a crowd-funded site called QMap which was aimed at a wider audience of soccer mums, white-collar workers and other 'normies' – feeding them improbable stories that they readily believed.

QMap attracted millions of visitors, earning $3,000 a month for its founder – who in 2020 was identified by fact-checking site

Logically.ai as Jason Gelinas. A few weeks later, Gelinas was fired from his job at Citigroup.[7]

Our previous two chapters focused on challenges faced by individuals and organizations in the 2020s. Before we continue, let's take a moment to assess the impact of the seismic changes in society we have described so far, changes that can lead a seemingly 'normal' Wall Street executive to champion an obscure cult which millions of people across mainstream America were quick to adopt.

The impact of 21st century lifestyles

In Chapter 3, we saw the impact that fear can have on people. Our 21st century lifestyle is also associated with other challenges to mental health, particularly our ability to accurately assess information. Workplace wellbeing must succeed in tackling this too if it is to support organizations and their people through the 2020s.

Challenges to perceptions of truth

Individuals have a choice. They can assess the validity of a suggestion by checking where it comes from and discussing it objectively with other people. Choosing this course of action requires specific skills. Self-confidence is needed to shape an opinion and skills in evaluation help to assess whether an opinion can be regarded as accurate. Communication skills allow opinions to be tested by others.

These steps amount to a process which an individual can use to decide whether new information can be trusted and accepted. However, since the arrival of smartphones and the prevalence of social media this process has been disrupted. All too often people choose a less reliable alternative. They choose to manage information through fast thinking, bias and easy acceptance.

In Chapter 3, we saw that we have a poor relationship with tech. In exploring the impact of this, it's apparent that in the 2020s the process of making accurate assessments has become harder for many people. This is because of three specific difficulties.

1. POOR MENTAL HEALTH LEADING TO COMMUNICATION PROBLEMS

A growing body of opinion accepts a correlation between high use of social media and damage to the mental health of teenagers and young adults. Many studies (e.g. Mehdizadeh, 2010; Kalpidou et al, 2011; Tazghini and Siedlecki, 2013) show a link between heavy use of social media and low self-esteem.[8] Rising levels of depression, loneliness and anxiety disrupt the developmental years of those in higher education – the employees of tomorrow.

Doubts about the value of reality can affect people who are overly interested in online galleries that present idealistic images of individuals and lifestyles. Employees who are frequently online may see a never-ending beauty parade of lifestyle choices apparently better than their own, from influencers' favoured products to idealized body shapes.

Psychology professor Matthias R Mehl suggests that what he calls the 'me-focused' approach to online content is 'not so great for your emotional health... it seems the more someone is posting about themselves, the less happy they are in real life'.[9]

A 'me-centric orientation', anxiety, depression and a shift from mainstream opinions of reality inevitably make it harder to be fully present with other people. Kristin Carothers, a clinical psychologist at New York's Child Mind Institute, noted that online interactions often lack emotion. When coming face-to-face with a person, frequent users of social media may 'miss some social cues'.[10] Moments of empathy and emotional intelligence in particular can be missed by people for whom fast thinking is the norm.

In the workplace, reduced empathy and emotional intelligence lead to a colder, less human way of working. In her book *Reclaiming Conversation*, clinical psychologist Sherry Turkle suggests: 'These days we hide from conversation. We hide from each other even as we're constantly connected to each other.'[11]

This leads to a transactional way of communicating. For example, someone from Generation X (born 1965-1980) sitting opposite someone from Generation Z (born 1997-2012) might ask them a question – only to receive a reply via email (these multigenerational issues are discussed further in Chapter 8, along with potential solutions). Similarly, back-to-back Zoom calls leave little room for incidental chat between meetings.

Business is about relationships, it's about team cohesion and human understanding. However, young digital natives – for whom social media, fast thinking and instant messaging have been present throughout their lives – may struggle with small-talk, eye contact, body language, empathy and emotional intelligence. The potential impact of this on relationship-building is hard to overestimate, particularly in the jobs of the future that will counter-balance AI by relying on fundamental human skills in empathy and communication.

2. SHRINKING ATTENTION SPANS

The average British adult checks their phone every 12 minutes during the waking day, according to 2018 research by the UK communications regulator Ofcom. With the subsequent expansion in working from home, that figure is likely to have increased.[12]

According to Harriet Griffey, author of *The Art Of Concentration*, we have adopted 'always-on, anywhere, anytime, anyplace behaviour, we exist in a constant state of alertness that scans the world but never really gives our full attention to anything. In the short term, we adapt well to these demands, but in the long term the stress hormones adrenaline and cortisol create a physiological hyper-alert state that is always scanning for stimuli'.[13]

This is an exhausting way of living. The deluge of incoming messages, tweets, posts, swipes, likes and status updates is tiring. We soon lose the will to respond to everything, which is perhaps why we regard phone calls as disruptive. In an age where ownership of a phone is ubiquitous, it's ironic that we only occasionally use them to phone anyone.

Instead of calls, direct messages feel safer and less intrusive. In truth, they are easier because we have no need to bother with the nuanced social norms that in-person contact demands, for example, employing the body language that shows we're listening.

Disengaging with people reduces their impact on us, shrinking them in our consciousness. By contacting the other person in a way that doesn't bother them – or bother with them – we skip the long chat and reassuring tone of voice that they might need. We send them a quick, transactional text that lets us stay absorbed in whatever it is we're doing in that moment. By keeping people out of sight and out of mind, we have more headspace for ourselves and our priorities.

The dismissive, always-on nature of the digital world creates a permanent, fast-thinking, ever-wary, short-term state of mind, a kind of lukewarm sensory-deprivation soup. In that state, it's easier to ignore meaningful contact, difficult questions, choices and responsibility.

According to Oxford University neuroscientist Professor Baroness Susan Greenfield, children's experiences on social networking sites 'are devoid of cohesive narrative and long-term significance. As a consequence, the mid-21st century mind might almost be infantilized, characterized by short attention spans, sensationalism, inability to empathize and a shaky sense of identity'.[14]

Leaders need people who can break free of this state of mind, people who are switched on, engaged and efficient. These abilities are under threat. We are finding it harder to concentrate. An employee can put their phone aside during work hours but an underlying low-attention span might still have an impact on their work.

3. CHALLENGES TO CRITICAL THINKING

The implications of a poor attention span for employers are bleak. Employees who lack the capacity for deeper, prolonged concentration are more prone to skim-reading, half-listening and being present but not fully engaged.

In a celebrated article for *The Atlantic* entitled 'Is Google making us stupid?', Pulitzer-nominated author Nicholas Carr wrote, 'I'm not thinking the way I used to think... Immersing myself in a book or a lengthy article used to be easy... That's rarely the case anymore. Now my concentration often starts to drift after two or three pages. I get fidgety, lose the thread, begin looking for something else to do. I feel as if I'm always dragging my wayward brain back to the text'.[15] This description might resonate with many of us.

A reduced attention span leads to damaging consequences for employers. When logical thoughts are cut short, choices can't be properly explored. Only by considering all the options with the eye of an objective critic can we make a reliable decision. This is critical thinking, on which decision making depends (this subject is explored in greater detail in Chapter 7).

A grasp of who to sell to or who to buy from, for example, comes down to an ability to assess the options and carefully construct an appropriate response. These are skills that demand attention and focus. Without them, decisions risk being reached through assumptions and flawed thinking.

Critical thinking is particularly important given the prevalence of online misinformation and disinformation where falsehoods are respectively carelessly or deliberately passed on. In our habitual fast thinking and distracted response to choices, there is less room for reflective thought.

Without knowing how to carefully evaluate what they read online, how can people offer opinions in the workplace that bring them trust and authority? How can they seek promotion to positions of responsibility?

Without critical thinking and a mature understanding of reality, individuals can fall victim to illogical beliefs – as demonstrated by Jason Gelinas. And without a sincere interest in meaningful communication with others, individuals can become trapped in their own wayward thoughts. They can sink towards biases and fallacious thinking.

Untangling human nature

Supporting everyone through company culture

Businesses are at the centre of social change. They always have been, of course, but in the 2020s change driven by tech is evolving faster than individuals and businesses can keep up with. Resilience is wearing thin. Organizations will need to evolve if they are to thrive in the 2030s.

Some 45 per cent of CEOs think their organization will no longer be economically viable by 2034 if it continues on its current course, according to PwC's 2024 global survey of CEOs.[16] PwC found that 'most of those CEOs feel it's critically important for them to reinvent their businesses for the future'.

Similarly, McKinsey found that only half of 2,500 business leaders surveyed said their company was 'well prepared to anticipate and react to external shocks, and two-thirds see their organizations as overly complex and inefficient'.[17]

How should businesses manage change? They will need solutions to:

- **poor working practices** that undermine workforce wellbeing
- **insufficient organizational resilience** in the face of global shocks
- **the impact of tech** on the mental health of their people

We saw (in Chapter 2) the ineffective response typical of many organizations. Current wellbeing options are often not fit for purpose. A radical approach to change must embrace the whole organization and its workforce. The most comprehensive way to achieve this is through company culture, which reaches everyone and does not depend on voluntary participation.

An assessment by the Boston Consulting Group (BCG) looked at companies going through a digital transformation. BCG found 'The proportion of companies reporting breakthrough or strong financial performance was five times greater (90 per cent) among those that focused on culture than it was among those that neglected culture (17 per cent)'.[18]

Culture is defined as an organization's values and behaviours that shape the way that things are typically done. Culture provides an overarching code of conduct, helping individuals to act instinctively in pursuing the organization's objectives.

Culture not only clarifies *what* is expected of people (ie, implementing strategy and goals), but also *how* things are done. For example, a collaborative culture supports effective teamwork. A poor culture, however, featuring an unhealthy level of internal competition can make individuals feel isolated.

Meeting fundamental needs

What should a healthy culture focus on? In getting the most from people, it helps to think about what makes them tick. This leads to questions about human nature which aren't always easy to answer. Of all the things that humans understand in detail, human nature isn't one of them.

Limited progress has been made through experiments, including one at an unidentified North American campus where people were given free money. Some were given $5, others $20. Participants were asked to rate their general level of happiness, then some were told to spend the money on themselves ('personal spending') while the rest were asked to spend it on other people ('prosocial spending'). Everyone had to spend it by 5 pm.[19]

At the end of the day, both groups were asked again about their level of happiness. It might be assumed that the happiest people were those who had been given $20 and the freedom to spend it on themselves. In fact, the people who spent the money on someone else were happier over the course of the day, and the amount of money they were given had no bearing on how they felt.

People like giving to others. The authors of this research recognized that 'the emotional benefits of giving might be dampened or eliminated in countries where many people are struggling to meet their own basic needs'. But they go on to say 'If, however, people derive emotional benefits from prosocial spending even in poorer countries, then this would provide evidence that the warm glow of giving may be a fundamental component of human nature'.[20]

The claim that giving is a core component of human nature is supported by earlier work. Aknin et al (2013) found evidence of a positive relationship between giving and happiness in 120 countries, implying that giving is important to people around the world.[21]

Having glimpsed a small part of human nature, what does the rest involve? In his monumental 18th century work, *A Treatise of Human Nature*, Scottish philosopher David Hume placed human nature at the very foundation of human enquiry, linking it with what he called the 'science of Man'.[22] Since then however, human nature has taken a battering. Pulled in this direction and that, developed by some, denied by others, we're still arguing about it today.

Given the inherent complications of defining human nature, let's start with an easier question: what do we live for? This isn't meant in a 'why do we bother with it all, where's the vodka?' kind of way – rather, what are we aiming to achieve? What is living ideally about?

Many people chase momentary highs in the hope that over time there will be more peaks than troughs, leading to a general balance of contentedness. Others prefer to skip the peaks and troughs and seek instead a steady plateau.

Either way, fundamentally people seem to share a preference for contentedness. They might not be able to reach it all the time, but that's beside the point. It's safe to assume that someone you've never met will prefer to aim for contentedness than not. Feeling happy is important to most of us, which in the workplace is better described as wellbeing.

Wellbeing then isn't just about better engagement or organizational resilience. It's about satisfying the most fundamental needs of people.

Five actions for contentedness

According to the New Economics Foundation (NEF), there are five things in particular that generally contribute to wellbeing.[23] Contentedness starts with personal interpretations of these five actions. They could apply to anyone, anywhere and they are joyfully free of charge.

The NEF's five actions are as follows, along with our own interpretations of them:

1 **Connecting**

This is about interacting with people you trust, which the NEF suggests includes your team at work. In our DNA, humans are social beings. People need to connect with others, especially through the indefinable but unassailable power of presence. Presence, being in the room with someone rather than at the end of a call, allows body language which includes – and this is the indefinable bit – a sense of immediacy, where reactions and responses can be instantly recognized and reciprocated more readily than through a screen or down a phone line. In a room, where it's easier to share immediacy, individuals quickly develop a sense of connection. Communication is straightforward. In a phone call or virtual chat, however, the other person hears the words that are spoken but they must work harder to connect, to show empathy and understanding. The devices and screens, that we are so fond of and are so prevalent, keep us one step removed from each other. Social connection is a core part of what it means to be human, which we sometimes forget at our peril.

2 Being active

The NEF suggests: 'Go for a walk or run. Cycle. Play a game. Garden. Dance. Exercising makes you feel good.' Physical wellbeing is a vital part of contentedness, particularly in moments when we might feel stressed or anxious – in other words, when negative thoughts threaten to get the better of us. By diverting negative energy into a physical activity, our mind can more easily find the peace needed to address unresolved issues. For example, it helps to untangle thorny problems by going for a walk. Some activities, like sport, allow us to connect with others, sharing the sense of immediacy noted above. It's about being part of something, not simply just part of the team – winning and losing together – but being part of an immediate connection where your presence is needed by other people. The closer the team, the stronger the accompanying sense of recognition and validation, along with contentedness and connection.

3 Taking notice

As we saw in Chapter 3, we have adopted a lifestyle that demands attention. When we are distracted (by tech for example), it's difficult to be present (for others) – the quality that people are looking for when seeking connection. The important thing to note here is that we don't trust people who aren't present, they deprive us of the elusive sense of immediacy, sometimes knowingly. For example, someone trying to sell us a car, while hawkishly watching other customers on the forecourt, is not present. Distracted and evasive, they may seem to be simply repeating a sales script rather than engaging with our questions and concerns. A deal is more likely to be closed when both parties feel there is trust – which only develops in a shared and personal experience. This is about participating in the moment. The NEF explains that we have a richer experience when we notice the world around us, particularly others. We might be distracted by tech, but only by noticing other people and being present with them can we nurture relationships and cement belonging.

4 **Continuous learning**

The world becomes more interesting the more we understand it. The more interested someone is in understanding, the more interesting they are to others. Learning – driven by interest and curiosity – broadens the mind and makes for fascinating individuals who are able to articulately express opinions on a range of subjects. Learning leads to new abilities and exciting opportunities. By developing new skills, we can begin to escape from doubts about when or whether bigger and better things will come our way. New abilities give us a chance to manage our career rather than waiting for a future that feels out of control and might simply sweep us up in its wake. Workplace training programmes, provided at an employer's expense, give individuals the chance to develop skills that can lead to pay rises and promotions. A commitment to learning keeps confidence high and fuels motivation.

5 **Giving**

Giving a gift is more rewarding than receiving something in return. The act of giving is to show something of who you are to other people and is therefore important to both self-identity and to connecting and belonging. Showing someone that you've spent time and attention on them immediately deepens the relationship and thus extends your value in their eyes. This is rewarding, physiologically. Neurotransmitters – chemical messengers – such as dopamine, serotonin and oxytocin 'reward' us when we give something to others, be it a thoughtful gift or just a few moments of our time.[24] It's possible that these neurological processes and habits develop at a very young age. Toddlers under the age of two showed greater happiness when they gave away tasty treats to a puppet than when they were given the same treats themselves.[25]

In the absence of a fully fleshed out analysis of human nature, these are components of wellbeing that could potentially shape company culture. A rounded approach to wellbeing has even influenced government policy. At the heart of New Zealand's so-called 'wellbeing budget' of 2019 was the recognition that all aspects of 'a good life' must be considered holistically.

'The conversation has changed,' said Girol Karacaoglu, former chief economist at the New Zealand Treasury. 'There's a realization that we need to worry about other things than income.'[26] Kirk Hope, chief executive of BusinessNZ added: 'Wellbeing is critical to business. You won't have a very productive workforce without it.'[27]

Wellbeing is important to individuals, businesses and even governments. In the workplace, perhaps an effective wellbeing strategy would simply support the NEF's five actions. Indeed, many companies already do support them.

These organizations encourage teamwork (connecting), they provide discounted gym memberships (being active) and they recognize the values of trust, learning and giving (CSR, for example). Yet disengagement is still spiking. Something isn't working. As we saw in Chapter 2, Oxford University's Dr William Fleming has shown that corporate wellbeing is failing.

The evidence for a new approach to wellbeing

On a level playing field, the core components of wellbeing are seemingly easy to adopt. So why isn't wellbeing working? Because organizations are not operating on a level playing field.

There are barriers to productivity, in particular:

- **poor working practices**, contributing to the four principal challenges to wellbeing (as noted in Chapters 2 and 3)
- **disruptions to mental health** caused by 21st century lifestyles, as discussed above

A successful approach to culture would accommodate the NEF's five actions. But it would also need to replace poor working practices and manage the impact of current lifestyles. In other words, a successful culture would support a better way of working. What would this look like in practice? In answer to this, we considered research by academics and corporations.

The need to belong

As we saw in Chapter 3, in 1995 social psychologists Roy Baumeister and Mark Leary published their seminal paper 'The need to belong: Desire for interpersonal attachments as a fundamental human motivation'.[28] Cited more than 30,000 times, this paper was the first to show that the desire to belong is a deeply rooted human motivation. Stemming from our ancestral origins, belonging is a fundamental need that permeates our thoughts, feelings and behaviours.

For Baumeister and Leary, 'belongingness appears to have multiple and strong effects on emotional patterns and on cognitive processes. Lack of attachments is linked to a variety of ill-effects on health, adjustment and wellbeing'. Their work has been supported by subsequent neurological research at MIT showing that enforced isolation provokes craving responses in the brain that mimic hunger.[29] In other words, the urge to associate with other people correlates with basic survival needs.

In the context of the workplace, it must be recognized that belonging is a fundamental need and that to go without it is likely to be detrimental to performance and even a potential cause of depression.[30] To perform at their best, people need to feel they belong to a group, that they are part of the team and are recognized and accepted as such.

Psychological safety

In her pioneering 1999 paper, Amy Edmondson, an expert in leadership at Harvard Business School, defined psychological safety as 'shared belief held by members of a team that the team is safe for interpersonal risk-taking'.[31] Edmondson refers to 'a team climate characterized by interpersonal trust and mutual respect in which people are comfortable being themselves'.[32]

As a concept, psychological safety is sometimes mistakenly assumed to offer entitlement to protection, as if it were a forcefield shielding an individual's right to say anything they wish – and everyone else in the room has to go along with it. The implication of this is that, ironically, psychological safety fails to make it safe to say anything, for fear of offending someone.

Another mistaken assumption suggests that you can start a meeting with a vague nod to things being 'you know, psychologically safe', then move on without any true commitment to what the phrase might actually involve.

Between these two positions there lies useful middle ground. Psychological safety is not a get-out clause, allowing an employee to resist or object to anything that makes them a bit uncomfortable – a tough assignment, for example.

Instead, psychological safety is the rejection of the kind of negative behaviour that makes it hard for someone to feel they belong in the room. Behaviour that shames or blames someone, or negates them by denying them a chance to speak or get involved, can be considered a threat to their psychological safety, affecting their performance and productivity.

Edmondson clarifies things in this way, 'If you change the nature and quality of the conversations in your team, your outcomes will improve exponentially. Psychological safety is the core component to unlock this.'[33]

The need for autonomy

In 2002, a paper by occupational behaviour specialists Nick Turner, Julian Barling and Anthea Zacharatos explained that work was shifting from regular hours and jobs for life to a 'larger number of hours worked and more temporary employment'.[34]

Critical of a 'do-more-with-less mentality that favours profits over the welfare of people', the authors believed the shift in the way that employees were being treated led to 'diminished choice and control'. People were being 'forced to take on hours and working arrangements that are against their wishes'.[35]

Favouring 'positive psychology at work' (the title of their paper), Turner, Barling and Zacharatos developed a model of 'healthy work' that built on ideas from early theorists on workplace wellbeing. Robert A Karasek for example had noted that 'workplace stress is an indicator of how taxing a worker's job is and how much control' an individual has over their tasks and duties.[36]

Turner, Barling and Zacharatos developed a concept of 'high-quality work' that envisaged new ways of working, beginning with a company culture that encourages 'employees to do meaningful work in a healthy way'. This should include jobs with high levels of control that allow employees to keep up with demands, helping them to exert choice which in turn encourages them to feel competent. The authors noted that 'typically, high amounts of job control are associated with increases in job satisfaction and decreased depression'.[37]

This model benefits organizations by enabling employees to 'face change with greater resilience and optimism' through jobs that give people 'autonomy, challenging work and the opportunity for social interaction'.[38]

For Turner, Barling and Zacharatos, a healthy way of working embraces autonomy for employees alongside 'transformational leadership', where leaders increase employees' awareness of the 'mission or vision toward which they are working', which develops motivation and interest in common goals.[39]

This revised approach to both jobs and leadership supports trust, engagement and belonging, which together contribute to higher levels of workplace wellbeing. Turner, Barling and Zacharatos finished their paper with the thought that 'these ideas are at the very heart of promoting healthy and positive work in the 21st century'.[40]

Collective intelligence

In 2010, Dr Anita Woolley, an expert in organizational behaviour, co-authored work showing that a group's 'collective intelligence' was higher in teams whose members understood each other.[41] More precisely, the paper by Woolley and her co-authors explained that this level of understanding was linked to:

- the average social sensitivity of group members
- the equality in distribution of conversational turn-taking
- the proportion of females in the group

These findings imply that teams work best when their members regard each other with empathy and understanding. When people give each other space – for example, by reading between the lines, perceiving unspoken concerns and listening to comments, ideas and solutions – they begin to work as a single unit with greater collective intelligence than a notional group of high-calibre individuals who are competing with each other.

Co-author Dr Thomas Malone said: 'Before we did the research, we were afraid that collective intelligence would be just the average of all the individual IQs in a group. So we were surprised but intrigued to find that group intelligence had relatively little to do with individual intelligence.'[42]

Ultimately, collective intelligence comes down to whether or not a group is made up of people who are high in social sensitivity. In other words, teams work better when there is psychological safety, with team members 'reading each other' with interest and respect. Teams can improve their collective intelligence by encouraging individuals to accommodate each other in their thinking.

Project Aristotle

In 2012, Google set up Project Aristotle with the aim of finding out how best to put a team together. According to Abeer Dubey, director of Google's People Analytics division, the company's top executives initially believed that building the best teams meant bringing specific individuals together; for example, people who shared similarities or who offered the right mix of abilities or who creatively sparked off each other.[43]

If two teams both exceeded their objectives, what might they have in common? Despite analysing the data for more than a year, patterns in membership were impossible to find.[44] Over time, it became clear that academic studies on the subject were pointing not to patterns but to 'group norms', the behavioural standards, team culture and unwritten rules that govern how people function when working together.

Project Aristotle researchers became interested in groups whose 'house rules' overshadowed dominant personalities by prioritizing the team, whether group norms were quietly adopted or openly expressed.[45] By identifying the norms that mattered most, Project Aristotle's leaders realized they could influence and improve Google's teams.

Researcher Julia Rozovsky found that what mattered most was how teammates treated each other. A little over a decade after Amy Edmondson's paper, psychological safety went from being a phrase once saddled with slightly fluffy connotations to becoming Google's missing piece of the puzzle. 'Just having data, that proves to people that these things are worth paying attention to sometimes, is the most important step in getting them to actually pay attention,' Rozovsky told the *New York Times*.[46]

The role of oxytocin

In 2017, neuro-economist Dr Paul Zak began to analyse the connection between trust in the workplace and economic performance. According to Zak, people at high-trust companies report:

- 74% less stress compared with people at low-trust companies
- 106% more energy at work
- 50% higher productivity
- 13% fewer sick days
- 76% more engagement
- 29% more satisfaction
- 40% less burnout[47]

In Zak's research on trust, individuals were designated as either senders or receivers. Both groups were paid for participating. Senders were asked to electronically send a receiver some (or none) of the money they'd been paid. They could choose how much – though both teams were aware that software would triple the amount that was sent to the receiver's account.

Receivers were then asked to choose whether to give some – or none – of the money back to the senders. This meant that the more money senders gave, the more they might get back – if they trusted the receivers to be kind.[48] Receivers who chose to be kind could claim personal trustworthiness.

Zak's research led him to the neurotransmitter oxytocin – a hormone involved in the exchange of information between brain

cells. Blood samples taken from both groups before and after decisions to send money showed that 'the receipt of money denoting
trust, but not money in general, causes the brain to synthesize
oxytocin'.[49] Zak's team also found that the amount of oxytocin
produced predicts trustworthiness – as indicated by the receiver's
return of money to the sender.

In one version of the experiment, volunteers who were given
synthetic oxytocin (via a nasal spray) were willing to send more than
double the amount of money than those who received a placebo. This
showed that the presence of oxytocin in the earlier results was no
coincidence but could be shown to be a cause of trust. To test whether
his findings were universal, Zak measured oxytocin in indigenous
people in Papua New Guinea and found the same results.[50]

In 2017, Zak published his findings in his book *Trust Factor: The
science of creating high-performance companies*, in which he discusses
eight management behaviours that foster trust:[51]

- **Recognize excellence** – leading to public recognition
- **Induce 'challenge stress'** – intensifying focus and strengthening
  social connections
- **Give people discretion in how they do their work** – trust them to
  work out solutions
- **Enable job-crafting** – allow people to shape their job based on
  things they care most about
- **Share information broadly** – openness and communication together
  reduce uncertainty
- **Intentionally build relationships** – building social ties at work
  leads to better performance
- **Facilitate whole-person growth** – high-trust workplaces help
  people develop personally
- **Show vulnerability** – when leaders ask for help, this stimulates
  oxytocin in others

Introducing social wellbeing

These papers, along with others on similar themes (cited throughout this book), share sentiments on belonging, trust, respect and psychological safety. Bringing these strands of research together, we realized there was significant overlap between them which had not been previously recognized. Authors tend to flag up their own unique findings rather than similarities with previous work.

The need for personal autonomy in a job highlights the importance of accepting, valuing and trusting individuals. The need to belong, and psychological safety, both focus on an individual's need to be accepted as a valid member of a group. Teams that recognize this – that accept and value individuals – develop greater collective intelligence than teams that don't.

Google found that when 'group norms' overshadowed dominant personalities, relying on the advantages of psychological safety, teams performed better overall, echoing earlier findings about collective intelligence.

Paul Zak gave scientific credence to the benefits of trusting people and encouraging them to build relationships. Zak found that high-trust companies hold people accountable but without micromanaging them. They treat people like responsible adults – supporting the earlier conclusions on autonomy.

In summary, our analysis of long-term workplace trends (as detailed in Chapter 2) and assessment of academic research together indicate that to improve workplace wellbeing an organization needs to:

- replace poor working practices by increasing autonomy and trust
- ensure that teams work with respect and psychological safety
- embed these 'group norms' into company culture
- thereby create a culture that encourages collective intelligence and a sense of belonging

These are the components of a company culture that would be capable of improving workplace wellbeing. Poor working practices that cause disengagement would be replaced with a better understanding of people. This would introduce a healthier, more meaningful approach to work. It would go some way to implementing the NEF's five ways to wellbeing, or at least would create an environment that would make them easier to adopt.

Such an environment would allow room for workplace learning, laying the groundwork for professional development that would tackle the impact of 21st century lifestyles. This would include training courses in critical thinking, future communication skills and leading through change (as detailed in Chapters 7, 8 and 9).

Above all, this approach to wellbeing – based on a meaningful analysis of engagement and implemented through a reappraisal of company culture – successfully brings the workforce together. This social approach to better ways of working is a concept we call **social wellbeing**.

Social wellbeing can be defined as the group of workplace behaviours that safeguard people, encourage engagement and protect productivity. Adopted by the board, supported by leaders, encouraged by managers and developed through a programme of learning, social wellbeing builds the organizational resilience that will protect businesses during the challenges that lie ahead.

Social wellbeing reimagines the impact of work. No longer would individuals be solely responsible for shouldering the burden of poor workplace practices, signing up to ineffective wellbeing initiatives in the absence of anything else. Instead, social wellbeing enables organizations to reclaim some of the responsibility for the outcome of the way they operate.

The route to long-term stability and competitive advantage, social wellbeing is the cornerstone of our strategy for managing the impact of the 2020s. Having introduced the theory, our remaining chapters will focus on developing social wellbeing in practice.

Notes

1 W Turton and J Brustein. QAnon High Priest Was Just Trolling Away as a Citigroup Tech Executive, 7 October 2020, Bloomberg Businessweek, www.bloomberg.com/news/features/2020-10-07/who-is-qanon-evangelist-qmap-creator-and-former-citigroup-exec-jason-gelinas (archived at https://perma.cc/5PVV-E5DB)

2 W Turton and J Brustein. QAnon High Priest Was Just Trolling Away as a Citigroup Tech Executive, 7 October 2020, Bloomberg Businessweek, www.bloomberg.com/news/features/2020-10-07/who-is-qanon-evangelist-qmap-creator-and-former-citigroup-exec-jason-gelinas (archived at https://perma.cc/83CD-M4LK)

3 W Turton and J Brustein. QAnon High Priest Was Just Trolling Away as a Citigroup Tech Executive, 7 October 2020, Bloomberg Businessweek, www.bloomberg.com/news/features/2020-10-07/who-is-qanon-evangelist-qmap-creator-and-former-citigroup-exec-jason-gelinas (archived at https://perma.cc/9LK3-QRMU)

4 BBC Trending. The saga of 'Pizzagate': The fake story that shows how conspiracy theories spread, 2 December 2016, BBC News, www.bbc.co.uk/news/blogs-trending-38156985 (archived at https://perma.cc/JUB7-V28A)

5 BBC News. Pizzagate: Gunman fires in restaurant at centre of conspiracy, 5 December 2016, www.bbc.co.uk/news/world-us-canada-38205885 (archived at https://perma.cc/DN7H-GX8E)

6 BBC Trending. The saga of 'Pizzagate': The fake story that shows how conspiracy theories spread, 2 December 2016, BBC News, www.bbc.co.uk/news/blogs-trending-38156985 (archived at https://perma.cc/UV62-F9XK)

7 K Gibson. Citigroup fires tech executive who ran popular QAnon website, 7 October 2020, CBS News Moneywatch, www.cbsnews.com/news/citigroup-fires-jason-gelinas-qanon-website/ (archived at https://perma.cc/WA4V-8UHY)

8 M Kalpidou, D Costin and J Morris. The Relationship between Facebook and the Well-Being of Undergraduate College Students, *Cyberpsychology, Behavior and Social Networking*, 2011, **14**, pp. 183–89; S Mehdizadeh. Self-presentation 2.0: Narcissism and self-esteem on Facebook, *Cyberpsychology, Behavior, and Social Networking*, 2010, **13** (4), pp. 357–64; S Tazghini and K L Siedlecki. A mixed method approach to examining Facebook use and its relationship to self-esteem, *Computers in Human Behavior*, 2013, **29** (3), pp. 827–32

9 B Stulberg. Self-absorption on social media is making us sick, 31 March 2021, The Growth Equation, thegrowtheq.com/self-absorption-on-social-media-is-making-us-sick/ (archived at https://perma.cc/N2E2-6JHA)

10 Z Feliciano. Is Social Media Hindering Our Face-To-Face Socialization Skills? 20 August 2015, Connecticut Health I-Team, c-hit.org/2015/08/20/is-social-media-hindering-our-face-to-face-social-skills/ (archived at https://perma.cc/3MKB-25PN)

11 S Turkle (2015) *Reclaiming Conversation: The power of talk in the digital age*, Penguin Books

12 Ofcom. Communications Market Report, 2 August 2018, ofcom.org.uk/
siteassets/resources/documents/research-and-data/multi-sector/cmr/cmr2018/
cmr-2018-narrative-report.pdf (archived at https://perma.cc/XK6V-UEGM)

13 H Griffey. The lost art of concentration: being distracted in a digital world, 4
October 2018, *The Guardian*, www.theguardian.com/lifeandstyle/2018/
oct/14/the-lost-art-of-concentration-being-distracted-in-a-digital-world
(archived at https://perma.cc/SSU9-R694)

14 P Wintour. Facebook and Bebo risk 'infantilising' the human mind, 24
February 2009, *The Guardian*, www.theguardian.com/uk/2009/feb/24/
social-networking-site-changing-childrens-brains (archived at
https://perma.cc/22LV-PUDV)

15 N Carr. Is Google Making Us Stupid? July/August 2008, *The Atlantic*,
www.theatlantic.com/magazine/archive/2008/07/is-google-making-us-
stupid/306868/ (archived at https://perma.cc/FG89-92YZ)

16 PwC. 27th Annual Global CEO Survey – Thriving in an age of continuous
reinvention, 15 January 2024, www.pwc.com/gx/en/issues/c-suite-insights/
ceo-survey.html (archived at https://perma.cc/UPY5-TSK2)

17 P Simon et al. The state of organisations, 2023, McKinsey, www.mckinsey.com/~/
media/mckinsey/business%20functions/people%20and%20organizational%20
performance/our%20insights/the%20state%20of%20organizations%202023/
the-state-of-organizations-2023.pdf (archived at https://perma.cc/5XZJ-MZY7)

18 J Hemerling et al. It's not a digital transformation without a digital culture,
13 April 2018, Boston Consulting Group, www.bcg.com/publications/2018/
not-digital-transformation-without-digital-culture (archived at
https://perma.cc/2DNP-LTBV)

19 E Dunn et al. Prosocial Spending and Happiness: Using Money to Benefit
Others Pays Off, *Current Directions In Psychological Science*, 2014, **23** (1)

20 E Dunn et al. Prosocial Spending and Happiness: Using Money to Benefit
Others Pays Off, *Current Directions In Psychological Science*, 2014, **23** (1)

21 L B Aknin et al. Prosocial spending and well-being: Cross-cultural evidence for
a psychological universal, *Journal of Personality and Social Psychology*, 2013,
104 (4), pp. 635–52

22 D Hume. A Treatise of Human Nature: Being an Attempt to Introduce the
Experimental Method of Reasoning into Moral Subjects, Wikisource, en.
wikisource.org/wiki/Treatise_of_Human_Nature (archived at
https://perma.cc/L8BW-9D99)

23 J Aked et al. Five Ways to Wellbeing, 22 October 2008, New Economics
Foundation, neweconomics.org/2008/10/five-ways-to-wellbeing (archived at
https://perma.cc/H926-ZWAV)

24 A Novotney. What happens in your brain when you give a gift? 9 December
2022, American Psychological Association, www.apa.org/topics/mental-health/
brain-gift-giving (archived at https://perma.cc/HTF5-AWEM)

25 L B Aknin et al. Giving leads to happiness in young children. *PLoS One*, 2012, 7 (6), e39211

26 A Jaquiery. New Zealand: Changing the Conversation on Well-Being, 26 January 2022, IMF, www.imf.org/en/News/Articles/2022/01/26/cf-new-zealand-changing-the-conversation-on-well-being (archived at https://perma.cc/NSZ4-RKNT)

27 A Jaquiery. New Zealand: Changing the Conversation on Well-Being, 26 January 2022, IMF, www.imf.org/en/News/Articles/2022/01/26/cf-new-zealand-changing-the-conversation-on-well-being (archived at https://perma.cc/NSZ4-RKNT)

28 R F Baumeister and M R Leary. The need to belong: Desire for interpersonal attachments as a fundamental human motivation, *Psychological Bulletin*, 1995, **117** (3), pp. 497–529

29 L Tomova et al. Acute social isolation evokes midbrain craving responses similar to hunger, *Nature Neuroscience*, 2020, **23**, pp. 1597–605

30 B M Hagerty and R A Williams. The effects of sense of belonging, social support, conflict and loneliness on depression, *Nursing Research*, 1999, **48** (4) pp. 215–19

31 A Edmondson. Psychological Safety and Learning Behavior in Work Teams, *Administrative Science Quarterly*, 1999, **44** (2), pp. 350–38

32 A Edmondson. Psychological Safety and Learning Behavior in Work Teams, *Administrative Science Quarterly*, 1999, **44** (2), pp. 350–38.

33 A Edmondson (2022) #136: The Resilient Surgeon S2: Dr. Amy Edmondson, Society of Thoracic Surgeons, www.sts.org/podcasts/136-resilient-surgeon-s2-dr-amy-edmondson (archived at https://perma.cc/BQ75-2PJ3)

34 N Turner, J Barling and A Zacharatos. Positive psychology at work. In C R Snyder and S J Lopez (Eds.) *Handbook of Positive Psychology* (2002), Oxford University Press

35 N Turner, J Barling and A Zacharatos. Positive psychology at work. In C R Snyder and S J Lopez (Eds.) *Handbook of Positive Psychology* (2002), Oxford University Press

36 R A Karasek. Job Demands, Job Decision Latitude, and Mental Strain: Implications for Job Redesign, *Administrative Science Quarterly*, 1979, **24** (2), pp. 285–308

37 N Turner, J Barling and A Zacharatos. Positive psychology at work. In C R Snyder and S J Lopez (Eds.) *Handbook of Positive Psychology* (2002), Oxford University Press

38 N Turner, J Barling and A Zacharatos. Positive psychology at work. In C R Snyder and S J Lopez (Eds.) *Handbook of Positive Psychology* (2002), Oxford University Press

39 N Turner, J Barling and A Zacharatos. Positive psychology at work. In C R Snyder and S J Lopez (Eds.) *Handbook of Positive Psychology* (2002), Oxford University Press

40 N Turner, J Barling and A Zacharatos. Positive psychology at work. In C R Snyder and S J Lopez (Eds.) *Handbook of Positive Psychology* (2002), Oxford University Press

41 A Woolley et al. Evidence for a Collective Intelligence Factor in the Performance of Human Groups, *Science*, 2010, **330** (6004), pp. 686–88

42 A Woolley and T Malone. Defend Your Research: What Makes a Team Smarter? More Women, June 2011, *Harvard Business Review*, hbr.org/2011/06/defend-your-research-what-makes-a-team-smarter-more-women (archived at https://perma.cc/3V7C-33J5)

43 C Duhigg. What Google Learned From Its Quest to Build the Perfect Team, 25 February 2016, *New York Times*, www.nytimes.com/2016/02/28/magazine/what-google-learned-from-its-quest-to-build-the-perfect-team.html (archived at https://perma.cc/25DP-GFSE)

44 C Duhigg. What Google Learned From Its Quest to Build the Perfect Team, 25 February 2016, *New York Times*, www.nytimes.com/2016/02/28/magazine/what-google-learned-from-its-quest-to-build-the-perfect-team.html (archived at https://perma.cc/25DP-GFSE)

45 C Duhigg. What Google Learned From Its Quest to Build the Perfect Team, 25 February 2016, *New York Times*, www.nytimes.com/2016/02/28/magazine/what-google-learned-from-its-quest-to-build-the-perfect-team.html (archived at https://perma.cc/25DP-GFSE)

46 C Duhigg. What Google Learned From Its Quest to Build the Perfect Team, 25 February 2016, *New York Times*, www.nytimes.com/2016/02/28/magazine/what-google-learned-from-its-quest-to-build-the-perfect-team.html (archived at https://perma.cc/25DP-GFSE)

47 P Zak. The Neuroscience of Trust, January-February 2017, *Harvard Business Review*, hbr.org/2017/01/the-neuroscience-of-trust (archived at https://perma.cc/E7UG-SKP3)

48 P Zak and K Nowack. The Neuroscience in Building High Performance Trust Cultures, 9 February 2017, Chief Learning Officer.com, www.chieflearningofficer.com/2017/02/09/neuroscience-building-trust-cultures/ (archived at https://perma.cc/MF7K-H4AC)

49 P Zak and K Nowack. The Neuroscience in Building High Performance Trust Cultures, 9 February 2017, Chief Learning Officer.com, www.chieflearningofficer.com/2017/02/09/neuroscience-building-trust-cultures/ (archived at https://perma.cc/MF7K-H4AC).

50 P Zak. The Neuroscience of Trust, January-February 2017, *Harvard Business Review*, hbr.org/2017/01/the-neuroscience-of-trust (archived at https://perma.cc/E7UG-SKP3)

51 P Zak (2017) *Trust Factor: The science of creating high-performance companies*, Harper Collins

PART TWO

PART TWO

6

Finding glue – social wellbeing in practice

In the years since the Covid pandemic, remote and hybrid working have provoked mixed reactions. Martin Sorrell, founder of advertising giant WPP and chairman of S4 Capital, initially found that the new working practices were effective. Support began to dissolve when it appeared that company culture was crumbling.

'Productivity levels and enthusiasm waned a bit and the lack of engagement on a face-to-face basis was an issue,' Sorrell told Bloomberg. 'If you are paying people to look at a screen, they'll end up going to the highest bidder. There's no glue.'[1]

Many organizations are struggling with culture. Misguided views about working practices and wellbeing aren't helping. For some businesses, hybrid has led to fragmented ways of working which has put a strain on interpersonal connection. Individuals are disrupted by 'fast thinking' and short attention spans. HR departments and business leaders can see things coming apart at the seams. What are the practical steps that keep people together in an organization? How do you find the glue?

The starting point is belief. What or who do your people believe in regarding their job? Do they believe their employer supports their short-term needs and long-term interests? Do they believe that they are trusted and are given the opportunity to develop their potential?

Do they feel their job has value? Are they able to freely express their ideas and feedback? Do they believe in the mission/vision of the company? Are they proud to participate in something bigger than who they are as an individual? If many of your people do not recognize most of these things, what can you do to improve company culture in the interests of protecting engagement and retention?

Reimagining culture

Two examples from sport share similarities in illustrating a culture of effective teamwork. The England men's football team under Gareth Southgate and the England men's test cricket team under Brendon McCullum both saw an upturn in fortunes after each implemented a new culture. The key to their success lay in team members developing a renewed, well-documented desire to represent their nation, playing with pride in a way that made the country reconnect with its elite players.

'Bazball'

Gareth Southgate prioritized the responsibility the England men's football team had to the country in how they approached the game itself. Compared with previous years, the team became a happier and more successful environment.

An even more extraordinary turnaround saw the fortunes of the England men's test cricket team soar to unexpected heights. Things were all the more remarkable considering where the team had been. In fact, in the months prior to June 2022, England had only won one of their previous 17 international test matches.

A group of talented players were transformed from a brow-beaten low into a team who began to produce something dynamic and effective. For fans, the end product – fuelled by enthusiasm and creativity – became infectious.

So, how did such change come about? Meet Brendon McCullum who took over as England coach in May 2022. McCullum, a laid-back New Zealander, realized that the fortunes of the team depended on a shift in culture that over time came to be known as 'Bazball'.

Before McCullum's arrival, the atmosphere behind the scenes had been marked by despondency, formality and occasional moments of despair. Ripping up the fusty sense of caution he had inherited, McCullum instilled a burning sense of hunger and ambition, fuelled by an off-the-field relaxed team spirit.

England's test cricket was no longer about resilience in the face of defeat. It developed into an all-out lust for success, embracing risk and creativity, flirting with danger, smooching with enjoyment. In short, it became enamoured with passion. Managing director Rob Key was responsible for long-term strategy and captain Ben Stokes oversaw the action on the pitch, but it was McCullum's vision that drove the crucial element of change.

For English test cricket, the stakes were high. Other, shorter, forms of the game were more popular with TV audiences. To save the test game commercially, England needed to ensure their performance was exciting, entertaining and, above all, successful.

Fortunately, McCullum's focus paid off. Within four months of his arrival, England had won six out of seven tests, their second-best haul in a home summer. They were even reaching their targets with such speed and ferocity that sometimes they had swathes of time to spare. The remarkable thing about this was that players who had been humiliated by India in Ahmedabad in March 2021 were achieving the stuff of legend in the summer of 2022. So how did McCullum and Stokes revitalize the team? And how can leaders elsewhere do the same for theirs?

Pursuing clarity, pride and ambition

McCullum didn't rely on new people, increased investment or a panicky sense of urgency. He focused instead on encouraging a better mindset, instilling a new approach to the challenges he faced. The changes were simple and very human.

One of the key shifts was to stop thinking only about results. The pressure to deliver had made the team function less well. McCullum instead focused on encouraging everyone in the team. Results remained as important as ever, but by keeping them in context they no longer dominated preparations at the expense of the mindset needed to win.

Another change involved sharper innovation and decision making (the implication being that the team had been doing roughly the same thing again and again and getting the same result). This was about creating an atmosphere of psychological safety. If Stokes was able to embrace risk-taking and encourage others to do the same without fear of failure then the team would play with more confidence, edge and ambition.

Stokes led by example, sometimes playing recklessly in order to give his teammates permission to express themselves. Cricket can sometimes be set in its ways and so a reckless approach was radical.

Sure enough, when Jonny Bairstow was dismissed playing an aggressive shot in the summer of 2022 Stokes turned to the team (who had been used to polite silence) and praised Bairstow for leading by example. Bairstow's resurgence in the rest of a record-breaking summer became the stuff of legend.

Secure in an atmosphere of trust and psychological safety, the team knew it was OK to take risks. In the workplace, those risks are usually interpersonal – such as expressing yourself in front of senior colleagues. Knowing you have the ear and support of everyone in the room makes it easier to share opinions that might otherwise be left unsaid.

The clarity, pride and ambition developed by Stokes's team created a sense of belonging so strong you could all but see it from space. England began to believe they could win from any scenario, no matter how far they fell behind in the early stages of a match. 'You go to bed in a completely different mindset than you would have previously,' said bowler James Anderson.[2]

In June 2022, after two days against New Zealand at London's legendary Lord's ground, England were struggling. Yet on the final day, with the match in the balance, McCullum announced, 'At no stage do we think about the draw here, this is all about the win. We don't want to ever shut down. We'll win more than we lose if we always go for the win.'[3] England won. They later won against India too, securing a record 378 for the loss of only three wickets, before going on to achieve victory over Pakistan.

Significant change and improvement begin by encouraging people to focus on achievement in a way that is both energizing and rewarding. Start by developing psychological safety. Data, tech and processes all have their place, but they support rather than supplant a human-centric culture.

Carefully creating culture

Company culture is a nebulous thing. Rather than a carefully created environment designed to fulfil a leader's vision, culture is usually what emerges from a ramshackle montage of snapshots in time – a thin thread weaving through a company's collection of unconnected decisions, incidents, triumphs and traumas.

For example, two middle-ranking managers, competing with each other in a way that some would regard as cold-blooded, might both eventually be promoted. As senior managers, they tolerate – or even encourage – the same atmosphere of internal competition and mistrust in which they themselves excelled. This tension shapes the company culture until it becomes 'the way we do things'.

Other organizations might take a less haphazard approach, carefully creating an environment that enshrines particular values. This form of culture can deliver positive dividends as proven by the Bazball experiment. Practical steps leading in this direction include:

- **Begin by deciding mid-term objectives** – on revenue, productivity, engagement and retention.
- **Resist temptations to focus only on results** – objectives are meaningless without support from your people.
- **Develop an atmosphere of psychological safety** – encourage the trust and respect that foster teamwork and cohesion.
- **Nurture a sense of belonging** – people who feel they are 'part of the bigger picture' will be more likely to commit to achieving company objectives.

Most people are likely to accept a culture of trust and sincerity. People who are trusted by their leaders are more likely to trust each other. In this atmosphere, they feel that they belong, that they're respected and are part of something. They become personally invested in their work and in their employer, and are more likely to meet or exceed their targets.

This is the strongest route to securing mid-term KPIs and long-term objectives. We don't pretend it's easy or straightforward, however training programmes will help managers and employees follow the path set by leaders. The initial set of actions, outlined above, represents a fundamental step towards a culture of social wellbeing.

This kind of culture, prioritizing people alongside profits, gives a clear sense of focus. It can survive the demands of hybrid working, indeed it supports remote working through a culture that centres not on a half-empty office building but on a way of working that people can buy into regardless of where they are based.

However, given the authenticity caveat that we discovered in Chapter 4, any attempt at delivering a new approach to culture will sink if punctured by insincere references to trust and respect that are aimed at nothing more than ticking boxes and sounding good.

Muscular mission statements that speak of 'power', 'dominating markets' or 'driving forward at all costs', raise questions about whether employees are being prioritized alongside profits. Such statements may not be able to accommodate a meaningful approach to wellbeing and vice versa.

Promises about wellbeing fall flat if a business refuses to deviate from unrelenting demands. And in today's workplace, one section of the workforce in particular doesn't get on well with empty promises.

Company culture fit for Generation Z

'Gen Z whisperers'

In 2022, a panel of six senior marketing executives were asked to name their biggest challenge. Each said the same thing: Generation Z.[4] In struggling to understand and motivate their youngest people, many organizations are seeking 'Gen Z whisperers' – i.e. advisers 'ranging from 20-something social media influencers and young employees to big consulting firms' as part of efforts to develop engagement and retention and capture new customers.[5]

Employers are struggling to connect with a generation that by 2030 will make up about 30 per cent of the US workforce.[6] Born between 1997 and 2012, Generation Z came of age in circumstances very different to their predecessors.

Since 2000, social change has been so swift that younger generations have a fundamentally different understanding of society compared with their older peers. In this context, generational misunderstandings are inevitable, though they're usually based on stereotypes and misassumptions. To some, Gen Z are digital natives, the embodiment of the future. To others, they are less resilient than older colleagues – a view that perhaps misses deeper truths.

Let's remind ourselves about some of the things that Gen Z had to face in their formative years. As a result of Covid, they were confined at home for 18 months – immersed in isolation at a critical time in their lives. This might explain doubts about their interpersonal skills. Alternatively, this issue may stem from their addiction to phones, bequeathed to them by older generations who sometimes wonder why Gen Z have an impersonal way of communicating.

As well as the pandemic, other potential causes of anxiety in younger people include tech, social media and the climate emergency, as we saw in Chapters 3 and 4. Coming of age in an unsettled period, Gen Z were not responsible for these developments yet are living with the challenging consequences. They are preparing for the future they will inherit by tackling social issues that they may feel older generations have been happy to let slide.

The global disruption that Gen Z has grown up with, coupled with their interest in breaking old taboos, have led many young people to reflect on their mental health more readily than their older colleagues.

Deloitte's 2024 survey of 22,800 people in 44 countries found that 'only about half of Gen Zs (51 per cent) rate their mental health as good or extremely good, while 40 per cent of Gen Zs say they feel stressed all or most of the time'.[7] These reactions may reflect Gen Z's experience of soaring rents, high student debt, a cost of living crisis and global uncertainty – on top of the deeper causes of anxiety noted above.

In a world that feels like it's spinning out of control, giving your all to a job might be less important than the struggle to find personal meaning, security and fulfilment. Consequently, for Gen Z, work is an extension of personal identity rather than a means to an end. Work is only meaningful if it reflects personal authenticity. It is something to be experienced, not endured.

Roughly nine in 10 Gen Zs (86 per cent) say 'having a sense of purpose in their work is very or somewhat important to their overall job satisfaction and wellbeing'.[8] Without this, they'll happily look for something else. A Bank of America report found that 25 per cent of Gen Z employees had switched jobs in the six months to April 2022.[9]

Interns who are bored on day one may not show up on day two if they've had a better offer elsewhere. Graduates are sometimes impervious to traditional inducements that depend on time served, such as promotions. New hires might be thinking more about travel plans than hoping that one day they'll make partner.

Companies are no longer able to pay a salary that enables young people to buy a home, a key factor in encouraging long-term stability and loyalty. Nor can they guarantee job security. Gen Z know that businesses ask loyalty of them yet can't guarantee it in return, and to them this smacks of inauthenticity.

For older demographics, Gen Z's approach to work flies in the face of experience. Boomers and Generation X (see Chapter 8) regard the daily slog of routine as the best way up the career ladder. For them, years of hard-won experience taught them about process and paper-trails and small cogs in big machines. To Gen Z, however, playing a small part in someone else's objectives isn't particularly attractive. They're reluctant to try and older groups struggle to persuade them.

Career ladders and property ladders aside, Gen Z would be happier taking a metaphorical elevator – taking a quicker alternative, enjoying the experience and sharing content as they go. They'll commit to their current role, but long-term loyalty is unlikely. As long as now is authentic, the future will look after itself, so the thinking goes.

This line of thought has several consequences. Less concerned about fitting in, in the eyes of their older peers Gen Z are seemingly impatient and irreverent. Half of Gen Zs (50 per cent) have rejected an assignment or project based on their personal ethics or beliefs.[10] Together, this stance and their focus on authenticity perhaps encourage Gen Z to feel entitled to the same level of respect enjoyed by more senior colleagues. When it comes to hierarchies and layers of management, Gen Z struggle to see what all the fuss is about.

Younger people prefer to focus on bigger thinking, such as employee advocacy. According to the Deloitte survey, 75 per cent of Gen Zs say that 'an organization's community engagement and societal impact is an important factor when considering a potential employer'.[11]

Responding to pressure

Gen Z's probing questions about an organization's stance on issues from gender to the environment can push the C-suite into decisions they would prefer to stay silent on. For a generation unrestricted by long-term loyalty, there's little sense of commitment – at least not enough to stop them using social media to expose companies that are slow to act on social issues.[12]

Six in 10 Gen Zs (61 per cent) believe they have the power to drive change within their organizations, particularly when it comes to workload, services offered to clients, learning and development, diversity and inclusion, wellness, social impact and environmental efforts.[13]

'These individuals are getting to the commercial heart of decision making, and the guts of a business, and it's really threatening', according to Alison Taylor, associate professor at NYU Stern School of Business. For Taylor, 'This generation is very difficult to impress. They have elevated expectations on everything from mental health to climate change... they're skilled on social media and they don't remember a time when companies were neutral on big issues.'[14]

Driven by new perceptions of identity, work, experience and progress, Gen Z are nudging employers into radical decisions and alternative ways of working. At the risk of being publicly exposed, either by Gen Z consumers or by their own workforce, companies feel the pressure to change.

Organizations reacting to this pressure have two choices. They can either try to keep up by hiring the 'Gen Z whisperers', individuals who are unlikely to offer a magic bullet. Alternatively, they can lead from the front and develop a tailor-made culture that accommodates not only Gen Z but all generations in the workplace, a culture of social wellbeing built on authentic, long-term principles.

Developing a culture of social wellbeing

Evidence of practical benefits

In the past, wellbeing was often overlooked by leaders, it sometimes being perceived as a luxury add-on to the demands of the business. However, social wellbeing supports competitive edge by accommodating the forces of change – including Gen Z.

In developing our approach to better working practices, we assessed long-term workplace trends (Chapter 2) and academic research (Chapter 5). We then looked for practical examples where actions related to social wellbeing appeared to be making a beneficial difference to organizations.

Paul Zak, who developed the trust experiments we saw in Chapter 5, has suggested that employees earn an additional $6,450 a year, or

17 per cent more, at companies in the highest quartile of trust compared with those in the lowest quartile.[15]

Trust and psychological safety support an inclusive approach to work, and it's been shown that diversity and inclusion lead to competitive advantage. A global study of more than 21,000 organizations found: 'For profitable firms, a move from no female leaders to 30 per cent representation is associated with a 15 per cent increase in the net revenue margin.'[16] According to research by software developer Cloverpop, diverse teams made better business decisions 87 per cent of the time.[17]

In looking for examples where social wellbeing could offer practical beneficial advantage, we were supported by our colleague Tom Cassidy. With an MSc in psychological coaching and a background in financial services, Tom has a close understanding of psychological research relating to business.

By finding practical examples of what we recognized as social wellbeing objectives, and supplementing them with conclusions drawn from our own research, we could develop a roadmap for our clients. This would guide them towards preparing their workforce and their business for the difficult years ahead.

The examples we found include the following.

NEW HOPE FOR HYBRID

Flexible work patterns such as hybrid can support work–life balance. However, since the pandemic, hybrid patterns have sometimes become bogged down in a head-scratching mishmash of fragmented teams, fractured morale and a diluted sense of direction. Leaders like Martin Sorrell have been concerned about losing the 'glue'.

There are definite advantages to working in an office. In 2022, Microsoft asked 20,000 people in 11 countries about their experience of hybrid working. Their results showed that 'people come in [to the office] for each other to recapture what they miss: the social connection of being with other people'.[18]

Connectivity – being with other people – is a key element of the work–life balance that's important to all generations, especially Gen Z and millennials (born 1981-1996). Together these two generations make up 42 per cent of the US population, compared to a combined 27 per cent for boomers and seniors.[19] Deloitte's annual Gen Z and

Millennial Survey found that, in both 2023 and 2024, work–life balance was this demographic's top consideration when choosing an employer and was also the 'top trait they admire in their peers'.[20]

Balance can include a hybrid pattern. But to maintain the essential qualities of connectivity and teamwork, effective hybrid must start from a mindset about how people work, not just where and when.

When people work remotely, leaders can help individuals take the team home with them, psychologically if not literally. By thinking about the team overall, rather than simply a timetable populated by individuals, managers can focus on who people feel connected to, regardless of who's working where.

The connectivity at the heart of social wellbeing guards against loneliness. It champions difference and diversity, and it's inclusive and forward-looking. This approach to hybrid accommodates work–life balance while still supporting a culture of teamwork and cohesion. This reduces the risk of individuals feeling isolated, which in turn can lead to demoralization and turnover.

DECISIVE DIVERSITY AND INCLUSION

In 2013, Qantas, Australia's national airline, posted a record loss of AUD 2.8 billion.[21] Fuel costs, engine issues and a labour dispute led to dire predictions. Yet within four years, CEO Alan Joyce had turned the business round from basket-case to an airline that was the envy of its global competitors.

Joyce not only dragged Qantas back from the brink but delivered a record profit of AUD 850 million. For good measure, Qantas boosted its operating margin to 12 per cent, won the 2017 World's Safest Airline award, ranked as Australia's most trusted big business and delivered shareholder returns in the top quartile of its global peers.[22] What was Joyce's secret? 'We have a very diverse environment and a very inclusive culture,' he said.[23]

Two-thirds of 10,000 leaders surveyed in 2017 cited diversity and inclusion as 'important' or 'very important' to business.[24] Boston Consulting Group found that companies with diverse management teams reported innovation revenue that was 19 percentage points higher than that of less diverse competitors.[25] This research echoed similar findings by others (including Cloverpop, 2017, as noted above).

When a young indigenous woman asked Alan Joyce whether she could ever lead Quantas, he replied, 'Well if a gay Irishman can become the CEO of Qantas then an indigenous lady can.'[26]

PROFESSIONAL DEVELOPMENT – UPSKILLING AND RESKILLING

Employees value professional development programmes, regarding them as an investment in their future. Both upskilling (enhancing performance in a current role) and reskilling (enabling a change in direction) can prepare people for changing work practices, such as AI. New skills also help to mitigate the impact of the digital age and its cost to mental health, attention spans and critical thinking.

In 2020, the World Economic Forum (WEF) noted: 'The top skills and skill groups which employers see as rising in prominence in the lead up to 2025 include groups such as critical thinking and analysis as well as problem solving, and skills in self-management such as active learning, resilience, stress tolerance and flexibility.'[27]

In 2023, new WEF evidence suggested that businesses see investing in learning and training on the job as 'the most promising workforce strategy for achieving their business goals'.[28] The WEF's 2023 research confirmed, as predicted in 2020, that organizations' top five needs in skills training from 2023 to 2027 are:

- analytical thinking
- creative thinking
- AI and big data
- leadership and social influence
- resilience, flexibility and agility[29]

For leaders, upskilling is important in an era when they are learning to loosen links with a newly flexible workforce while still maintaining a tight rein on cohesion, engagement and morale. Reskilling is helpful in finding new ways to implement ingrained experience, for example developing communication techniques to suit younger generations.

For employees, upskilling is the route to promotion and new opportunities. Reskilling will become increasingly important as AI reshapes the workplace. Both will involve a high degree of focus on the skills that humans excel in and which AI struggles with.

Deloitte forecasts that so-called 'soft skill-intensive occupations' will account for two thirds of all jobs by 2030.[30] This likely explains why – according to the WEF – 'socio-emotional skills steadily increased their share of learning hours from 2017 to 2023'.[31]

Training opportunities in upskilling and reskilling demonstrate investment in individuals, recognizing talent and potential. They are also the natural outcome of a reimagined approach to appraisals.

UPDATING APPRAISALS

Antiquated review systems, described by one writer as an 'annual rite of corporate kabuki', are on their way out.[32] Annual appraisals, condemned by managers and staff alike, have been abandoned by more than a third of US companies.[33]

Leading tech businesses including Adobe, Google, Juniper Systems, Dell, Microsoft and IBM have replaced once-a-year conversations with regular feedback. So too have professional services companies such as Deloitte, Accenture, PwC and KPMG, as well as Netflix, Gap and Lear. They are switching to systems that favour:

- **Ongoing feedback** in which problems can be resolved quickly and effectively instead of focusing on work done a long time ago.

- **A shift from accountability to learning.** Rather than dwelling on what went wrong in the past and who was at fault, better to think about the skills that will ensure things go well next time.

- **Human assessments.** Reduce the reliance on data by focusing instead on human analysis.

- **Better interpersonal connections**, including efforts by leaders to get to know their team through informal chat sessions.

- **Renewed focus on coaching**, with mentors and managers helping people to improve their performance.

- **Feedback from a range of sources** so that employees know their future rests on more than one opinion.

- **Employees setting their own goals**, in partnership with their manager.

ONBOARDING – LIKE UNBOXING A NEW PHONE

Traditionally, new hires were quietly merged into a team. According to behavioural scientists Daniel M Cable, Francesca Gino and Bradley R Staats, onboarding procedures were usually aimed at absorbing 'joiners' into company culture.[34] Better instead, however, to 'unbox' joiners, with the flourish reserved for that fanfare moment when you take a glossy new phone out of its packaging.

Traditionally, new people were expected to keep their personal values and creativity under wraps, at least while they were at work. Much has changed under the influence of Gen Z. Priorities in personal identity at work now also mean more to older generations too, especially since the pandemic.

Recognizing this, HR professionals are increasingly acting on research by Cable, Gino and Staats. This advocates a more personal approach to onboarding, with new hires encouraged to express creative ideas and talents on the job from day one.

Cable, Gino and Staats took their research to Wipro, a business process outsourcing company, where they were able to compare the organizational (i.e. traditional) approach to onboarding with the new, personal model. Wipro found that onboarding processes that emphasized personal identity rather than company culture led to stronger connectivity, better job retention, higher productivity rates and fewer cases of human error.

Developing skills for social wellbeing

By blending data-driven research (detailed in Chapter 5) with everyday experience (as noted above), we assembled a practical understanding of social wellbeing which for us means company culture that:

- offers credible psychological safety, respect, trust and belonging
- ensures these values are supported by all, from the board to the interns
- demonstrates commitment through recognition, inclusivity and work–life balance

- accommodates flexibility in thinking, prioritizing people rather than process
- offers pathways towards improvement through skills training and promotions

Next, we needed to roll everything up into a comprehensive training programme that we could give to clients. Social wellbeing had been developed in response to their difficulties with engagement. Now that we could offer them a viable solution, we had to design skills modules that would transform our conclusions into a programme of effective, practical steps.

We developed four training modules. The first is social wellbeing, which can be imagined as the base of a pyramid, propping up the other three.

Social wellbeing applies to everyone across the business, from the C-suite down. Understood as the set of behaviours that tackle underlying causes of disengagement, social wellbeing provides a meaningful alternative to the ineffective initiatives that people are losing faith in.

Social wellbeing sets the tone for our three remaining modules. These include two specific skillsets that address the impact of 21st century lifestyles. In particular, they give key staff the skills prioritized by organizations in the 2020s, as noted by the World Economic Forum and listed above. These two skillsets are:

- agile thinking
- future communication

Finally, the fourth module – at the top of the pyramid – is aimed specifically at leaders and gives them the skills to lead through change. These four training modules, reimagining culture from the ground up, together offer the future skills that will prepare businesses for the years ahead (Figure 6.1).

By helping organizations develop a culture that leads to beneficial results, we are effectively rolling out a re-interpreted Bazball for business, packaged into tangible, practical steps. Together, these can be expressed as a formula (Figure 6.2).

FIGURE 6.1 Future skills solutions – at a glance

Leading through change

Helping leaders manage uncertainty while boosting motivation and company culture

Future communication

Helping people get the most from AI and create compelling narratives from data

Agile thinking

A dynamic approach to critical thinking, supporting creativity, collaboration and flexibility

Social wellbeing

Building a strong company culture by improving trust, psychological safety and engagement

FIGURE 6.2 A formula for Bazball for business

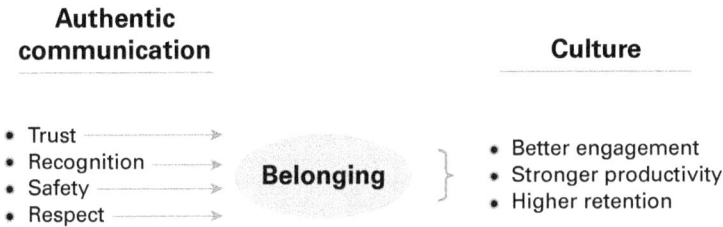

Authentic communication

- Trust
- Recognition
- Safety
- Respect

Belonging

Culture

- Better engagement
- Stronger productivity
- Higher retention

Exploring our four modules in detail, let's begin with the foundation stone of social wellbeing itself. This consists of five courses, developed in initial training sessions by our long-time colleague Julia Davies. Designed to help leaders and employees work together in building a better environment at work, our courses include the following themes and ideas.

How leaders create culture

Intangible assets such as human capital and culture are estimated to comprise on average 52 per cent of a company's market value.[35] Culture is a significant part of an organization's worth. With this in mind, writer Simon Sinek said: 'Customers will never love a company until the employees love it first.'[36] How much do your people love yours?

An organization without a clear outline of the culture it aspires to can't expect HR to rustle up a quick-fix solution. It's bigger than that. Culture starts with the board, who must ask themselves whether current management styles inspire the behaviours they expect.

We don't aim to give organizations a shopping list detailing the specifics of the culture they could or should develop. Instead, we prefer to help clients navigate their own way forward. Our toolkit starts with a focus on objectives, shaped by the organization's values.

Culture is a matter of communication. Leaders need to be crystal clear in their messaging, showing in practice the values they advocate in theory (showing how rather than showing off).

By building culture 'top-down', leaders reward 'champions' – who help to shape things at a grassroots level. Leaders keep people on track, and encourage and reinforce through reward and recognition. Success can be measured by assessing whether employees feel that communication, respect and a sense of belonging are as meaningful and effective as leaders hope.

How to create psychological safety

At first glance, psychological safety seems like a simple source of reassurance to those who stand to gain from it. In practice, however, it's a double-edged sword that must be carefully managed.

At its simplest, psychological safety amplifies people in the room who might otherwise be overlooked. Leaders adopting it as best practice aim to ensure that everyone benefits from an equal platform, enjoying the chance to be heard while feeling free from fear of shame or humiliation. Psychological safety helps people cut through so they can make their presence felt.

There is, however, a risk that individuals may brandish it in pursuit of their own comfort, using it to fend off comments they mistakenly perceive as an attack. When this happens, other people dare not say the 'wrong thing' for fear of censure. Leaders trying to champion safety without giving in to demands for comfort can feel like they're caught in a sword fight on a tightrope.

In our course on psychological safety, the 'anti-fragility' work of social psychologist Jonathan Haidt inspired an exercise where we ask participants to think of a personal example of significant learning.[37] Rather than a moment in a classroom, most people think of a time when they had to juggle many demands and were forced to quickly learn how to cope with pressure.

The incident they remember might not have been an easy experience. But that's the point. We learn more when we are stretched and overcoming challenges than we do when we're doodling and thinking about lunch. Psychological safety isn't about seeking comfort, it's about making the most of opportunity. Expressing your opinion, fighting for your corner and overcoming challenges are part and parcel of working life. Being entitled to victory is not.

Our course also seeks to help leaders find balance in these complex issues. They can do this in conversation with employees, whether separately or as a team. In discussing a 'contracting agreement', there is expectation on both sides. Employers offer security, benefits and recognition to employees who offer time, effort and loyalty. As part of this agreement, leaders can remind people that psychological safety and accountability go hand in hand.

Hybrid working practices

It used to be taken for granted that an employer would provide an employee with somewhere to work for five days a week. Since the pandemic, offices and five days a week have been subject to new arrangements.

Centralized culture, teamwork and personal contact have all evolved. To create a culture fit for the 2020s, it's important to understand how a team can benefit by both coming together and being apart.

In the office, it helps to recognize proximity bias. In a call that includes people in the room and others working remotely, who is more likely to be given air-time? Usually those in the room. Recognizing this and acting on it will help to even things out.

Fearful of losing the 'glue', many businesses are showing concerns about their people working from home. This comes despite widespread experience during the pandemic of people committing to 'deep work' away from a busy office.

Ultimately, effective team culture in a hybrid setting thrives on:

- communication
- behaviour
- purpose
- values

A team charter, clarifying purpose, strategy and goals is helpful, particularly if it includes commitments to ideal behaviours and the communication that supports them. For example, in a hybrid setting, cliques, misunderstanding and rushed decisions can be avoided by ensuring key conversations only take place during meetings arranged in advance. Meetings should only be held when necessary, avoiding back-to-back calls so that working from home can be just that.

Building social confidence

Social wellbeing supports an individual's ability to sustain self-respect so that they may show their authentic self to others. This is the basis for strong professional relationships at work. Self-respect is deepened by life experience. It comes from being self-aware, and feeling dependable and reliable to yourself when you are tested by life.

Self-respect is supported by inner triumphs, not showy goals. It is not comparative; in other words, it's not earned by feeling better than someone else. It is the starting point of our respect for others, enabling us to value their own self-respect.

Self-respect nurtures self-confidence, strengthening our sense of identity and enabling us to build an image of ourselves as someone with valuable experiences, positive traits and human shortcomings, all of which we are ready to recognize and accept without judgement.

Self-respect for our abilities and belief in our professional competence both reduce vulnerabilities such as impostor syndrome. Both also contribute to a sense of authenticity – which is what others seek and value in their communication with us.

The tricky bit in all of this is that we each have our own personal preferences and foibles, a contradictory collection of strengths and weaknesses. Office politics – in which we try to amplify our strengths, hide our weaknesses and hope no-one spots our efforts – is always something of a minefield. Transactional calls (whether phone or virtual) that squeeze out warmth and empathy create many opportunities for misunderstanding.

Many of the wrinkles in office politics relate to the clash between too much self-confidence and too little. At the heart of this it helps to think about self-esteem, the rich mix of identity behaviours that include components such as:

- self-respect
- authentic identity
- feeling of belonging
- sense of competence

Self-esteem is vulnerable to others' opinions of us. No-one wants to be tainted with a reputation for incompetence, which can be triggered if we mishandle office politics. To safeguard against this, an understanding of self-confidence must allow for the demands of workplace social interaction.

The social human at work

As well as strengthening the relationship between employer and employees, social wellbeing also builds authentic communication between peers. Respect, tolerance, empathy and patience help to deflate potential conflict. Ultimately, allowance for human foibles reduces fear, pressure and tension – the negative emotions that blunt the sharp edge of meaningful, creative engagement.

Skills in personal impact, networking and difficult conversations can help to repair and preserve workplace connections and relationships. So too can awareness of common errors in thinking, such as the logical fallacies that can potentially lead to mistakes in our relationships with others.

Multigenerational communication is particularly vulnerable to misunderstanding if handled without care. This is especially so when natural human connection is neglected in favour of functional, transactional process. Humans are prone to characteristics and variability and only by accepting this can we manage the ebb and flow that all relationships experience.

In encouraging better understanding of other people, it helps to begin with a sense of our own humility. This is achieved by balancing the needs of the self with the needs of those around us. In conversation, it's good to give a little of ourselves, revealing something that shows we're just as human as everyone else. By quietening the self and giving space to grace and curiosity, we can value others and accept the impossibility of perfection – in them and in ourself.

At the start of the book, we looked at some of the harsh realities of life in the Industrial Revolution, a time when huge mechanical looms noisily clattered back and forth, posing great dangers to small hands. Children, darting in and out of the machines, scooped up loose cotton and tended to the moving parts, sometimes suffering serious injury.

They could expect to be blamed for getting too near to the unguarded, steam-powered machinery that they were expected to get near to. Responsibility for the outcome of harsh, physical conditions was dumped on their shoulders.

Today, around the world, fewer children tend machines. Adults, meanwhile, might face conditions that impact their mental health, including long hours, excessive workloads and a clattering rate of working. Responsibility for managing this often falls to individuals.

Individuals, though, are also members of a team, a team that perhaps expected them to work in this way. As such, does the team not owe them more than this? As in the past, so too now the direction of travel is change. The changes we advocate focus on culture.

Organizations are recognizing the benefits of protecting the team. Rather than isolating individuals, exposing them to the giddy work-rate of the digital age and letting them cope with the fallout alone, businesses are shouldering more of the responsibility, for example softening in their approach to work–life balance. And they are reaping rewards in return.

Social wellbeing offers a blueprint for this strategy. It serves as a roadmap for the future, for organizations and the people they employ. In the next chapter, we'll discover more practical examples of how to implement the skills it depends on.

Notes

1 I Anghel. Workers resisting the office grind are suddenly lonely at home, 15 June 2023, Bloomberg, www.bloomberg.com/news/articles/2023-06-15/how-work-from-home-or-remote-jobs-impact-productivity-staff-happiness (archived at https://perma.cc/7ZFA-7PQV)

2 S Wilde. How Ben Stokes and Brendon McCullum inspired England's summer of Bazball, 13 September 2022, *The Times*, www.thetimes.com/sport/cricket/article/how-ben-stokes-and-brendon-mccullum-inspired-englands-summer-of-bazball-g7680zj3p (archived at https://perma.cc/9DS5-4Y8W)

3 S Wilde. How Ben Stokes and Brendon McCullum inspired England's summer of Bazball, 13 September 2022, *The Times*, www.thetimes.com/sport/cricket/article/how-ben-stokes-and-brendon-mccullum-inspired-englands-summer-of-bazball-g7680zj3p (archived at https://perma.cc/NL5V-NX6J)

4   A Raval. Making sense of Gen Z: employers seek answers on managing younger workers, 16 June 2024, *Financial Times*, www.ft.com/content/ee6fb86c-d2c6-4bc3-ac5c-e7bd7a1db1d4 (archived at https://perma.cc/VHU2-DPSA)

5   A Raval. Making sense of Gen Z: employers seek answers on managing younger workers, 16 June 2024, *Financial Times*, www.ft.com/content/ee6fb86c-d2c6-4bc3-ac5c-e7bd7a1db1d4 (archived at https://perma.cc/P6KH-STA2)

6   K Dubina. Projections overview and highlights, 2020-30, October 2021, US Bureau of Labor Statistics, www.bls.gov/opub/mlr/2021/article/projections-overview-and-highlights-2020-30.htm (archived at https://perma.cc/ATZ8-MCNV)

7   Deloitte. Gen Z and Millennial Survey: Living and working with purpose in a transforming world, 2024, www.deloitte.com/global/en/issues/work/genz-millennial-survey.html (archived at https://perma.cc/99A8-LD55)

8   Deloitte. Gen Z and Millennial Survey: Living and working with purpose in a transforming world, 2024, www.deloitte.com/global/en/issues/work/genz-millennial-survey.html (archived at https://perma.cc/2YLR-ZR82)

9   D Tinsley. US labor market: changing for the better? Bank of America Institute, content.fortune.com/wp-content/uploads/2022/05/who-is-benefiting-from-the-us-labor-market-may-2022.pdf (archived at https://perma.cc/VZ2C-HWSB)

10   Deloitte. Gen Z and Millennial Survey: Living and working with purpose in a transforming world, 2024, www.deloitte.com/global/en/issues/work/genz-millennial-survey.html (archived at https://perma.cc/8YP2-2BXP)

11   Deloitte. Gen Z and Millennial Survey: Living and working with purpose in a transforming world, 2024, www.deloitte.com/global/en/issues/work/genz-millennial-survey.html (archived at https://perma.cc/2HH8-6AJX)

12   A Raval. Making sense of Gen Z: employers seek answers on managing younger workers, 16 June 2024, *Financial Times*, www.ft.com/content/ee6fb86c-d2c6-4bc3-ac5c-e7bd7a1db1d4 (archived at https://perma.cc/5LWP-6JKX)

13   Deloitte. Gen Z and Millennial Survey: Living and working with purpose in a transforming world, 2024, www.deloitte.com/global/en/issues/work/genz-millennial-survey.html (archived at https://perma.cc/25DM-FTUG)

14   A Raval. Making sense of Gen Z: employers seek answers on managing younger workers, 16 June 2024, *Financial Times*, www.ft.com/content/ee6fb86c-d2c6-4bc3-ac5c-e7bd7a1db1d4 (archived at https://perma.cc/9ZDM-2GY3)

15   P Zak. The Neuroscience of Trust, January-February 2017, *Harvard Business Review*, hbr.org/2017/01/the-neuroscience-of-trust (archived at https://perma.cc/3R9B-9P6F)

16 M Noland, T Moran, and B Kotschwar. Is Gender Diversity Profitable? Evidence from a Global Survey, February 2016, Peterson Institute for International Economics, www.piie.com/sites/default/files/documents/wp16-3. pdf (archived at https://perma.cc/PKD8-5ZN6)

17 E Larson. Diversity + Inclusion = Better Decision Making At Work, September 19 2017, Cloverpop, www.cloverpop.com/blog/infographic-diversity-inclusion- better-decision-making-at-work (archived at https://perma.cc/T6P4-XW26)

18 Microsoft WorkLab. Work Trend Index Special Report: Hybrid work is just work, are we doing it wrong? September 2 2022, www.microsoft.com/en-us/ worklab/work-trend-index/hybrid-work-is-just-work (archived at https:// perma.cc/6WGG-SY25)

19 J Leichenko. How well do you know Gen Z and Millennials? 23 February 2023, Kantar, www.kantar.com/north-america/inspiration/consumer/how-well- do-you-know-gen-z-and-millennials (archived at https://perma.cc/ XD8T-EDZB)

20 Deloitte. Gen Z and Millennial Survey: Living and working with purpose in a transforming world, 2024, www.deloitte.com/global/en/issues/work/genz- millennial-survey.html (archived at https://perma.cc/52VK-B8DD)

21 J Bourke. The diversity and inclusion revolution: Eight powerful truths, 22 January 2018, Deloitte Insights, www2.deloitte.com/us/en/insights/deloitte- review/issue-22/diversity-and-inclusion-at-work-eight-powerful-truths.html (archived at https://perma.cc/UPJ2-4TD9)

22 J Bourke. The diversity and inclusion revolution: Eight powerful truths, 22 January 2018, Deloitte Insights, www2.deloitte.com/us/en/insights/deloitte- review/issue-22/diversity-and-inclusion-at-work-eight-powerful-truths.html (archived at https://perma.cc/VDE8-8U5C)

23 J Bourke. The diversity and inclusion revolution: Eight powerful truths, 22 January 2018, Deloitte Insights, www2.deloitte.com/us/en/insights/deloitte- review/issue-22/diversity-and-inclusion-at-work-eight-powerful-truths.html (archived at https://perma.cc/9NFM-WMW7)

24 B Walsh et al. Rewriting the rules for the digital age: 2017 Deloitte Global Human Capital Trends, Deloitte, www2.deloitte.com/content/dam/Deloitte/us/ Documents/human-capital/hc-2017-global-human-capital-trends-us.pdf (archived at https://perma.cc/UWN5-2LFC)

25 R Lorenzo et al. How diverse leadership teams boost innovation, 23 January 2018, Boston Consulting Group, www.bcg.com/publications/2018/how-diverse- leadership-teams-boost-innovation (archived at https://perma.cc/4D84-SK8V)

26 K Hope. Why it's important to be yourself at work, 21 June 2016, BBC News, www.bbc.co.uk/news/business-36574837 (archived at https://perma.cc/ L9QV-U3UF)

27 K Schwab et al. The Future of Jobs Report 2020, 20 October 2020, World Economic Forum, www.weforum.org/reports/the-future-of-jobs-report-2020 (archived at https://perma.cc/3T4Z-7MX5)

28 S Zahidi. Future of Jobs Report 2023, 30 April 2023, World Economic Forum, www.weforum.org/publications/the-future-of-jobs-report-2023/ (archived at https://perma.cc/BXN2-G9EX)

29 S Zahidi. Future of Jobs Report 2023, 30 April 2023, World Economic Forum, www.weforum.org/publications/the-future-of-jobs-report-2023/ (archived at https://perma.cc/BXN2-G9EX)

30 J O'Mahony and D Rumbens. Soft skills for business success, Deloitte, www2.deloitte.com/au/en/pages/economics/articles/soft-skills-business-success.html (archived at https://perma.cc/3HD8-H2F9)

31 J O'Mahony and D Rumbens. Soft skills for business success, Deloitte, www2.deloitte.com/au/en/pages/economics/articles/soft-skills-business-success.html (archived at https://perma.cc/SE7Z-KFM3)

32 J McGregor. The corporate kabuki of performance reviews, 14 February 2013, *Washington Post*, www.washingtonpost.com/national/on-leadership/the-corporate-kabuki-of-performance-reviews/2013/02/14/59b60e86-7624-11e2-aa12-e6cf1d31106b_story.html (archived at https://perma.cc/K865-6KK7)

33 P Cappelli and A Tavis (2016) The Performance Management Revolution, *Harvard Business Review*, hbr.org/2016/10/the-performance-management-revolution (archived at https://perma.cc/B7HX-Q2BF)

34 D M Cable, F Gino and B R Staats. Breaking them in or eliciting their best? Reframing socialization around newcomers' authentic self-expression, *Administrative Science Quarterly*, 2013, **58** (1), pp. 1–36

35 D Haigh. Brand finance global intangible finance tracker 2018, Brand Finance, brandirectory.com/reports/global-intangible-finance-tracker-gift-2018 (archived at https://perma.cc/W37Y-2URN)

36 S Sinek (2017) *Leaders Eat Last: why some teams pull together and others don't*, Penguin

37 G Lukianoff and J Haidt (2018) *The Coddling of the American Mind: How good intentions and bad ideas are setting up a generation for failure*, Penguin

7

Agile thinking

Sending people back to the moon, as some countries plan to do, is all very exciting. But how can they be sure of bringing them home again?

China, Russia and America have all indicated an interest in sending people back to the harsh environment of the lunar surface, where visitors would need to be protected from searing temperatures, intense radiation, zero atmospheric pressure and an absence of oxygen. Low gravity doesn't help either. Getting to the moon is one thing, surviving there and coming home is another.

The reasons for going back to the moon are hard to pin down. There's much talk about science, education, exploration and other humbug disguising the fact that the impetus for such missions is political. It always was.

Efforts to get to the moon began in 1962 when President Kennedy put it on America's to do list in a speech at Rice University in Texas. Kennedy was seeking to demonstrate US ingenuity, though he seemed a little vague – announcing that America would go to the moon and 'do the other things'.

Ingenuity, from the plot of *Romeo and Juliet* to the development of AI, begins with the spark of an idea that flickers with the possibility of accomplishment, fulfilment, recognition and reward. Ingenuity stems from a creative process that can be broken down into steps and adopted as habit. After love, it's possibly just about the best thing we can do with our mind.

Choosing to think

The process is fundamentally about the way we think. It ensures that we carefully examine an idea and assess it with the eye of a critic, holding it to the light before discarding or developing it. This is critical thinking, which at our company Working Voices we call **agile thinking** since it relies on the mental agility to think with an open mind and a spark of creativity.

Agile thinking lies at the root of all good decisions and subsequent actions. The fusion between emotion (in the form of inspiration) and reason (logical process), agile thinking transforms visionary inspiration into practical reality. It's about choosing to think, evaluating thoughts, assessing what to react to and deciding on next steps.

This is the process that transformed a politician's speech into a space mission that took people from a Florida launchpad to the moon's Sea of Tranquillity. The whole venture would have been an embarrassing shot in the foot if it had ended in fatal failure. NASA had to get three men and a 'lunar lander' capsule into space, requiring a rocket the size of a 36-storey building. The rocket was assembled and launched by thousands of technicians – none of whom would be on the moon to get the crew home again.

In their absence, what creative ingenuity could be relied on to bring the men back? How can you be sure that when you hit the 'get me home' button you'll safely leave the moon?

The failsafe solution lay in two chemicals that when allowed to mix would be guaranteed to create an explosion so strong it would blast the crew's lunar lander up into space and send them on the journey home. Critical thinking can be relied on, even in perilous situations.

Today, in our age of online falsehoods and conspiracies, clear-thinking analysis safeguards truth, enabling teams to share understanding of what's real and what's not. In recent years businesses have, slowly, begun to recognize the increasing threat to clarity of thought and perceptions of reality. In 2014, we developed training sessions in critical thinking. We knew we were on the right lines when in 2020 we finally sold one.

Training can enhance skills in finding reliable clarity and common ground. People will always come to their own conclusions, but training will help them do so logically so that their conclusions are more likely to be viable, balanced, defendable and robust. Clarity leads to credibility, respect, trust, influence and recognition, values that in turn lead to promotions, pay rises and new opportunities.

The process of agile thinking starts with recognizing the value of an idea and then shapes it into something worth sharing. This is a better bet than failing to think, resisting the effort to evaluate and giving in to the crowd.

Wrestling with complexity

Truth isn't always as popular as we might expect. Some of us readily notice truth's sweet scent and can follow it through a forest of complexity. Others may not see the wood for the trees. Around the world, millions of people let objective truth wither in the glare of nonsense about 'deadly vaccines', 'Marxist liberals' and secret cabals supposedly running government.

How did we get to a point where truth could be so easily discarded? What are the implications for employers of widespread confusion diluting our grip on reality? And what can be done in response?

The central point at the heart of these questions is not the truth of this or that issue. It's about the process of consistently reaching accurate, objective understanding. Objective truth can be hard to see. Our own subjective viewpoints all too easily get in the way. It's sometimes hard to escape our own individual perspective and see the simple truth, especially when truth isn't that simple.

To give an example, the influence of the European Union on pre-Brexit Britain can be described in many competing ways according to whom you ask. In an issue as complex as this, differing views may all contain accuracies. Yet, prior to the UK vote on Brexit in 2016, it was hard for many people to see truth in the 'other side's' position.

No initial opinion can be regarded as the last word on a subject, particularly on complex issues. Other opinions are available. By adopting an agile approach to the way we think, we are more likely to get beyond our own limited perspective and burrow through the layers of complexity in search of objective truth.

In fact, our ability to nimbly assess the value of competing opinions can be played to our advantage, as we shall discover. However, this isn't always easy to do. Comparing and contrasting competing lines of thought can be scary. To explain all of this a little more, let's briefly open up your head and take a quick look at your brain.

Taking a quick look at your brain

The brain's many parts have evolved over millions of years. They include the frontal lobes that support reasoning. Other parts form a set of structures known as the limbic system which can throw up strong emotional reactions. In our daily actions, the frontal lobes usually take the lead, though substances such as alcohol can reduce their impact.

Connected by neural circuits (information highways linking the parts of the brain), mental messages pass rapidly within and between the brain's structures. When a thought arises in one part of the brain, another part might throw up a competing idea, offering us alternative options or possibilities. A sense of fulfilment about saving a pot of money might be quickly followed by a spontaneous urge to blow the cash in Vegas, in turn followed by sensible thoughts about planning a calm holiday.

A simmering mishmash of bickering urges isn't particularly healthy, so – to preserve the brain's energy – an almond-sized part of the limbic system known as the hypothalamus tries to subconsciously maintain order and balance, with varying levels of success.

A job offer for example can lead to a sense of excitement or concern about change or both. These competing interpretations can be confusing, leading to anxiety about how to respond. Confusion and anxiety can lead to fear. Immobilizing and corrosive, fear is always a threat.

We can manage fearful reactions by ignoring their impact and calmly assessing our options, for example looking at the pros and cons of changing jobs. This calls for a mental process in which we carefully examine and compare the alternatives before eventually making an informed decision.

Alternatively, we can give in to fear and follow its clamouring urge to abandon any analysis of pros and cons. It's easier and quicker to jump to a conclusion that makes us feel safe and certain. If we reject the job offer, the fear goes away. In giving in to fear, however, we lose the ability to make effective decisions which means we may also miss out on valuable opportunities. The process of critical thinking helps people reach safe conclusions and override instinctive feelings that might otherwise lead them astray.

The divisive impact of fear

Accepting the easiest option

Some people prefer to give in to fear and accept the easiest option rather than make calm comparisons. This can be a dangerous practice. Individuals who are reluctant to carefully think about choices may not be able to escape their biases and assumptions. This is an unreliable approach to decision making. Online, this habit is open to exploitation by groups looking for new recruits. By swelling their numbers, political 'tribes' and their leaders seek to become more influential.

Today, we are more tribal than we were in the post-war period when political parties in the UK and US weren't really that far apart. At that time, there was rule by consensus. Paternalistic, middle-of-the-road politicians from opposite parties shared a similar outlook. Neither side wholeheartedly scrapped decisions made by the other or filibustered their way to obstructing vital bills.

Voters too shared broad understanding. Restricted to a limited number of TV channels, people watched the same news and entertainment. Many millions of people would watch the same thing on TV at the same time, reinforcing a coherent version of reality that most individuals were happy to accept. Fundamentally, people shared similar perceptions of truth.

Of course, the past was far from perfect. Acceptable 'reality' could be intolerant of people perceived as different, reinforcing attitudes of 'them and us'. Radical social change, a rise in international travel and the development of the internet could potentially have made us more understanding and open-minded than we were in the past. The populations of most developed countries enjoy more openness and choice than before. Yet we are fearful and fragmented.

Today, huge TV audiences watching the same show are far less common. We have fewer moments where millions of us experience similar reactions and conclusions at the same time. There are news channels that specifically target just one section of the audience. The internet divides us as much as it brings us together.

Social media encourages closed chat groups and echo chambers. Heated comments and emotional responses raise the temperature, deepening divisions and stoking fear. Polarized opinion leads to mistrust and suspicion, especially when fanned by misinformation and deliberately deceptive disinformation. Some groups question whether NASA ever put a man on the moon at all.

Voters not only struggle to understand 'the other lot' but may even doubt their validity, as if alternative opinions are threats along with the people who hold them. In times of fear and uncertainty, it's reassuring to fall back on a perspective that doesn't demand careful assessment or the need to accept something new.

Fear works in other ways too. The global financial crisis that began in 2007 unnerved banks and businesses. At the time, we visited a client whose finance traders were feeling too nervous to trade. Unable to decide between actions that could lead to luck or loss, they were effectively paralyzed by fear.

Sinking into groupthink

Biases, misassumptions and mental paralysis can be contagious. In the grip of fear, people seek safety by following the crowd, readily rushing towards the accepted viewpoint – sometimes without stopping to find out what makes it correct. This leads to groupthink, where no-one challenges the prevailing opinion. There's no need to challenge it. Groupthink is not about accuracy. It's about unity and the security it offers.

Again, the financial crisis offers a clear example. In the early 2000s, rising numbers of US mortgages were sold to people who were unlikely to pay them off. So-called 'subprime mortgage debts' owed to banks were bundled together into mortgage-backed securities and sold to other banks, spilling over into the credit market as well as domestic and global stock markets.[1] But the practice of selling bad debt for good money was never going to last forever, as many in the industry well knew.

And yet, as if putting their hands over their ears and singing so they wouldn't hear reality knocking on the door, bankers continued to dump derivatives and other financial chicanery on to investors without much thought for the risks. It was as if they were splashing in the surf, jumping en masse on a single battered airbed that was about to give way at any moment. The rest of us meanwhile trusted that the banks were as safe as houses.

We delivered a training session in 2006 when one of the participants, a banker, explained that derivatives include contracts that repackage bad debt. 'The amazing thing is,' he said, his eye glinting with pride, 'we take trash, in the form of unpaid mortgages from hard-up Americans, and after we package it up to sell to investors it gets triple-A ratings.'

'Great, isn't it?' he beamed, looking for a poetic metaphor to give his thoughts a little lustre. 'It comes in as garbage and we sell it as birthday cake.' This was helpful, though we thought it was worth checking whether he was actually saying that money was being made from loans that were unlikely to be paid back? 'Yep,' he said, still beaming. This needed to be challenged. How did the bosses feel about it – surely they were wise to the folly at play here? 'Well,' he said, 'by the time it hits the fan, they'll all be on their yachts.'

It seemed that people at this bank did not have a clue about the sizeable impact of unthinking groupthink. Then in 2007 the consequences struck all of us, like an iceberg looming out of the darkness, and banks began sinking soon after.

The 2007–08 global financial crisis was fuelled by a combination of groupthink and greed that outweighed calm and careful assessment. The International Monetary Fund estimated that large US and European banks lost more than $1 trillion from toxic assets and bad loans between 2007 and 2009.[2] The impact of this created international spikes in fear and alarm, contributing to a rise in populist politics and tribalism which still reverberates around the world in the 2020s.

Truth is in trouble as soon as we reject a plural approach to thinking, dismissing alternative opinions and the people who hold them.

Individuals who readily abandon an agile way of thinking often find that their opinion quickly hardens into 'fact', which helps them fit into safe groups of familiar people who feel the same as them.

The stronger the opinions they share, the more the group feels united and secure. And so they feed their fears with more outlandish 'facts' – eventually succumbing to delusion. This can take different forms. In 2007, bankers clung to magical thinking, believing their businesses would be OK. Other groups also succumb to fantasy, among them the conspiracy theorists we met in Chapters 3 and 5.

Mistrusting expertise

One of the global problems we face today is our general inability to address complex challenges, such as protecting international supply chains and tackling the climate emergency. By their very nature, complex issues can only be addressed when we are prepared to appreciate or at least acknowledge competing needs and pressures.

To get closer to understanding the impact of a complex issue, like escalating energy prices or dwindling resources, it helps to rely on a thinking process that's curious, tolerant and accommodating of alternatives. It's important to allow careful understanding to develop, rather than fall back on comforting but limited thoughts. Closed minds aren't open to new ideas.

Reactions influenced by caution, fear and unfamiliarity can be held in check by an ability to think for ourselves. This is a skill that doesn't come easily to everyone. We don't teach our children how to think critically. Common sense isn't as common as you'd hope.

Not only do we sometimes lack the patience to develop careful comparisons but also we are not much good these days at trusting experts who might be able to help us. This is a departure from the past. In days gone by, we had wise men and wandering stars. Later, there were learned monks who in turn gave way to scientists, explorers, thinkers and engineers. In times when few people could read or write, it was hard to ignore the opinion of someone with a quill and a command of Latin.

Today, however, while experts may be highly qualified and peer reviewed, they're sometimes sidelined by a 'me' culture that can be superficial and overbearing. Eminent scientists are still trying to persuade many politicians about the need to protect the environment, meanwhile anyone with a half-baked opinion can easily spread it through social media platforms and like-minded followers.

Unless we stem fake news, reclaim accuracy and renew our trust in experts, organizations will be compromised by a workforce divided by individual interpretations of reality. Leaders need employees who can rise above digital distractions, polarized opinion or fearful reactions. They need open-minded people who can keep a cool head and pursue logical lines of thought that lead to reliable decisions.

Understanding agile thinking

An agile way of thinking helps us develop informed opinions, make good decisions and communicate them more effectively. These are the steps that pave the way to successful actions. Agile thinking is an essential tool to anyone who needs to assess the options available in managing complex issues like risk analysis or change management.

Agile thinking cuts through sentiment and bias. It supports reliable conclusions and gives individuals the confidence to present their case, 'steel-manning' their thoughts with arguments as solid as if they were made of steel.

Pursuing these thoughts, our colleague Andrew Day developed practical support that evolved into four courses in agile thinking. An expert in bringing specialist ideas to non-specialist audiences, Andrew has a degree in philosophy and years of experience in giving people skills in critical thinking. He began by acknowledging that such skills allow people to do several things at once:

- **Pause before being overwhelmed** by fear or committing to a hasty decision, giving you a chance to objectively review things.

- **By objectively reviewing the options, you can consider possible alternatives** including those suggested by others which you yourself might have missed.

- **Having considered all the options** and assessed the advantages of each, you can feel confident about your final preference.

Using this outline as a starting point, Andrew broke it down into four different routes towards solutions and decisions. By being able to skip between them, leaders and managers can disrupt groupthink, manage cognitive limitations, show confidence in actions and trust their creativity.

These skills can help people break out of old habits in decision making and problem solving and rely instead on creativity, collaboration and a scientific sense of analysis. Leaders skilled in agile thinking are able to jump – or 'toggle' – between these mindsets, maintaining swift and effective flexibility in flipping between them when tackling a problem. Our courses on these four alternatives include the following themes and ideas.

Creative thinking

Creative thinking flourishes in an environment of freedom and tolerance. This is typical of creative companies – TV indies, ad agencies, design consultancies, etc. – but less easy to establish in sectors such as banking, insurance and accounting. Of course, the former live or die by their creativity while the latter are subject to greater compliance and regulation. Nevertheless, the point still stands: as a method of analysis there is value in creative thinking, whether you're in television or banking.

Creativity needs room to breathe. Compliant, regulated freedom is ineffective. To build authentic freedom into company culture, two criteria are necessary:

- A 'let's get it done' atmosphere of functional process needs to be suspended.
- There needs to be psychological safety, empowering people to suggest ideas.

In this environment, ideas and conversations emerge then veer off at tangents. Unless you have a supremo on your team delivering unbridled perfection at the first attempt, excellence won't run from a tap. It will trickle out of unexpected thoughts, dead ends and idle speculation – all of which must be permitted.

Divergent thinking such as this is one side of the coin. The other requires converging ideas into tangible proposals within deadlines and budgets. Leaders nimbly shifting between divergent and convergent ideas will be able to make the most of both in creating timely, effective solutions.

An element of creative freedom is especially important to younger people, many of whom have shown creative agility in building, curating and sharing social media galleries and channels. It's what they've grown up with. Organizations that choose to overlook this life experience are missing out on one of the key characteristics of the age in which we live.

We don't all need to 'move fast and break things', as was once popular at Facebook. But it certainly helps to think a little more innovatively than we might be used to and be a little less concerned about the consequences. This is a point made by Waguih Ishak, chief technologist at tech multinational Corning:

> I recall a scientist who had just returned from a conference in Japan and who barged into my office with a fierce determination to immediately begin work on a new (at the time) kind of laser that promised very low-cost computer interconnection.
>
> He had just met the inventor of the laser and had gone through a back-of-the-envelope analysis showing its feasibility. He assembled a small team of engineers and technicians and reached out to a couple of professors who had already started work in the same area.
>
> The lesson? If he had not insisted on going to the conference; if I hadn't broken the rules and let him travel; if we hadn't given him the resources to start the work; and if he had not asserted that the best time, however painful, to rethink the company's direction was during a down cycle, we would not have been the first company to develop this widely adopted technology.[3]

During periods of slow growth, leaders depend on people who can think creatively, people who have the confidence to reach into themselves and find something new. Leaders who are ready to listen to such thoughts, whether their own or other people's, will be able to consider a valuable range of solutions and opportunities – one or more of which might just prove effective in the long-run.

Scientific thinking

Creativity is a response to a known problem. Sometimes, however, the problem is not clearly defined. When your numbers are down on last year, an accurate explanation can take time to discover.

Multinational organizations need to be able to explain the complexities they encounter. They need to pitch concepts to clients, develop plans under multiple constraints and create metrics to analyse market conditions. In the words of astrophysicist Dr Moiya McTier: 'These are some of the most commonly requested skills in job postings by tech, finance and consulting companies, yet most candidates don't have formal training in any of them. Know who does? Scientists.'[4]

Scientific method starts with an assumption – a hypothesis. This is regarded with suspicion until it can be proved. It's tested against the available evidence and if it stands up to scrutiny only then can the hypothesis be accepted. If it doesn't measure up, it's abandoned or adjusted and the process repeated. Eventually a hypothesis is found that fits the evidence and this is accepted as the correct explanation.

Scientific thinking is related to other types of analysis such as inference and problem solving. Columbia University psychologist Deanna Kuhn highlights its connection to argumentative thinking, which relies on evidence in persuading others of the validity of an argument.[5]

Scientific thinking is not about science itself or even scientific aptitude. It's broader than that. For Kuhn, it's better described as 'knowledge seeking', a definition that 'encompasses any instance of purposeful thinking that has the objective of enhancing the seeker's knowledge'.[6] Scientific thinking is something people do, not something they have. It relies on the kind of rigorous, evidence-based thinking that is essential to science but not specific to it.

For these reasons, scientific thinking is actually engaged in by many people rather than a rarefied few. So how do you do it? Moiya McTier offers three simple steps, paraphrased here:[7]

1 **Learn to distinguish between observables and assumptions.**
   As we've seen, the brain makes 'fast thinking' assumptions (heuristics). For example, through a window we see blue sky and sunshine and so we assume it's warm, though when we get outside we find it's

surprisingly cold. Similarly, do you know for sure that the client is happy with your product or are you assuming so based on their buying record? Mistakes can be avoided by asking good questions.

2 **Be guided by questions rather than your task.**
Scientists move slowly, only taking the next step when they're sure of the last. The rest of us tend to gallop towards achieving the task. If the numbers are down on last year, then maybe we need to sell more products. Better however to ask questions at each step of the way. Why were the numbers down? Let's answer that before racing towards a remedy.

3 **For every question, create a working hypothesis.**
How will you know when a question has been correctly answered? Scientists pursue scientific method, repeatedly asking new questions until they find an explanation that fits the facts. When your numbers are down, you might assume that sales are lower. This hypothesis fits the facts but it's only part of the story. Sales are lower, but not by much. A new hypothesis will need to include other factors too.

Beware. The brain craves certainty and will try to interpret something as either 100 per cent likely or 0 per cent likely. This is related to the physiological flight or fight response. It's about binary choices, action or inaction, and it doesn't easily accommodate more nuanced perceptions.

By closely looking at the evidence, you might find that the issues at stake are more complicated than had been assumed. Maybe your sales figures are only a fraction of the bigger picture. Fractions are complicated for the brain, leading to anxiety about uncertainty and indecision and prompting a temptation to grasp at straws. This urge is best restrained by asking more questions and reshaping your hypothesis.

There's not much point berating the sales team when on closer inspection the data reveals a complex mix of factors including higher inflation, tougher export regulations and teething issues in hybrid working. By rigorously and accurately finding causes, you're more likely to adopt appropriate reactions.

Collaborative thinking

Effective teamwork requires all involved to share a collaborative spirit. It's down to leaders to set the tone, ensuring that teams remain mindful of their members. Otherwise, individuals with the most social capital are free to take centre-stage. These are the people with the most influence, or the most friends in the room or simply the loudest voice.

Dragged along in their wake, the team becomes a disparate group of individuals who are no longer effective as a single unit. As a group, everyone appears to be agreeing and working together but in truth much of their potential remains untapped.

With honesty and creativity effectively trimmed, the group is likely to be limited to conclusions that are shaped by just one or two individuals and approved by groupthink. People simply go along with what's been said since dissent will likely be batted away.

Groupthink is a loss to the organization. People who are paid to contribute are not able to give their all. Overlooked and struggling to participate, their intellectual capital is unrecognized and unused. If individuals had felt able to speak up in support of the strongest ideas rather than the loudest voices, more options would have been considered by the team and more solutions would be available.

By creating an atmosphere of psychological safety, all individuals will be in a better position to contribute rather than just the chosen few. This requires a sense of collaborative thinking, a spirit of empathy that validates a broad spectrum of opinions.

Professor of management at MIT, Dr Thomas Malone (whom we met in Chapter 5) found that groups make better decisions than individuals when they combine the different perspectives, skills and knowledge of their members. 'In our research,' Malone told *The Economist*, 'we found that groups in which the members were more socially perceptive were more collectively intelligent, presumably because they were able to work together more effectively.'[8]

According to Malone:

> Just putting a bunch of smart people together doesn't guarantee that you'll have a smart group. You might guess that from your own experience: most of us have seen plenty of groups of smart people who couldn't get anything useful done. But if just having a bunch of smart people in a group isn't enough to make the group smart, what is?

For Malone and his co-researchers, groups made up of socially perceptive people are more likely to be effective because they accommodate a range of opinions. However, Malone found that effectiveness also depends on the degree to which group members feel able to participate equally in conversation.

In favouring intellectual diversity, socially perceptive people are open to alternatives. However, for true collaboration to thrive, these alternatives need to be considered by the group as a whole. Individuals may need to step back from their own pet theory. This requires intellectual humility, which has been defined as a 'method of thinking that involves being genuinely open to learning from other people and simply accepting that you might be wrong'.[9]

Intellectual humility, a key feature of true collaboration, requires people to be ready to revise and even reverse their opinions in the light of new suggestions or updated information. This element of the collaborative process helps teams break out of silo thinking and make the most of the talent in the room. By remaining actively curious about your blind spots – things you've missed or were reluctant to accept – you become more receptive to alternative (and possibly better) solutions suggested by other people.

The fundamental elements of collaborative thinking, among them psychological safety, social perceptiveness and intellectual humility, lead to more than just effective teamwork. Embedded within company culture they open the way to a collaborative spirit across the organization, increasing the collective intelligence of the business as a whole. Collaborative thinking is therefore not just about better meetings, it's about social wellbeing and a better way of working.

Flexible thinking

Sometimes it might be tempting to dismiss suggestions that challenge current processes. This is a natural reaction. It's about preserving order and maintaining familiarity by correcting something that risks disrupting the 'way we always do things'.

This feeling is a reaction to things being out of place and causing a low-level sense of irritation, similar to hearing a duff note in a song. Pretending to ignore it leads to cognitive dissonance, in other words it jars with your understanding of how the song is 'supposed' to sound like.

This form of irritation can be problematic. In a meeting, it can overshadow a new idea that might be valid but may be rejected simply because it jars with the pre-existing understanding of things.

Negative emotion such as frustration can influence the more rational side of your intellect. The trick here is to recognize the emotions at play, step round them and allow yourself to take a more flexible approach to the new suggestion. Flexibility is about making room for novelty and alternatives.

In a paper entitled 'Psychological flexibility as a fundamental aspect of health', psychologists Todd Kashdan and Jonathan Rottenberg argued that mental strength is best understood through a lens of psychological flexibility.[10] For Kashdan and Rottenberg, this kind of flexibility includes being able to:

- recognize and adapt to various situational demands
- shift mindsets or behavioural repertoires
- be aware, open and committed to behaviours that are congruent with deeply held values

Building on their work, Professor Elaine Fox, head of psychology at the University of Adelaide, found a growing realization that mental agility is essential for wellbeing and resilience. In her 2022 book *Switchcraft: How agile thinking can help you adapt and thrive*, Fox argued that it's important to know when and how to flexibly switch between opinions and beliefs.[11]

According to Fox: 'We never know when we might fall ill, a lover might leave us, or we might lose our job. To optimize our psychological adjustment, then, we must duck and dive and adapt to our ever-changing world – using what I call switchcraft.' For Fox, a key part of flexibility is the intellectual humility that is essential to collaborative thinking:[12]

Those who are intellectually humble show a willingness to reconsider even their most cherished beliefs when faced with new evidence; tend not to get overly defensive when challenged; and strive for accuracy without undue regard for protecting their own worldview. While it flies in the face of typical cognitive processing – which is of course heavily influenced by self-interest, in-group pre-conceptions and our experiences – intellectual humility is a mindset that seeks out the truth of a situation.[13]

It's essential to consider things from other perspectives; it's also important to understand the relationships between perspectives. Together, these create a 'latticework' of mental models which we can 'toggle' between at will.

In his well-known 1994 speech, Berkshire Hathaway's long-time vice chairman Charlie Munger – often referred to as Warren Buffett's right-hand man – said, 'You can't really know anything if you just remember isolated facts… If the facts don't hang together on a lattice-work of theory, you don't have them in a usable form. You've got to have models in your head. And you've got to array your experience – both vicarious and direct – on this latticework of models.'[14]

Fox's book and Munger's speech are variations on a similar theme: only by flexibly toggling between mental perceptions and understanding the relationships between them can you see the bigger picture and act accordingly.

The benefits of agile thinking

We are all of us subject to biases and assumptions. Agile thinking helps people put aside distracting emotions and past experiences when deciding on an appropriate course of action.

By equipping individuals with a range of strategies, agile thinking is an adaptable approach to problem solving. Rather than a single, one-size-fits-all solution, think of it as a toolkit, offering many benefits such as:

- **accelerated decision making** – better ability to find new options and assess which are relevant
- **ability to tackle complex problems** – going back to fundamentals to find underlying factors and potential solutions
- **deeper engagement and support** – ensuring that colleagues are more closely involved and empowered

- **flexibility in attitude and workflow** – leading to less reliance on dogma and process

Those skilled in agile thinking find that certainty is an end point reached with others in their team, not a starting point that excludes people and possibilities. Above all, they discover that agility is a mindset as much as a methodology, an opportunity to put ego aside and focus on what, rather than who, is right.

As we saw in our previous chapter, analytical thinking and creative thinking are the two leading skills that organizations are focusing on in the 2020s.[15] Opening the way to clarity of thought, resilience and leadership, they reliably support effective decisions and actions. To ensure these aren't derailed by disruption, a second set of future skills is just as important, as we shall discover in our next chapter.

Notes

1 R Barnes. The Fuel That Fed the Subprime Meltdown, 27 August 2023, Investopedia, www.investopedia.com/articles/07/subprime-overview.asp (archived at https://perma.cc/SK3D-KH3K)

2 Reuters. FACTBOX-U.S. European bank writedowns, credit losses, 5 November 2009, www.reuters.com/article/banks-writedowns-losses-idCNL5541556 20091105?rpc=44 (archived at https://perma.cc/5U5G-B79M)

3 W Ishak. Creating an innovation culture, 28 September 2017, McKinsey Quarterly, www.mckinsey.com/capabilities/strategy-and-corporate-finance/our-insights/creating-an-innovation-culture (archived at https://perma.cc/C53D-U89N)

4 M McTier. Want to thrive in the future of work? Practice scientific thinking, 17 May 2018, Fast Company, www.fastcompany.com/40570969/want-to-thrive-in-the-future-of-work-practice-scientific-thinking (archived at https://perma.cc/2282-KFBJ)

5 D Kuhn. What is Scientific Thinking and How Does it Develop? In U Goswani (Ed.) *Handbook of Childhood Cognitive Development* (2013), Wiley-Blackwell

6 D Kuhn. What is Scientific Thinking and How Does it Develop? In U Goswani (Ed.) *Handbook of Childhood Cognitive Development* (2013), Wiley-Blackwell

7 M McTier. Want to thrive in the future of work? Practice scientific thinking, 17 May 2018, Fast Company, www.fastcompany.com/40570969/want-to-thrive-in-the-future-of-work-practice-scientific-thinking (archived at https://perma.cc/2282-KFBJ)

8 The Economist. Why collaborative thinking beats individual smarts, 18 June 2018, www.economist.com/open-future/2018/06/18/why-collaborative-thinking-beats-individual-smarts (archived at https://perma.cc/482K-63DN)

9 B Resnick. Intellectual humility: the importance of knowing you might be wrong, 4 January 2019, Vox.com, www.vox.com/science-and-health/2019/1/4/17989224/intellectual-humility-explained-psychology-replication (archived at https://perma.cc/YQ2W-QTKN)

10 T B Kashdan and J Rottenberg. Psychological flexibility as a fundamental aspect of health, *Clinical Psychology Review*, 2010, **30** (7), pp. 865–78

11 E Fox (2022) *Switchcraft: How agile thinking can help you adapt and thrive*, Hodder and Stoughton

12 E Fox. Why intellectual humility matters, 28 July 2022, The British Psychological Society, www.bps.org.uk/psychologist/why-intellectual-humility-matters# (archived at https://perma.cc/2CG2-DUWF)

13 E Fox. Why intellectual humility matters, 28 July 2022, The British Psychological Society, www.bps.org.uk/psychologist/why-intellectual-humility-matters# (archived at https://perma.cc/D4A7-8Q3F)

14 C Munger. A Lesson on Elementary, Worldly Wisdom As It Relates To Investment Management & Business, 1994, USC Business School, speakola.com/corp/charli-munger-widom-business-usc-1994 (archived at https://perma.cc/JV6T-U2YN)

15 S Zahidi. Future of Jobs Report 2023, 30 April 2023, World Economic Forum, www.weforum.org/publications/the-future-of-jobs-report-2023/ (archived at https://perma.cc/BXN2-G9EX)

8

Future communication

In the first few weeks of 2020, Britain – like many countries – took a sudden dive into the deep end of Covid. On 23 March the UK went into lockdown, though by then it was too late to prevent the pandemic sweeping across the country. By May, the *British Medical Journal* was describing the UK's death toll as 'the worst in Europe'.[1]

Lockdown restrictions were eased in the summer, though by the autumn the rate of infections was rising once again. By that point however there was a sense of familiarity. The natural rhythm of life was beating once again, drowning out concerns. On the evening of Saturday 31 October, people were either heading out to Halloween parties or settling down to watch *Strictly Come Dancing*, the BBC's TV dance extravaganza.

Just as *Strictly* began, in a sparkling blaze of sequins and glitter, a government broadcast cut in featuring the chief medical officer Professor Chris Whitty in a sombre suit, accompanied by the chief scientific adviser and one of the UK's recent prime ministers.[2] For seven long minutes, Whitty numbed his audience with an impenetrable set of slides consisting of tiny print and a fog of detail, such as shown in Figure 8.1.[3]

Briefing people as if they were in a government seminar, Whitty treated a primetime audience of 16 million mums, dads, kids and their grannies to a smorgasbord of detail designed by and for experts.[4] And just in case we hadn't had enough, he handed us over to the government's chief scientific adviser, Patrick Vallance, who came at us with his own take on the slides.

FIGURE 8.1 Geographical spread of Covid-19 in England

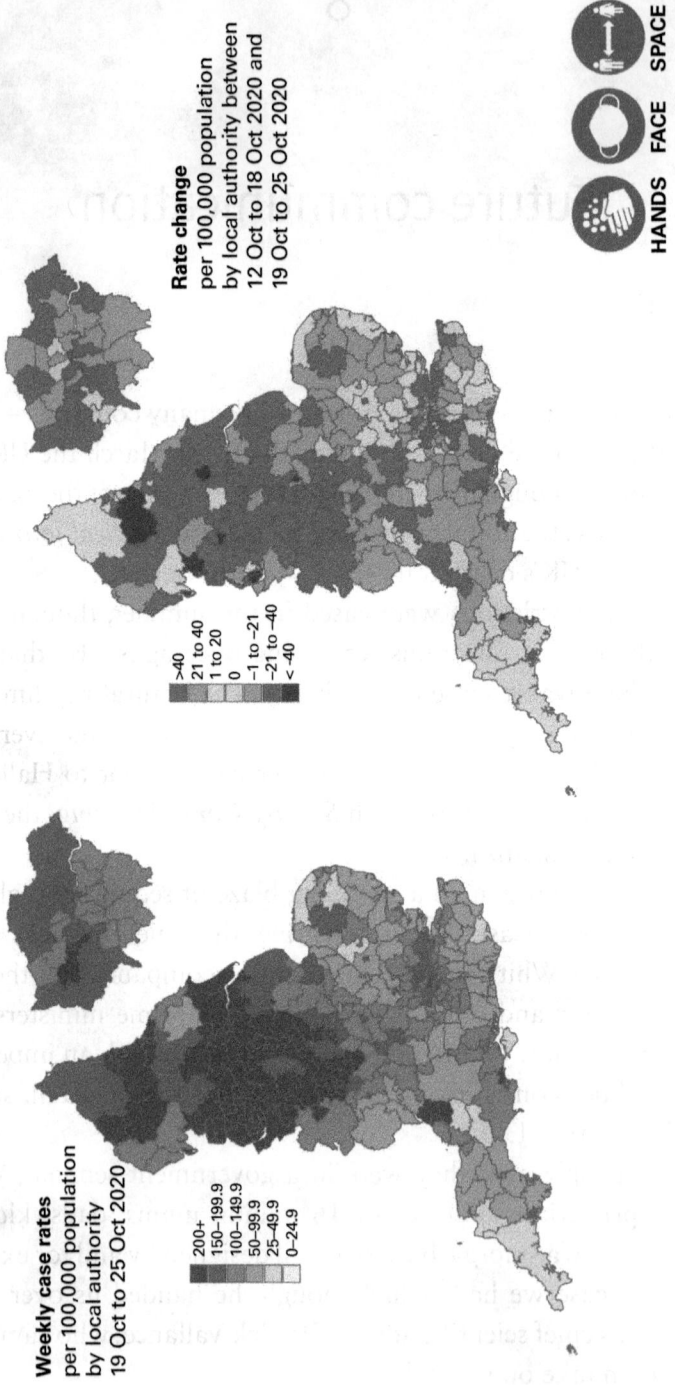

Weekly case rates
per 100,000 population
by local authority
19 Oct to 25 Oct 2020

200+
150–199.9
100–149.9
50–99.9
25–49.9
0–24.9

Rate change
per 100,000 population
by local authority between
12 Oct to 18 Oct 2020 and
19 Oct to 25 Oct 2020

>40
21 to 40
1 to 20
0
–1 to –21
–21 to –40
< –40

HANDS   FACE   SPACE

SOURCE Data from Pillar 1 and 2 testing. Figure by Outbreak Surveillance Team, Public Health England, and ONS 2019 mid-term population estimates. Contains National Statistics data © Crown copyright and database right 2020.

Vallance in turn handed over to the prime minister, Boris Johnson. At nearly 18 minutes into the press conference, Johnson finally got round to announcing the reason for the broadcast. For only the second time in modern British history, the entire population was being instructed to stay at home under lockdown rules.

This was a significant and troubling moment in the lives of millions of people. The focus of the message should have been delivered earlier in a clearer way while Johnson and his team still held the attention of those watching. The scientific evidence was essential, of course, but it was only playing a supporting role.

Messaging is meaningless if it goes unheard. Unaware they had left the audience behind, Whitty and co pressed on with their slides, oblivious to the reaction on social media:[5]

> Like WHAT is this supposed to mean? Without the key information it's literally just lines.
>
> I feel like I'm in Specsavers having an eye test.
>
> 70 inch tv and can [only] read it from 2 feet away.
>
> I feel like I was watching a spoof comedy. Such a strange briefing!!!!!
>
> Next slide please – honestly. Such a shambles.

To get such a challenging message across to millions of people, the story ought to have begun with a clear announcement followed by a simple explanation about the rising rate of infections. The opening deluge of impenetrable data was too much for most people. It squandered their initial interest and offered them little more than a Halloween horror show. It's a mistake that's easily repeated.

Communication skills for the future

Organizations, like governments, thrive on big data – on everything from historic trends and product performance to market variables and real-time updates. There are market advantages for those who are able to interpret this information astutely. This means spotting trends and opportunities ahead of the competition, which comes down to talented people translating the numbers into meaningful suggestions.

Big data is easily available thanks to the ongoing advances in tech. But data is only part of the equation. For interpretation, decisions and actions you need people. Tech is only a means to an end, a tool for the benefit of people. To exploit its potential, people need future skills in communication so that they can make the most of tech's far-reaching capabilities.

In Chapters 5 and 6, we looked at the fundamentals of interpersonal communication including trust, respect and psychological safety. We saw that social wellbeing, as the basis of company culture, touches everyone from the board to the interns. It is the bedrock that supports productivity, resilience and retention.

Social wellbeing is also the basis for advanced abilities that build upon it, in particular the future skills needed by key individuals. In Chapter 7, we saw that the first of these skills, agile thinking, helps people reach reliable conclusions. Here in this chapter, we'll discover the communication skills that are needed in the 2020s to best express and share conclusions, particularly those drawn from data.

Future communication skills include a broad spectrum of abilities, in particular:

- **Communicating with AI** – by creating effective prompts, employees will be able to make the most of chatbots and data analysis tools.

- **Managing with AI** – leaders can advocate AI by using it to save time in routine tasks, meanwhile safeguarding balance in the relationship between people and tech.

- **Storytelling with data** – transforming data into a clear narrative by following storytelling structure and thinking about the audience.

- **Next level engagement** – learning to create 'sticky' stories that stay with people long after your presentation has finished.

- **Multigenerational communication** – reducing workplace tension and misunderstanding by building bridges between generations.

Using storytelling to catch attention

Communication is not just saying what you want to say, it's about being understood by other people. In their broadcast in October 2020, Whitty and Vallance failed to appreciate this.

Whether you're explaining data in a meeting, giving a major presentation or getting to know a new colleague, the fundamentals of communication start with thoughts about the person or people you're communicating with. For example, you might think about building rapport through eye contact, maintaining a warm approach and having something meaningful to say.

Future communication skills include finding something to say by using AI and managing data. How are your numbers best understood, assessed and shared with other people?

As we've seen, humans are social. We have a fundamental need to communicate, to belong and to connect with others. Throughout human history, connections in families and groups have been developed through stories. Indeed, cognitive psychologist Jerome Bruner suggested we are 22 times more likely to remember a fact when it has been wrapped in a story.[6]

Storytelling is a central part of what makes us who we are. It is a human trait, a skill that will be a core component of communication in the future just as much as when we were daubing rudimentary paint on to cave walls in our ancient past.

For a while, it was believed that the world's oldest cave paintings were more than 40,000 years old. In 2024, it was revealed that the oldest is actually more than 50,000. Telling a story that features three human-animal hybrids and a wild pig, the painting was found in Indonesia and may have been created by some of the first people to have got that far from their ancestors' point of origin in Africa.

'Storytelling is a hugely important part of human evolution and possibly even helps to explain our success as a species' according to archaeologist Adam Brumm who jointly led analysis of the painting.[7] The precise meaning of ancient images is often unclear, but their significance can still be perceived thousands of years after they were created. Even the simplest outline of a hand tells a timeless story of someone saying, 'I am, I came here and I shall be remembered'.

Transforming data into a story helps to ensure it's understood by others. Best to begin by asking yourself a question. What do you or your audience need to know? Perhaps they need to see how current performance figures compare with last year, or the projected impact of inflation. Perhaps you just need to tell people that 'the numbers are in, and here's what they show'. Even this approach begins with a question; in this case: 'What's the bigger picture?'

Questions are helpful because they demand an explanatory answer. Explanations are stories and stories are easy to follow, which is important when decisions and actions are at stake. A four-step process starts with data which needs to be interpreted so that appropriate decisions can be made and actions taken:

1 data comes in as a stream of numbers

2 analysts' questions lead to interpretations

3 responses are selected by decision makers

4 actions are assigned to team members

These steps can be represented like this:

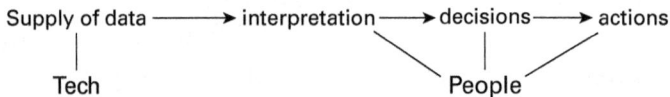

Supply of data ⟶ interpretation ⟶ decisions ⟶ actions

Tech   People

The conclusion here is that even in a workplace with the most advanced AI, people dominate 75 per cent of the processing of data.

In the Covid broadcast of October 2020, data was allowed to dominate. It had been interpreted and decisions had been made. The UK was returning to lockdown, but the poor performance in communication overlooked the audience – whose actions might mean the difference between higher or lower death rates.

Organizations risk overlooking the relevance of people through an over-reliance on tech. Tech can interpret the numbers – for example determining who's buying what among your clients. Decisions and actions can also be outsourced to tech. An increase in demand for a particular product at a specific location could automatically lead to units being diverted from another location, removing people from the decision making process altogether.

However, problems arise when organizations readily default to tech and reduce the relevance of people. This can happen in the misguided belief that AI is key to some 'futuristic' way of working in which employees are routinely relegated to a secondary role. Leaders who take this line of thought might act as if they've seen a vision of what's to come, much like the blind man in *Monty Python's Life of Brian*, who proclaims with rapturous wonder that 'I was blind and now I can see' before plunging into a giant hole that he hadn't seen.[8]

Cutting too many people out of the process of interpretation reduces the influence of human nuance, experience, bravery, imagination and foresight. This can lead to a rise in inflexible process, a loss of understanding through storytelling and a limited response to unexpected challenges.

Structuring a story

When creating a narrative – for a presentation, for example – your story doesn't need to be a potential movie script. It just needs to include a basic structure. The clearest stories have a beginning, middle and end – a principle that may sound obvious but is easily overlooked.

Effective communication expands on this basic structure with a dash of emotion, such as a sense of confidence, disappointment or optimism. Structure, emotion and audience awareness together make up the secret sauce of future communication. Let's explore each a little further.

Beginning, middle and end

Think of how a child might talk about a film, something along the lines of: 'You know, the princess and a man, who was noisy and the car park was full. And then the ticket machine… but in the beginning the turtle was cross. The noisy man dropped his popcorn on us. The start was scary.'

This is a jumbled set of reactions, as you'd expect from a child. Their thoughts have not been pulled together into a coherent account that can be understood by someone else. You can't relate much to the film they're describing. This story is not a review intended for a listener, it's simply a bubbling rendition of the young storyteller's exciting experience.

Information is easier to follow when it's presented with structure:

- **Beginning**: set the scene so that you and the audience are on the same page. You're simply creating a level playing field. No twists, no turns, just a bare introduction.

- **Middle**: the level playing field is not all it seems. Whether it's good news or bad news, there's some ruffling disturbance – which is why you're here, telling people about it.

- **Ending**: What response does the disturbance require? Bring the facts together by summing everything up in a decisive conclusion that includes possible decisions and actions.

Here's a set of facts brought together in a story so powerful it's been told in one form or another for a century or more. It has a beginning, middle and end, it's soaked in emotion, and at only six words long it's hard to beat:

For sale: baby shoes. Never worn.

This is a story that's often attributed to Ernest Hemingway, but it probably predates him.[9] It's based on data (two shoes) that has led to action (a decision to sell). The power at the heart of this story does not come from 'corporate writing' – the tendency to use overly long words strung together in a meandering sentence. Instead, the story's strength lies in decisive events told with structure and simplicity. The beginning, middle and end are each no more than two words long.

In a presentation, you're not looking to rival Hemingway. Nevertheless, assembling data and evidence into a structured story is not just a helpful tip, it's the only way to ensure that people will quickly grasp the point you want to make.

Adding emotion to your story

A spark of emotion can help the driest set of numbers catch attention. While structure leads the audience logically towards your conclusion, emotion makes it easier for them to follow your thinking and accept your findings.

Emotion helps to reveal something more than the bare bones of the data; something buried, something that humans are able to discern far better than AI. Data can be gathered by AI, even presented by AI, but what underlying story does it see? People are better able to, as journalists say, look for the 'story behind the story'.

An organization's retention data might have improved, but the real headline is the reason behind the better numbers: the shift in company culture thanks to a range of factors that the data doesn't show. Similarly: 'Because productivity is up, we can offer more to clients.' Or: 'Because footfall is down, we should try something new.'

The sales figures might be up. This might feel like a cause for congratulations. But other data might show that the story behind the story is more complicated than things seem. Tough decisions are necessary. A joyful sense of triumph will only make it harder to land your difficult conclusions. Instead, presenting the seemingly positive figures with wary caution indicates the direction you're taking long before you get to your conclusion. This lays the groundwork for the tough note you plan to finish on.

The story behind the story shapes your conclusion, which in turn indicates the emotion you need to adopt from the beginning, an emotion that sets the scene. It's what people will be looking for right from the start. They will be reading between the lines, looking for clues, listening to the tone of your presentation to see whether things are good, bad or middling.

See the bigger picture. Build your understanding into a structure, then use a touch of emotion to underline your conclusions.

Think of your audience

A common mistake in storytelling, perhaps the most common, is to forget your audience. For example, it's easy to imagine they are thinking about the same things that you are in the same depth of detail.

In your mind, your audience are right there with you, primed with the same facts and the same familiarity with the subject. Usually, however, they're not. People settling down to an episode of *Strictly* are not thinking about infection data to the same extent as the chief medical officer.

When explaining something, whether to one person or many, it's easy to forget the extent of knowledge you have compared to them. You are likely to know more, on this specific subject at least, which is why you're giving the presentation.

They might need to understand your numbers. But they probably also need to think about 100 other things. You might not be their first priority. Grabbing and holding their attention is vital if you are to make your story stick.

They could perhaps look at the data themselves, but they want to hear your take on things. It's not just your numbers they want to hear, it's you and your interpretation of the story. They want to see what you know, which means building rapport with them.

It helps to think of your audience not as a homogeneous collection of colleagues, but as one person, someone who's all too human: mismatched socks, thinking about lunch, a bit distracted and sometimes misunderstanding stuff. Help them along, one step at a time, through empathy and emotional intelligence – both of which were absent in the Covid broadcast of October 2020.

Whitty, Vallance and Johnson had a structure of a story. New data had come in, and it didn't look good. New measures were necessary.

They even wrapped it up in plenty of emotion – their sombre tone and stark words made it clear that this was a time of difficulty and resilience. But they struggled to bring the audience along with them, which in a presentation can be an expensive mistake to make.

Future communication skills in practice

Using AI to enhance communication

Given the rapidly expanding reach of technology, it's no longer just analysts who need to interpret data. Major clients are preparing employees across a range of departments, particularly HR – giving them the skills they need to work with AI and make data-led decisions.

When chatbots were first rolled out in late 2022, there was an initial sense of concern among employees, as if they were coming face to face with an uncertain future. People were getting their first glimpse at the tech that some feared would one day take their job away. According to one estimate, around 80 per cent of the US workforce could have at least 10 per cent of their work tasks affected by the introduction of large language models (i.e. chatbots).[10]

These initial concerns have since been deepened by additional difficulties. Using large language models requires a skill that for many people flies in the face of traditional company culture.

AI performs at its best when given specific questions and tasks. These must come from employees who will use AI in everything from writing reports to researching presentations, so the thinking goes. However, this will require people to develop a creative, entrepreneurial way of thinking – which some will struggle with. Many employees have spent years working in a compliant environment. They have been trained to respond to requests rather than create prompts for AI systems.

When training employees to work with AI, we find that many struggle to develop the mindset they need for systems that demand a certain level of creativity. One of the difficulties stems from the fact that people are being encouraged to think more creatively so that they can become better at using a tool that does their thinking for them.

Compliance and conformity in company culture will have to be managed if people are to creatively harness the power of AI. Organizations that favour both centralized control and compliant individuals will need to think more about trust and creativity. People who feel safe, respected and trusted are more likely to develop the creative confidence that will help them make the most of AI.

These are some of the issues that have shaped our course on communicating with AI. Aimed at employees, it seeks to help people develop AI literacy. This has been defined as 'a set of competencies that enable individuals to critically evaluate AI technologies; communicate and collaborate effectively with AI; and use AI as a tool online, at home and in the workplace'.[11]

AI literacy can help with:

- **Research** – e.g. supporting a client who's looking for better performance in their investment portfolio.
- **In-depth feedback** – e.g. discovering how different asset classes are affecting fixed income positions in specific international locations.
- **Collaborative problem-solving** – e.g. predicting concerns and questions from a client that can then be distributed to team members for further research.

AI will have an impact on jobs. AI literacy, however, will help employees strengthen their position. Nevertheless, much depends on their employer's view of the fragile relationship between people and tech. For leaders, managing with AI involves various conflicting factors.

Using AI when managing people

As we've seen, tech has the potential to supply data, interpret it, make appropriate decisions and initiate automated responses. Tech does not get tired, expect to be paid, complain or need time off.

Tech is an attractive prospect for organizations looking to cut costs. There is no doubt that jobs will be lost to tech, as we saw in Chapter 3.

However, organizations benefit from people in ways that tech will never truly replicate. Data and AI-generated content needs to be managed by people (through prompts), evaluated (through human assessments of accuracy), kept in context (by people who can see the story behind the story) and presented (by individuals who have in-depth personal experience).

Tech is only one side of the relationship. Organizations whose people remain a meaningful part of the equation will stay ahead of competitors who prioritize one asset rather than two. 'Humans add the most value to complex tasks by identifying and understanding outliers and nuance in a way that it is difficult to imagine a model trained on historical data would ever be able to do,' warned Jim Covello, Head of Global Equity Research at Goldman Sachs.[12] People inject authenticity into their organization – which tech can barely measure but which is abundantly clear to Generation Z, whether customers or employees.

In order to safeguard the balance between people and tech, leaders must fend off C-suite attempts to save money by cutting back on uniquely human skills and experience. In support of this, a shift in company culture towards trust and respect will help people work creatively with tech. This in turn will allow tech to be used to its full potential, in support of business objectives.

Employees not yet ready to engage with tech will depend on leaders who can give them the training that will bring them up to speed. By monitoring the relationship between people and tech, leaders can protect their teams and maintain collective intelligence. The alternative involves an over-reliance on tech and an erosion of the critical skills in agile thinking that are a key investment for organizations preparing for the future.

These issues are rooted in company culture and must be addressed alongside investment in AI. For organizations that get this right, there lies the tantalizing prospect of human ingenuity supported by technical capability – leading to optimum performance and growth.

For many organizations, these thoughts lead to three central questions:

1 In focusing on 'whole work processes' – from product conception through to delivery – what does the relationship between people and AI look like when functioning at its best?

2 Once competitors resolve similar questions, what direction will the wider industry take? What will the future look like and how can an organization keep its competitive edge?

3 With these questions in mind, what form of AI should leaders be investing in now and how should they prepare their people for the road ahead?

Our trainers are often asked by clients what the future holds in store. However, the world is still in the foothills of AI. Things will never be this simple again. Surrounded by steep climbs and false summits, it's hard to accurately predict the peak of AI achievement.

Nevertheless, we are clear that organizations do not want to be left behind. Those that imagine this means throwing everything at AI are looking in the wrong direction. They risk being left behind not by AI but by the potential of their people to make the most of what AI can offer.

As part of this thinking, leaders must prepare their people, advocating AI by using it themselves. By using AI to complete administrative tasks, leaders can give more time to other priorities.

AI systems can be used to track performance metrics, set goals and provide personalized development plans for team members. They can help draft agendas for meetings, track attendance, transfer handwritten notes into a meaningful paper record and list key action points.

AI can supply the briefing notes that help in managing up and it can break down complex project management tasks into smaller chunks. In the words of Rob Thomas, chief commercial officer at IBM, 'AI may not replace managers, but the managers that use AI will replace the managers that do not.'[13]

Counting on data

We were asked by a client to help a key employee whose work was 'really important'. We agreed, though the client seemed to feel that we'd missed something. 'No, you don't understand,' they hissed in a tone somewhere between secrecy, triumphalism and panic. 'It's really important! His analysis is legendary, we make a huge amount of money off him. It's just that during the morning call, he's so boring that people just switch off. We could make even more money off him if people didn't nod off when he spoke.'

The employee in question was easy-going, but took the view that data was 'just numbers', stats to be fed to other people. He knew which stats were significant and why, and assumed that so would everyone else. We helped him see that his understanding of data was invaluable and should be shared with other people in addition to the data itself.

He hadn't grasped that his job was about telling a story – giving meaning to data by spelling out how to cash in on his analysis. It's the difference between just reading out a list of stats – leaving people in mystified darkness – and shedding light on the mysteries they explain.

So how do you make numbers interesting for other people? Our trainee said he wasn't sure, so we asked him to think of his young children. How did he speak with them in a way that caught their attention? As soon as he began talking about his kids, he dropped the work persona and became 'dad' and immediately his voice became much more animated.

Holding on to this, we returned to thoughts about his job. By infusing his explanations with a greater sense of clarity and delivering them in an animated way, our friend was better able to hold people's attention and the client was better off.

Reeling off a list of numbers is a routine task that can be given to AI. Interpretation, however, involves the uniquely human skill of ownership in which the numbers are perceived as a story – created, developed and owned by someone imaginative enough to see the business possibilities on offer.

Better this than relying too heavily on AI, giving the last word to data when an honest human interpretation might be more insightful and therefore more valuable.

In 2015, the England cricket team coach Peter Moores relied on numbers as part of his preparation for the Cricket World Cup. Following his team's humiliating exit from the competition, Moores was saddled with the perception that he'd become preoccupied with statistical analysis. When asked to explain what had happened, Moores was said to have told a TV interviewer: 'We will have to look at the data' (though it has been suggested that his actual comment was: 'We will have to look at it later').[14]

The following year, the US was embroiled in a general election campaign, and we were invited to observe Hillary Clinton's team in action. 'Aren't you worried about Trump,' we asked a senior adviser. He replied, 'No Republican can get to 270 [electoral votes, necessary to win].' How could he be so sure? 'The data!' he replied emphatically. Trump went on to win.

Information must be managed so that an accurate story can be developed that makes the most of data while keeping it in context. Our course on this was designed by Paul Hill, author of many of our communication courses and one of our specialists in storytelling.

One client told Paul that he presented data by first putting his slides together and then working out his story. Paul explained the need to construct a story first, complete with meaningful conclusions. Only then can useful slides be created to illustrate key points. Thinking about the slides first, without initially building them into a story, usually falls flat as demonstrated by the 2020 Covid briefing.

Graphics, graphs and charts supplement your story, illustrating it and making it easier to grasp the point you're making. But they are not the story itself.

Next-level engagement through 'sticky stories'

Having looked at the basics of storytelling, an advanced set of skills borrows from a phenomenon that is tantalizing, elusive and worth its weight in gold. Some stories fall flat and some linger on. A precious few go viral.

Narratives presented in the workplace don't need to go viral but they do need to easily and memorably command attention. Our colleague Gene Douglas developed a course that helps participants understand the secrets of getting and keeping attention so that they can enhance their storytelling and increase audience engagement. Based in our New York office, Gene has more than 20 years' experience as an educator and specializes in helping people get their message across.

In looking at some of the ideas that inspired Gene's course, let's begin with some numbers:

- Research in 2016 found that approximately 35 million PowerPoint presentations were given each day.[15]

- In their book *Made to Stick: Why some ideas survive and others die*, brothers Chip and Dan Heath suggested that, 'After a presentation, 63 per cent of attendees remember stories. Only 5 per cent remember statistics.'[16]

- Molecular biologist Dr John Medina noted in his book *Brain Rules* that speakers start to lose the audience's attention after around 10 minutes.[17]

Here's a story. A paint manufacturer is giving a presentation on new products, including a quick-drying formula. Giving a presentation under the title 'Paint drying' might be a tough ask. How to make it particularly memorable? The objective here is to create something that can be quickly understood, remembered and discussed.

In his 1976 book *The Selfish Gene*, biologist Richard Dawkins discussed evolutionary processes that copy and repeat information. Over time, some information is selected and retained by genes (sharp eyesight in hawks for example). This is selective retention and occurs, Dawkins suggested, in cultural evolution too – not through genes but via what he called memes: for example, tunes, catchphrases, fashions and technologies.[18]

Memes are memorable – meme-rable, as Gene Douglas suggests. Memes are a useful way of quickly getting to the emotion you want people to feel. A funny image, a useful quote, a picture of a familiar scene from a film all help to lift your story and give it a little zing.

The more familiar the memes, the easier it is to remember them and the story they illustrate. This is because you are engaging your audience on a personal level, exploiting their familiarity with cultural references, making yourself easy to relate to.

Dr Jonah Berger touches on similar thoughts in his book *Contagious*, in which he sets out his 'STEPPS' model:[19]

- **Social currency** – make people feel like insiders
- **Triggers** – encourage discussion so that people are triggered to return to your idea
- **Emotion** – focus on feelings rather than function, 'when we care, we share'
- **Public** – we imitate others, particularly when we see that an idea has wide acceptance
- **Practical value** – 'news you can use', expertise gets handed on even after the presentation
- **Stories** – narratives are memorable, making it easier for your ideas to travel

Complex ideas are easier to understand if they are said with simplicity and supported with familiar memes. To help your story land with impact, think about psychological responses. How do you want your audience to feel? Perhaps you want them to remember your conclusions long after you've finished. An edgy conclusion will help, something that leaves them thinking.

A useful checklist might look like this:

- Present your ideas with simplicity, sticking to one key focus.
- What psychological response do you want to induce?
- Memes can help to set the tone.
- End by giving your audience something to react to – keep them talking.

Audience participation helps too, from shared anecdotes to Q&A sessions. Our story about paint drying began with the numbers. Maybe it could also have started with someone from the audience being invited to use the quick-drying formula to paint a board at the front of the room. For all the power of the sales figures, at the end of the brief presentation the presenter could memorably prove their point by approaching the newly painted board and leaning on it.

Issues and solutions in multigenerational communication

Future communication skills might seem to focus on tech and managing numbers. In fact, they're about empathy with people. The rise of AI can potentially create a divide between people and tech. Human skills in interpretation and narrative help to maintain balance in the relationship.

Narratives are useful for anyone designing a presentation. Teams and organizations can jointly shape a narrative together too, sharing a story and building understanding – not in an individual presentation but through an ongoing culture of empathy. This is especially important for organizations disrupted by division and imbalance.

Fragmented teams – struggling with hybrid patterns or the rise of AI – can develop a shared narrative about achieving objectives. Similarly, different generations within the workforce, who might harbour unhelpful caricatures of one another, can share a narrative focusing on inclusion and empathy.

Multigenerational communication involves more than the complexities of Generation Z, as explored in Chapter 6. At the moment there are four generations in the workplace. Let's identify who's who.

When soldiers returned home from the Second World war, there was a sudden boom in birthrates. Baby boomers (born 1946–1964) are the oldest generation in the workforce. They were followed by Generation X (born 1965–1980), millennials (born 1981–1996, also known as Generation Y) and Generation Z (born 1997–2012, also known as 'zoomers'). Generation alpha, born in or after 2013, are still in school so we'll put them aside for now.

In the very broadest of generalizations, each generation has its own traits and characteristics:

- **Boomers** are noted for their strong work ethic. They value professional relationships developed by building rapport through face-to-face meetings and phone calls. They favour a hierarchical structure and may not be the most flexible members of the workforce.

- **Generation X** seek autonomy at work and value the flexibility this relies on. For Generation X, efficient working involves face-to-face contact and consistent forms of communication; for example, one email address rather than messaging via three different apps.
- **Millennials** have grown up in the digital age and prefer interactive platforms like messaging apps. They seek purpose-driven work, rapid career progression and work–life balance, though their achievements can sometimes be undermined by a reputation for entitlement.
- **Generation Z**, as we saw in Chapter 6, differ from their older colleagues in their expectations and preferences. For them, meaningful work is ideally delivered through authentic actions now rather than via long-term planning and patience.

Boomers have spent years building workplace relationships. They suspect that younger generations not only lack interpersonal skills but struggle to even see the need for them. Meanwhile, Generation X managers want Generation Z to be part of the team – doing what's asked of them and feeling connected to their peers by, for example, talking to them rather than WhatsApping them from a neighbouring desk.

Millennials may want to act quickly, but might feel hamstrung by Generation X's deliberative need for process, complete with emails and paper trails. Millennials' interpretation of efficiency includes flexible schedules with a hybrid pattern that boomer leaders and Generation X managers may be reluctant to accept. Generation Z, meanwhile, sometimes struggle to accept protocol and process and may not stick around long enough to try.

Marci Alboher, vice president at CoGenerate, a nonprofit focused on bridging generational divides, said: 'We're seeing younger workers go digital nomad or taking early-career pauses, mid-career folks returning to school to reskill, parents taking breaks and people of all ages juggling care responsibilities… [which] results in workplaces with a combination of people of all stages needing to partner, support each other and collaborate with whomever is nearby – across a lot of lines of difference, including age.'[20]

Picking a way through potential flashpoints, our course on multigenerational communication offers practical examples of psychological safety focusing on language, listening and shared objectives. Seeking to deflate the misunderstandings and tensions that lead to conflict, the course includes starting points for meaningful discussion such as perceptions of behaviour and values. For example, older generations might conclude that:

> Young people don't use polite forms of address to older/senior colleagues – the way we did when we were young. This raises questions about behaviour.

> Young people do not respect older/senior colleagues. This leads to concerns about values.

It may be, however, that young people's values are similar to previous generations but are shown through different behaviour. This may lead to questions about whether we can reliably infer values from behaviour. Understanding behaviours in more detail may lead to alternative judgements.

It can be helpful too to question assumptions about earned versus entitled behaviours, responsibilities and rights, commitment and balance, and group needs and personal priorities. We encourage participants to think less about stereotypes and more about people they know.

The rise of AI has made tech more accessible, offering new tools to broader sections of the workforce. This has come at a time when organizations are stretched by the many challenging factors we have covered in the book so far, from global threats to multigenerational tension. There is wide scope for workplace misunderstanding and friction, whether stemming from honest difficulties in explaining data or from darker thoughts about 'that generation'.

While workplaces will always echo with familiar healthy tensions, an empathetic culture of tolerance will bring people together, release human potential and keep tech in check. This way of working can be protected by surefooted skills in communication, the tangible side of company culture. For leaders, these skills are essential in difficult times of change and uncertainty, as we shall see in our next chapter.

Notes

1   E Mahase. Covid-19: UK death toll overtakes Italy's to become worst in Europe, 6 May 2020, *British Medical Journal*, www.bmj.com/content/369/bmj.m1850 (archived at https://perma.cc/BG3U-8XSA)

2   10 Downing Street. Coronavirus press conference (31 October 2020), BBC1, www.youtube.com/watch?v=7B1sBUdQeio (archived at https://perma.cc/6MK2-WHD7)

3   COBR. Slides and datasets to accompany coronavirus press conference, 31 October 2020, Cabinet Office Briefing Room, assets.publishing.service.gov.uk/media/5f9db0ae8fa8f57f3db056b7/Slides_to_accompany_coronavirus_press_conference-_CMO-_31_October_2020.pdf (archived at https://perma.cc/G6HY-Z5BA)

4   N Wilkes. Strictly Come Dancing ratings top 10 million, 1 November 2020, MediaMole, www.mediamole.co.uk/entertainment/strictly-come-dancing/news/strictly-come-dancing-ratings-top-10-million_420692.html (archived at https://perma.cc/U5HV-4LB9). Other sources give a higher audience figure for the press conference, for example: M Lawson. 2020 vision: How Covid news topped the TV ratings, 23 December 2020, *The Guardian*, www.theguardian.com/tv-and-radio/2020/dec/23/tv-news-2020-covid-ratings-dominic-cummings (archived at https://perma.cc/P2W7-PHAD)

5   A Hanman. 31 October 2020, X, x.com/arianehanman/status/1322618591699705863; H Brocklehurst. 31 October 2020, X, x.com/harrisonjbrock/status/1322612664267407360 (archived at https://perma.cc/9BY6-7MEF)

6   J Bruner (1987) *Actual Minds, Possible Worlds*, Harvard University Press

7   S Thou. Oldest known picture story is a 51,000-year-old Indonesian cave painting, 4 July 2024, *The Guardian*, www.theguardian.com/science/article/2024/jul/03/oldest-picture-story-cave-painting-indonesia-record-51000-years (archived at https://perma.cc/87BS-ETRS)

8   *Monty Python's Life of Brian* (1979), montypython.50webs.com/scripts/Life_of_Brian/19.htm (archived at https://perma.cc/JH5Q-A3CZ)

9   D Haglun. Did Hemingway Really Write His Famous Six-Word Story? 31 January 2013, Slate.com, slate.com/culture/2013/01/for-sale-baby-shoes-never-worn-hemingway-probably-did-not-write-the-famous-six-word-story.html (archived at https://perma.cc/56U4-N49T)

10   T Eloundou et al. GPTs are GPTs: An Early Look at the Labor Market Impact Potential of Large Language Models, 21 August 2023, arXiv, arxiv.org/abs/2303.10130 (archived at https://perma.cc/QV4J-VNMN)

11   D Long and B Magerko. What is AI Literacy? Competencies and Design Considerations, CHI '20: Proceedings of the 2020 CHI Conference on Human Factors in Computing Systems, doi.org/10.1145/3313831.3376727 (archived at https://perma.cc/LN7G-WGD3)

12 A Nathan. Gen AI: Too much spend, too little benefit? 27 June 2024, Goldman Sachs, www.goldmansachs.com/intelligence/pages/gen-ai-too-much-spend-too-little-benefit.html (archived at https://perma.cc/U8WY-P2ZH)

13 A Mok. Managers who use AI will replace managers who don't, says an IBM exec, 9 May 2023, *Business Insider*, www.businessinsider.com/ibm-managers-who-use-ai-will-replace-those-who-dont-2023-5?r=US&IR=T (archived at https://perma.cc/AP9Q-SX8M)

14 P Newman. Peter Moores on the World Cup debacle and being dumped as England coach: 'Bitter? No, I want them to become heroes', 22 June 2015, Mail Online, www.dailymail.co.uk/sport/cricket/article-3134863/Peter-Moores-World-Cup-debacle-dumped-England-coach-Bitter-No-want-heroes.html (archived at https://perma.cc/JM3C-XW9T)

15 Poll Everywhere. 10 little-known facts about PowerPoint, 29 November 2016, blog.polleverywhere.com/powerpoint-infographic (archived at https://perma.cc/5S4G-FQDA)

16 C Heath and D Heath (2007) *Made to Stick: Why some ideas survive and others die*, Random House

17 J Medina (2009) *Brain Rules: 12 principles for surviving and thriving at work, home, and school*, Pear Press

18 R Dawkins (1976) *The Selfish Gene*, Oxford University Press

19 J Berger (2014) *Contagious: How to build word of mouth in the digital age*, Simon & Schuster

20 K Mitra. What to Know When Five Generations Share an Office, 24 January 2023, *Time*, time.com/charter/6249581/what-to-know-when-five-generations-share-an-office/# (archived at https://perma.cc/V5LA-U4CZ)

9

Leading through change

In the 2004 Olympics, US champion swimmer Michael Phelps won six gold medals and two bronze, equalling the record for most medals won at a single Games. Four years later, in Beijing, he aimed to repeat his success, once again competing in eight Olympic swimming events.

In the first race, Phelps won gold in the 400-metre individual medley. He won gold again in the 4×100-metre freestyle relay. In his third event, the 200-metre freestyle, Phelps broke his previous world record by nearly a second, winning his third gold. He was on target to win the medals he wanted. But when Phelps dived into the pool at the start of his fourth event, the 200-metre butterfly, his goggles began to leak. At just 25 metres into the race, he was effectively blinded.[1]

For lesser mortals, a typical first reaction in that situation would be to somehow fix the problem, either by adjusting the goggles or keeping your head above water. But the knee-jerk desire 'to do something' disrupts cool, calm thinking and can be counterproductive. In fact, often the best solution in a crisis is not something you come up with there and then, as Phelps already knew.

Phelps later revealed that when preparing for a competition his mental training included visualization:

> Getting up to a meet, I would visualize probably a month or so in advance just what could happen, what I want to happen and what I don't want to happen because when it happened I was prepared for it.
>
> So you know, when I go into 2008 and in the 200 fly, my goggles fill up with water the first 25. And I am blind for 175 metres. I revert back to what I did in training and counted my strokes. And I knew

how many strokes I take the first, second, third and fourth 50 of all of my best 200 flies. So I reverted back to that and I was ready for that because I was mentally prepared for it.[2]

His preparation paid off. Defeating silver medalist László Cseh by almost seven-tenths of a second, Phelps set a new world record and won his fourth gold of the Games, his tenth overall – more than anyone else in the modern era. Phelps went on to win four more golds in Beijing. He eventually retired in 2016, with a tally of 28 Olympic medals including an astonishing 23 golds, comfortably taking the title of most decorated Olympian of all time.[3]

Throughout his career, Phelps relied on mental as well as physical preparation, learning to 'visualize' at a young age so that he could prepare for the unknown. This is different to agile thinking, which is helpful in choosing from a range of options. In the face of disruptive change and uncertainty, when choices and control become severely limited, something else is needed.

Dealing with disruption

Preparing for change

Often, change can be anticipated, for example in the wake of a merger or acquisition, or a rethink of the business model or pressures from a new senior leader. In contrast, unanticipated change might stem from global events or something closer to home like the impact of a new competitor or the departure of a key supplier.

Either way, change has the appearance of a mystifying force that's hard to quantify, impossible to measure and challenging to manage. An often repeated narrative suggests that '70 per cent of change programs fail to achieve their goals' (e.g. Ewenstein et al, 2015).[4] In fact, this stat was shot down in 2011 by Dr Mark Hughes, who surveyed a range of papers that included it and found 'there is no valid and reliable empirical evidence to support such a narrative'.[5] Change need not be doomed to failure.

Managing change begins with identifying the nature of the problem: change, complexity and uncertainty are not the same thing; each demand their own appropriate response. The first step is to diagnose the root of the issue and assess its immediate impact on a team or organization.

Various systems of recognizing unknowns have been developed over time, leading to an alphabet soup of acronyms. In the late 1980s, we had VUCA (volatility, uncertainty, complexity and ambiguity). Later, came BANI (brittle, anxious, non-linear, incomprehensible), now we have RUPT (rapid, unpredictable, paradoxical, tangled).[6]

We're not short on theories about recognizing disruption, which is ironic given that recognizing it isn't usually the problem. Disruption doesn't hide quietly behind the sofa. Pushing aside familiarity, disruption can quickly overwhelm us. When things are crunching to a halt, the immediate issue is how to manage them, which is a subject that VUCA and the rest don't have much to say about.

Phelps has the answer. Leaders have a better chance of navigating uncertainty when they prepare in advance, using moments when they're in control to prepare for times when they're not. At its simplest, preparing in advance can mean writing a plan, deciding how to implement it and sharing it with those involved. We advise clients to go further than this. For us, planning in advance is about developing mindsets and building organizational resilience.

According to change consultants Deborah Rowland, Nicole Brauckmann and Michael Thorley, the force that has the 'greatest impact on change outcomes is our primary need to belong'.[7] For Rowland and her co-authors, belonging is defined as 'the desired emotional outcome in an organization in which each individual is invited to be fully themselves in community with others, with no parts of themselves hidden – and is essential to making change happen'.[8]

Analysing 77 recent examples of change management, Rowland and her co-authors found that the top 12 per cent examples of effective change featured leaders who paid significant attention to belonging. In practice, this meant encouraging people to feel secure and involved while also helping them break free from outdated ways of working in order to allow room for novel solutions.[9]

For us, belonging is a cornerstone of social wellbeing, as noted in Chapter 5. A strong culture of social wellbeing and a clear sense of belonging go hand in hand. Belonging is a key part of organizational resilience, settling disruption and softening the impact of change and uncertainty.

Preparing for uncertainty

Uncertainty seemingly shakes the floor and rattles the furniture. It can be overwhelming, making all that seems familiar feel out of place and threatening. In such moments, negative emotions are hard to manage, as if experience and talent have been temporarily deleted or at least lost in a fog of confusion.

Uncertainty is interpreted by the brain as a threat, prompting feelings of anxiety and an urge to do something, anything, to restore order. This urgent need to act triggers rushed attempts to try one thing then the next in the hope that something will work.

At this point, the press of psychological energy risks spinning faster and faster, tumbling into anxiety and perhaps even racing towards panic. Our colleague Tom Cassidy has noted: 'In business there is a bias towards action; nevertheless a useful rule of thumb in times of difficulty is don't make things worse.'

Managing this level of uncertainty involves a two-step process.

Firstly, in order to focus on a sensible course of action, it helps to take a moment and recognize the presence of negative emotions. This makes it easier to break free from their grip and step out of their gravitational pull. For Tom Cassidy: 'It's important to get past the inside view, the tendency to ask questions like why's this happening to me. Better instead to adopt an objective outside view, such as focusing on how the problem might have been tackled before.'

It helps to get past the assumption that leaders must always have an answer. Satya Nadella, CEO of Microsoft, suggested that leaders must shift from a 'know it all' to a 'learn it all' approach,[10] building on the concept of growth mindsets developed by Stanford psychology professor Carol Dweck.

After breaking out of the sense of fearful alarm, it's easier to begin the second step in the process which involves managing the problem itself. There are various ways to approach this, which can be used individually or together depending on circumstances. In all of them, the aim is the same: to create the conditions in which you can play to your strengths. For example, leaders can rely on:

- **Advance planning**
  In moments of unexpected change, a pre-prepared plan softens anxiety by offering an immediate 'go-to' course of action, buying time to tackle the issue in detail. Change that has been anticipated similarly demands a clear sense of vision, from the outset, so that employees know the direction of travel and can adjust accordingly.

- **Communication**
  A plan isn't much good sitting forgotten in a drawer or on a desktop. Share it with others through preparation and practice. Give your team the floor. By opening up the plan to ideas from other people, you'll be able to refine it in ways you might not have thought of and you'll secure buy-in from those you'll rely on in the heat of the moment.

- **Talent**
  Manage uncertainty by breaking the problem into sections that can be given to the team or individual best qualified to tackle them. When made in advance, such decisions help to lighten the load in moments of unplanned change. Planned change meanwhile may meet resistance which demands skills in motivation in order to retain the support of key individuals.

- **Leadership**
  Give yourself options by keeping an agile mindset, perhaps retaining a narrow focus in some areas while staying open and creative in others. Build support by creating opportunities for minor achievements and breakthroughs, and allow time and space for these to be recognized.

Developing organizational resilience

In response to the disruption associated with change and uncertainty, we developed five courses aimed at strengthening organizational resilience. A brief selection of their concepts and solutions is presented here.

Leading through change

After analysing change management at more than 100 companies, John P Kotter, a Harvard professor of leadership, noted that in 'almost every case' organizations were responding to challenging markets. Kotter found: 'Change involves numerous phases that, together, usually take a long time. Skipping steps only creates an illusion of speed and never produces a satisfying result.'[11]

Kotter realized that many of the companies he assessed made common mistakes that can be paraphrased as:

1 **Not starting with enough urgency** – a problem that affected well over 50 per cent of the companies Kotter looked at.

2 **Not creating a powerful enough guiding coalition** – change can fail without the support of a 'minimum mass' of leaders.

3 **Lacking a vision** – without a clear picture of the future, change can become bogged down in tedious depths of detail.

4 **Under-communicating the vision 'by a factor of 10'** – the essential support of hundreds or thousands of people can only come through effective communication.

5 **Not removing obstacles** – resistance to change in individuals and organizational structure has to be identified and overcome.

6 **Not systematically creating short-term wins** – maintain momentum through change by finding and rewarding opportunities for short-term successes.

7 **Declaring victory too soon** – change needs to sink in across the business, a process that can take many years.

8 **Not anchoring changes in the corporation's culture** – change sticks when it 'seeps into the bloodstream of the corporate body'.[12]

Whether change is chosen or thrust upon you, it can cast every-thing – even familiar things – in a new light and leave you feeling that today nothing feels like it did yesterday. Running a team is hard when you're struggling to find your feet.

As Kotter noted, change comes in phases. First reactions can be messy, conflicting and a potential cause of tension. Managing them begins with recognizing their presence and allowing time and space for them to unfold. In this regard, change shares similarities with grief which can also be broken down into specific phases, as psychologists Elisabeth Kübler-Ross and David Kessler showed.[13]

Our course on leading through change explores some of the emotions involved and emphasizes that people work in different ways. Emotions might not start and stop in a neat sequential pattern. Rather, they come and go unexpectedly, progressing and regressing depending on circumstances. For some people, reactions to change might include:

- **Phase 1: Shock** – nervous, disorientated, lonely, confused, worried, anxious, uncertain
- **Phase 2: Curiosity/honeymoon** – creative, innovative, resourceful, in denial, numb
- **Phase 3: New rhythm** – optimistic, settling in, 'phoney adjustment', false certainty
- **Phase 4: Rainy days** – melancholy, thoughtful, guilty, low self-esteem
- **Phase 5: Cabin fever/restlessness** – frustrated, bored, distracted, agitated, angry, disruptive
- **Phase 6: Hope** – optimistic, growing, looking ahead, resilient, building anew

Consequently, when managing change, leaders may need to take these emotions into account. Appropriate responses include:

- **Phase 1: Reassurance** – empathy, honesty, regular check-ins
- **Phase 2: Guidance** – direction, communication, clarity
- **Phase 3: Short-term goals** – clear feedback, realistic optimism
- **Phase 4: Personal connection** – support, motivation, energy
- **Phase 5: Engagement** – encouragement, inspiration to keep going
- **Phase 6: New skills** – acknowledging journey achieved, structure, planning

Fundamentally, managing change is an exercise in empathy and communication in which leaders are mindful of key phases in human emotion and are ready to respond accordingly.

Leading through complexity

Complexity can be defined as the consequences (often chaotic) arising from problematic events – the pandemic for example. This is different to tasks (often mundane) that are merely complicated, such as getting to grips with tax law or developing an algorithm. Complicated tasks usually have rules and procedures while complex situations do not, so it's important to know which of the two you're up against.

Like crossing a messy room in the dark, tiptoeing through complexity's tangled mess can't be done by following rules. By approaching a complex situation as if you're managing something that's complicated, you risk looking for procedures and processes that simply aren't there. Instead, solutions typically emerge through trial and error. Finding them requires mental flexibility, humility and a willingness to learn and adapt.

Preparing in advance helps to reduce mistakes or delays in the event of a crisis. For example, in an emergency on an aircraft, we might rush forward towards the exit, losing time in the struggle to get there. If we'd taken a moment to plan ahead, however, we might have noticed another exit right behind us.

Leading through complexity begins with putting plans in place and being ready to implement them with creative flexibility. By accepting rather than denying the impact of complex events, we can break the whole into manageable parts. One way of doing this is through the Cynefin framework, as described by management consultants David Snowden and Mary Boone.[14]

Developed by Snowden in 1999 while he was at IBM, Cynefin (a Welsh word, pronounced 'ku-nev-in', meaning something akin to home – as in habitat, acquainted, familiar), allows leaders to consider a complex issue by assessing it through specific perspectives. In their article, Snowden and Boone described five perspectives – or 'contexts' – that enable leaders to break an issue into manageable chunks:

The [Cynefin] framework sorts the issues facing leaders into five contexts defined by the nature of the relationship between cause and effect. Four of these – simple, complicated, complex and chaotic – require leaders to diagnose situations and to act in contextually appropriate ways. The fifth – disorder – applies when it is unclear which of the other four contexts is predominant.

Using the Cynefin framework can help executives sense which context they are in so that they can not only make better decisions but also avoid the problems that arise when their preferred management style causes them to make mistakes.

Judy Kruger and Romeo Lavarias, experts in emergency manage-ment, used the Cynefin framework in understanding people's reactions to wearing a mask during the pandemic.[15] Using a mask could be considered a simple procedure. It became complicated when conflict-ing advice was given by healthcare professionals on which masks to wear, when and how.

The issue became complex when it ran into concerns about civil liberties. It then became chaotic when people violated the rules of shops and businesses by refusing to wear a mask. Complex and chaotic though it was, managing the situation was essential if people were to limit the impact of Covid. Kruger and Lavarias concluded that the Cynefin framework should be used to enhance communica-tions and decision making when trying to make sense of a rapidly unfolding situation.[16]

Managing uncertainty

In the grip of overwhelming complexity, it can be hard to respond immediately. Yet, though it might feel like you've been caught in the bright glare of oncoming headlights, it's risky to stand still in the face of danger. Uncertainty, however, is more like cautiously walking along a clifftop in fog. You can stop whenever you want, but if you want to make progress you'll need to keep tiptoeing forward – know-ing that out there somewhere is a cliff edge but also a safe destination.

Here's an example. In 2024, Britain, the US, Canada and France joined other nations in marking the anniversary of D-Day. Eighty years earlier, General Dwight D Eisenhower was in command of more than a million soldiers, sailors and airmen who were tasked with liberating occupied Europe from the Nazis.

The battle was due to begin on 5 June 1944 with a surprise attack on the French coast. More than 175,000 soldiers would secretly cross the Channel at night and attack at first light before the enemy realized what was happening.

The day before the operation, everything was ready – apart from the weather. It was too stormy. If the soldiers were sent into action the next morning, their small landing craft would be swamped and many men would drown. Eisenhower couldn't give the order to go, nor could he delay for too long either. Thousands of soldiers now knew about the secret mission. If the attack didn't launch soon, the Nazis might hear of the plan, they would reinforce the beaches and many more men would die.

Eisenhower was uncertain about whether to delay. If so, for how long? The weather forecasters were worryingly vague. Conditions might be better on 6 June, or not. They just didn't know. They looked to Eisenhower for a decision, and so did everyone else.

Managing uncertainty is usually a consequence of a shortage of information, sometimes perhaps a single though critical piece of the puzzle, like a weather report. The solution lies in recognizing the shortfall and working around it so that decisions and progress aren't delayed. More on this in a minute, but first let's enjoy a moment from the film *Ocean's Eleven*, when Brad Pitt gives Matt Damon advice on his role in the big heist:

> You look down, they know you're lying! And up, they know you don't know the truth. Don't use seven words when four will do. Don't shift your weight, look always at your mark but don't stare, be specific but not memorable, be funny but don't make him laugh. He's got to like you then forget you the moment you've left his side. And for God's sake, whatever you do, don't, under any circumstances…

Pitt breaks off to answer someone else and Damon – and the rest of us – are left to guess whether what he was about to say would mean the difference between glittering riches or 20 years in jail. We've been guessing ever since.[17]

When you've been left to guess about something, find clarity by recognizing and managing your relationship with uncertainty. Three tips will help:

- After recognizing fear and concern, and resisting the urge to do something, find something concrete to focus on. What are the things you know for certain, what are your strongest cards? Focusing on strengths will encourage calmness and clarity of thought.

- Identify what you're uncertain about. Big concerns, when seen in context, might well turn out to be smaller issues than you'd initially imagined. Accept these and move on. Better to move forward with limited facts than stay stuck while you wait for missing information.

- Moving forward is a better bet than paralysis, where someone is frozen by their initial concerns and by doubts about how to respond. By moving forward, thinking about action and outcomes, you escape uncertainty's grip and can begin to restore a sense of control.

Stress can bottle up troubled thoughts and feelings. As a leader, it's important to communicate concerns and intentions. Keep your mind moving and avoid paralysis by focusing on what you know for sure, communicating clearly and working with others where you can.

Delaying the D-Day operation hours before it was due to begin, Eisenhower repeatedly asked for weather updates. Waiting for better information when there was none available demanded level-headed patience and a readiness to go to plan B.

The operation needed a precise set of weather conditions along with specific morning tides. If the attack didn't go ahead in early June the next weather window wouldn't come for two weeks, far too long to keep the men on ships. But if they were allowed to go ashore in England's ports, the secret could leak to Nazi spies. Eisenhower had to make a decision. Finally, late at night, news came that the storm was finally passing. Eisenhower gave the command to attack on 6 June – and the rest is history.

Leading with bounded optimism

Optimism is about believing in what's possible. It's not always easy to find solutions in which you can justifiably believe. But there's a greater chance of discovering them with optimism than without. When bounded by facts and evidence, optimism can lead you towards meaningful options and away from the falsehoods that come from unbounded optimism.

A lack of realistic optimism can lead to the negative state of mind that writer Jim Collins calls the Stockdale Paradox. This is a concept he developed after interviewing Vice Admiral James Stockdale, a former US navy pilot who had been shot down over Vietnam in 1965.[18]

The most senior naval officer held in the Hỏa Lò Prison, the infamous 'Hanoi Hilton', Stockdale spent eight years in captivity not knowing when or if he might be released. Despite being tortured more than 20 times, Stockdale told Collins: 'I never doubted not only that I would get out but also that I would prevail in the end and turn the experience into the defining event of my life, which, in retrospect, I would not trade.'[19]

A solid case for optimism then? Not quite. Stockdale believed it was essential that optimism should be tempered with facts. Collins wanted to know who didn't make it out? He later wrote,

> 'Oh, that's easy', Stockdale said, 'the optimists. Oh, they were the ones
> who said, we're going to be out by Christmas. And Christmas would
> come, and Christmas would go. Then they'd say, we're going to be
> out by Easter. And Easter would come, and Easter would go. And
> then Thanksgiving, and then it would be Christmas again. And they
> died of a broken heart.' Then he turned to me and said, 'This is a very
> important lesson. You must never confuse faith that you will prevail in the
> end – which you can never afford to lose – with the discipline to confront
> the most brutal facts of your current reality, whatever they might be.'[20]

Inspired by the potential of bounded optimism, we developed a course for leaders who may find themselves confronted by difficult challenges with no clear end in sight. This work was led by our colleague Maria Kassova. The daughter of a diplomat, Maria grew up in many different countries, frequently moving school and developing the resilience and positivity to cope with change.

There's much online content about optimism, some of which is a pessimistic comment on the state of our collective sanity. Leaving aside references to dreams, candles, kittens, hilltops, sunsets and ideas about positive thoughts leading to positive rewards by lunchtime, there's another approach to optimism that sidesteps this fantasy-industrial complex. The optimism we favour focuses instead on a tangible strategy for leaders and their organizations.

Optimism learned as a skill can serve as a useful tool in escaping the paralysis associated with stress. Learned optimism challenges pessimistic thoughts and negative self-talk. Learning optimism as a skill is an idea that stems from the work of US psychologist Martin Seligman, who suggested that psychology was only half formed. Seligman believed that while there is a solid body of evidence about diagnosing and treating mental trauma, there is little focus on the other, more optimistic, side of life.[21]

Of course, there's a fine line between reality and magical thinking. The latter leads to overtly optimistic images of a future where everything's just dandy. That's not our focus here. Nor is it helpful to cling to doom and despair. Pessimism in the workplace isn't going to do much for morale in the face of change and complexity.

Uncertainty can affect a team as a whole and even make itself felt across the entire organization. Leaders are responsible for limiting the impact of negative fallout arising from adverse circumstances. In addition to rising above stress and seeking solutions, leaders need to help others maintain focus and direction so that the team can keep going without uncertainty knocking them off course.

Leaders can't ignore reality, but they can put it into context. By shaping an optimistic narrative for their people, leaders can more easily maintain motivation. A glimmer of optimism, supported by objective reasoning and evidence, can offer solid cause for hope and help people keep things in perspective.

Optimism can be a great source of energy when rooted in authentic values, such as:

- accurate interpretation of facts and data
- trust in people's capabilities

- honesty in communication
- readiness to accommodate other people's ideas
- grit and self-belief
- realistic appraisal of future outcomes

Bounded optimism, grounded in reality, encourages a growth mind-set that can lead to solutions. For example, in a meeting someone may suggest something that at first glance might not seem helpful. However, a response shaped by bounded optimism may build on the suggestion's potential. The suggestion itself might not work but perhaps it can be developed into something more.

At Working Voices, we encourage people to give a 'yes, and...' response to suggestions. Ideas are received with positive affirmation, opening the way to additional (hence the 'and') constructive thoughts that take things further on. It's a simple phrase, but it's effective in building cohesion. It's what our colleague Julia Davies calls radical open-mindedness.

Inclusive leaders

In 2019, Jack 'Farva' Curtis was the commanding officer of a squadron of US navy EA-18G Growler aircraft. When he took the job, Curtis brought with him a large map of the US that he'd had in his previous office at the same squadron. The map was dotted with dozens of small pins which visitors would usually ask about.[22]

Curtis would tell them that the pins didn't represent airports he'd visited or cities. In fact, they told a story of leadership, inclusivity and unity. 'Those pins represent what makes my organization strong', Curtis wrote; 'that they're dispersed so widely around the map underscores the point'.[23]

A routine task in both this and his previous roles involved meeting new members of the team for an introductory chat, regardless of their rank or time in service. He would begin by asking them to take a pin out of the jar and stick it in their home town on the map.

As the number of pins increased, Curtis's intention was easier to see, 'I point out that we come from different cultures, different values, different educations, different family dynamics, different spiritual or faith traditions, and many of us have different motivations to serve. But, and this is the key, now we're all here – at this squadron – which means we now have a shared purpose, and all those differences... they're features, not flaws'.[24]

Sailors would tell Curtis that they had never worked with a Black person before, or knowingly met someone who was gay. Some felt they were in unchartered waters, others felt isolated. Nevertheless, all were now part of the same unit.

In explaining their shared priorities, Curtis would bring them to understand that their joint purpose was respect. 'My expectation from them is to extend the same Day One respect to their new shipmates. But I go further. Not only do we start with my respect, but we pair it with trust. I explain that from the moment we meet I trust them. This strikes some of them as odd because we've been told for so long that trust is earned over time. That's true, but it's also true that sometimes you just have to start with the presumption of trust and go from there if you hope to have it reciprocated.'[25]

Tolerance, respect and trust bring a team together, which ultimately as their leader is what Curtis was looking for. 'We're stronger because we come from everywhere.'[26]

We seek to encourage similar values through our two courses on inclusive leadership. Both developed by our colleague Gene Douglas, these courses focus on company culture. The first maps out the fundamentals: defining inclusivity goals and developing choice architecture (in which decision-making processes encourage cultural change, leading to an inclusive workplace).

Our second course focuses on the critical link between inclusion and wellbeing. Looking at the health and wellbeing options offered by many large companies, Gene noted that research suggests 83 per cent of large organizations fail to address the important link between wellbeing and diversity, equity and inclusion.[27]

In looking at diversity and inclusion in general, Gene explained that he 'wanted to reframe the discussion in a way that links issues of inclusion and exclusion to wellness and wellbeing – topics everyone understands and that cross all demographic lines. As a person of colour, and a professional who teaches topics of inclusion and unconscious bias, it seemed wise to point out the connections between inclusion and health, productivity and overall team morale'.

Gene's priorities were:

1 highlighting the link between institutional health and the wellbeing of employees

2 offering practical, actionable strategies for individuals, teams and organizations

This course encourages dialogue around inclusion and wellbeing through concepts such as the 'four As of mindful coping', as developed by the Mayo Clinic:[28]

- **Avoid**: Avoid stress by planning ahead. Take control of your surroundings; learn to say no; avoid excluders, when possible; make mindful responses.

- **Alter**: Take ownership of what you can control and make alterations or upgrades. Clarify boundaries; communicate respectfully and openly; respectfully ask others to alter their behaviours; initiate positive changes, where possible.

- **Accept**: Accept what you can't control, work to change what you can. Talk with someone; forgive; commit to positive self-talk; learn from mistakes.

- **Adapt**: Adaptive behaviour teaches us how to cope. Look at the big picture; practise wellness strategies; focus on what's working; adjust expectations and reframe issues; if necessary, move to a healthier environment.

Ultimately, Gene designed a course that helps participants better understand the links between inclusion, wellness and the health of an organization and its people. This understanding leads to dialogue that implements change. 'If we can get some of the approach strategies implemented on an organization level and normalize these steps,' Gene said, 'that would be a real triumph.'

Change, complexity and uncertainty share much overlap. Whether self-induced or unexpected, their unsettling disruption can cause negative first reactions. These demand an acute level of management, often just when crucial information, staff or familiar routine may be unavailable.

While it's important to identify which of the three you're up against, all require a vigorous two-step response that subdues challenging emotions and kickstarts the management processes that will restore stability. Managing disruption relies on a broad range of skills, none more important than communication.

Think of travelling on a train. Your plans depend on arriving at your destination on schedule; however, the train has come to a halt in the middle of nowhere. It's stuck at a red light and has been stationary for some time. When neither the driver nor anyone else tells you what's going on, it can be frustrating.

An explanation would not change anything; a few words from the driver aren't going to put you back on schedule. But communication in moments of disruption is essential. Uncertainty can quickly spiral into irritation and tension. When you don't know the extent of the problem, silence sounds like disinterest and a lack of leadership.

In the workplace, silence is just as unhelpful, adding to tension and prompting questions about whether the root problem is down to external difficulties or internal failings.

When leading through change, you might feel you don't have any useful information to give your team. You'll update them when you're ready. But this contributes to tension and is not an excuse for a lack of communication. People need to know there's someone at the wheel, keeping an eye on what's coming down the track, someone who's ready to respond. More than just supplying information, communication is about presence, reassurance and keeping the team together.

Difficult moments often arise from deficit, for example a breakdown in planning, market information, client confidence or similar. Whatever's been lost, leaders can compensate by relying on what they still have – for example the trust, respect and commitment of their team. When they need their people more than ever, leaders must maintain cohesion and morale through communication and clarity.

Communicating comes first, even when there's nothing to communicate. To find something to say, leaders can fall back on their advance planning. Expect the unexpected and prepare in advance, developing a plan for transformation or even just for continuity. This can be broken down into components, allowing room for flexibility and easy wins and openly shared with key individuals.

Within the team, psychological safety and a sense of belonging will develop resilience and encourage novel ideas from a range of voices. In unsettled times and unfamiliar circumstances, new solutions may prove valuable. It's not about whether an idea is immediately worka-ble; it's more about whether everyone's working well enough as a team to build on initial ideas and transform them into viable proposals.

Developing a plan in advance is important but it's only a single part of the process. More significant is the team's underlying motiva-tion, cohesion and willingness to engage. Developing this mindset in advance brings the team together long before disruption settles in. Building respect, trust, safety and belonging is social wellbeing in action, it is the route to organizational resilience.

More than simply an antidote to poor working practices, social wellbeing is a positive force that ensures employees can cope with the emotional fallout that comes from change. It enables people to bounce back faster so that they can quickly restore stability under the guidance of communicative leaders. In our final chapter, we'll discover other practical benefits of social wellbeing and take a look at how some of these have been adopted by major multinationals.

Notes

1 N Srivastava. "My Goggles Filled Up With Water"- Michael Phelps Swam Blind for Over 175m to Achieve One of His Biggest Career Achievement, 6 June 2022, Essentiallysports.com, www.essentiallysports.com/us-sports-news-swimming-news-my-goggles-filled-up-with-water-michael-phelps-swam-blind-for-over-175m-to-achieve-one-of-his-biggest-career-achievement/ (archived at https://perma.cc/2W4L-EG8D)

2 I Deokule. "My goggles fill up with water... I counted my strokes" – Michael Phelps on how he swam 'blind' at the 2008 Olympics, 13 March 2024, Sportskeeda, www.sportskeeda.com/us/olympics/michael-phelps-swam-blind-2008-olympics (archived at https://perma.cc/35Q2-3T7Z)

3 World Aquatics. Michael Phelps, www.worldaquatics.com/athletes/1001621/michael-phelps/medals (archived at https://perma.cc/CNR3-A2PQ)

4   B Ewenstein. Changing change management, 1 July 2015, McKinsey, www.
mckinsey.com/featured-insights/leadership/changing-change-management
(archived at https://perma.cc/M645-WH6T)

5   M Hughes. Do 70 Per Cent of All Organizational Change Initiatives Really
Fail? *Journal of Change Management*, 2011, **11** (4), pp. 451–64

6   NicLim. A Comparative Analysis of VUCA, TUNA, BANI, and Pre, During,
and Post Crisis Decision Making, 31 July 2023, Medium.com, medium.com/@
dreamydsire/a-comparative-analysis-of-vuca-tuna-bani-and-pre-during-and-
post-crisis-decision-making-a5648058dea3 (archived at https://perma.cc/
FFN9-UCN5)

7   D Rowland, N Brauckmann and M Thorley. How to get your team on board
with a major change, 4 August 2022, *Harvard Business Review*,
hbr.org/2022/08/how-to-get-your-team-on-board-with-a-major-change
(archived at https://perma.cc/9EBG-MBKQ)

8   D Rowland, N Brauckmann and M Thorley. How to get your team on board
with a major change, 4 August 2022, *Harvard Business Review*,
hbr.org/2022/08/how-to-get-your-team-on-board-with-a-major-change
(archived at https://perma.cc/9EBG-MBKQ)

9   D Rowland, N Brauckmann and M Thorley. How to get your team on board
with a major change, 4 August 2022, *Harvard Business Review*,
hbr.org/2022/08/how-to-get-your-team-on-board-with-a-major-change
(archived at https://perma.cc/9EBG-MBKQ)

10 gdowns. Satya Nadella: 'The Learn-It-All Does Better Than the Know-It-All',
23 January 2019, *Wall Street Journal*, www.wsj.com/video/satya-nadella-the-
learn-it-all-does-better-than-the-know-it-all/D8BC205C-D7F5-423E-8A41-
0E921E86597C.html (archived at https://perma.cc/YYM5-UHP7)

11 J P Kotter. Leading change: why transformation efforts fail, May-June 1995,
Harvard Business Review, hbr.org/1995/05/leading-change-why-transformation-
efforts-fail-2 (archived at https://perma.cc/WB5K-AL6A)

12 J P Kotter. Leading change: why transformation efforts fail, May-June 1995,
Harvard Business Review, hbr.org/1995/05/leading-change-why-transformation-
efforts-fail-2 (archived at https://perma.cc/WB5K-AL6A)

13 E Kübler-Ross and D Kessler (2005) *On Grief and Grieving*, Simon & Schuster

14 D Snowden and M Boone. A Leader's Framework for Decision Making,
November 2007, *Harvard Business Review*, hbr.org/2007/11/a-leaders-
framework-for-decision-making (archived at https://perma.cc/NVM3-3QNQ)

15 J Kruger and R Lavarias. Application of the Cynefin Framework to
COVID-19 Pandemic, 23 February 2022, DomesticPreparedness.com,
www.domesticpreparedness.com/healthcare/application-of-the-cynefin-
framework-to-covid-19-pandemic/ (archived at https://perma.
cc/6QUV-RZS5)

16   J Kruger and R Lavarias. Application of the Cynefin Framework to COVID-19 Pandemic, 23 February 2022, DomesticPreparedness.com, www.domesticpreparedness.com/healthcare/application-of-the-cynefin-framework-to-covid-19-pandemic/ (archived at https://perma.cc/6QUV-RZS5)

17   IMDb. Ocean's Eleven (2001) Brad Pitt: Rusty Ryan, www.imdb.com/title/tt0240772/characters/nm0000093 (archived at https://perma.cc/6X8L-J5CL)

18   J Collins (2001) *Good to Great*, HarperCollins; extract from JimCollins.com: jimcollins.com/concepts/Stockdale-Concept.html (archived at https://perma.cc/2K79-WLU4)

19   J Collins (2001) *Good to Great*, HarperCollins; extract from JimCollins.com: jimcollins.com/concepts/Stockdale-Concept.html (archived at https://perma.cc/2K79-WLU4)

20   J Collins (2001) *Good to Great*, HarperCollins; extract from JimCollins.com: jimcollins.com/concepts/Stockdale-Concept.html (archived at https://perma.cc/2K79-WLU4)

21   M Seligman (1991) *Learned Optimism*, Knopf

22   J Curtis. The Map on the Wall, 23 August 2019, From the Green Notebook, fromthegreennotebook.com/2019/08/23/the-map-on-the-wall/ (archived at https://perma.cc/USL8-3PBQ)

23   J Curtis. The Map on the Wall, 23 August 2019, From the Green Notebook, fromthegreennotebook.com/2019/08/23/the-map-on-the-wall/ (archived at https://perma.cc/USL8-3PBQ)

24   J Curtis. The Map on the Wall, 23 August 2019, From the Green Notebook, fromthegreennotebook.com/2019/08/23/the-map-on-the-wall/ (archived at https://perma.cc/USL8-3PBQ)

25   J Curtis. The Map on the Wall, 23 August 2019, From the Green Notebook, fromthegreennotebook.com/2019/08/23/the-map-on-the-wall/ (archived at https://perma.cc/USL8-3PBQ)

26   J Curtis. The Map on the Wall, 23 August 2019, From the Green Notebook, fromthegreennotebook.com/2019/08/23/the-map-on-the-wall/ (archived at https://perma.cc/USL8-3PBQ)

27   C Michalak and M Jackson. Supporting the Well-Being of Your Underrepresented Employees, 4 March 2022, *Harvard Business Review*, hbr.org/2022/03/supporting-the-well-being-of-your-underrepresented-employees (archived at https://perma.cc/44UG-M7NC)

28   D Sparks. Mayo Mindfulness: Try the 4 A's for stress relief, 24 April 2019, Mayo Clinic, newsnetwork.mayoclinic.org/discussion/mayo-mindfulness-try-the-4-as-for-stress-relief/ (archived at https://perma.cc/A99B-BLGE)

10

Working sustainably

Here's the story so far. Victorian industrialists weren't big on well-being. Employees were fined for letting material get into the machinery while trying to save their fingers; meanwhile shareholders received a 38 per cent dividend. Children were caught in fatal accidents in coal-mines, factory women developed phossy jaw, rest breaks didn't exist and exploitation at work was a fact of life.

We – employers and employees – are not those people anymore. Who have we become?

Workplace relationships fit for the 21st century

After the horror of the First World War, the Versailles Treaty enshrined a commitment to social justice. No longer would someone's labour be regarded as a soulless commodity. In industrialized nations, politics was broadening, accommodating new voters and new voices.

As a consequence of these developments, many workplace practices became morally and legally unacceptable. Employers needed to find other ways to manage the workforce in order to meet their objectives. And so began a partnership, a dialogue between employer and employee.

Scientific Management favoured less stick and more carrot – in the form of rest breaks and organized training. Abraham Maslow gave us ideas about motivation, which Douglas McGregor developed into Theory X and Theory Y.

Theories abounded, occasionally leading us backwards. The rank and yank system of 'Neutron Jack' Welch had something Victorian about it. It might have supported short-term gains but its impact on morale undermined the long-term interests of the business.

Dehumanizing workplace practices are counter-productive; they go against the direction of travel and do not represent the best of human potential. As soon as Welch moved on from General Electric, ranking and yanking was dropped.

There are better ways of getting the best from people, beginning with dialogue shaped by mutual need. In challenging markets, organizations need to do what they can to stay competitive. Their successes protect employees, who need security, career development, a sense of accomplishment and personal fulfilment. Employers and their people have much to offer each other. Mutual support leads to strong organizations that benefit all involved along with their families and communities.

Over time, the relationship between employer and employee became closer, more relaxed, more informal. First names and less formal clothes became acceptable, reflecting social trends.

Then the 2007–08 global financial crisis sounded alarm bells in economies around the world. Pushed into a defensive, fortress mentality, organizations prioritized tough financial constraints, pulling up the drawbridge on a softer, more human outlook. Smaller budgets, cautious planning, new compliance and tighter cost-cutting required people to work longer hours and make do with less. Previously, the warm smell of coffee suggested cosy informality. After 2008, it was mainly about the caffeine.

When fatigue set in, organizations responded with wellbeing perks including free fruit bowls and table tennis in the lobby (though, at least one global bank took away the fruit bowls, fearing they sent a misleading message about 'plenty'). For organizations focused on surviving tougher markets and financial instability, wellbeing was not a priority. Perks were largely symbolic, no more than optional extras for individuals.

Many businesses showed little interest in finding better ways of working. Little was said about sharing wellbeing responsibilities between employer and employee. Individuals were left to take responsibility for the impact of the long hours that their employer asked of them.

Offices were redesigned to feel less formal – not for the sake of comfort but to encourage people to feel at home and stay longer at work. And once Blackberries and smartphones arrived, and people could be reached 24/7, home was no longer the escape it had once been.

Work and home were blurring into a single fuzzy world, a space where individuals were never beyond the reach of their employer. With less opportunity to break free from an organization's encircling walls, it became harder to hide from expectation.

Working practices often overlooked fundamental human needs for recognition and connection. This was compounded by a rise in technology that disrupted the very way we think and, ironically, left us feeling disconnected. Technology enabled some companies to extend control over their people, monitoring their keystrokes and compromising the autonomy that is central to an engaged sense of fulfilment.

Fatigue deepened and disengagement set in. Gallup found that 77 per cent of employees were either not engaged or actively disengaged.[1] The World Health Organization recognized 'burn-out', defining it as:

> A syndrome conceptualized as resulting from chronic workplace stress that has not been successfully managed. It is characterized by three dimensions:
>
> - feelings of energy depletion or exhaustion;
> - increased mental distance from one's job, or feelings of negativism or cynicism related to one's job;
> - reduced professional efficacy.[2]

Then came Covid, bursting underlying tension in the employer/employee relationship and reinvigorating ideas of social justice from a hundred years earlier. This time, people didn't need an international treaty to give them confidence. Covid led to a psychological shot in the arm for many, giving them new resolve. In the Great Resignation, millions voted with their feet.

In the mid-2020s, organizations are struggling with disengagement and retention issues. These difficulties are compounded by 21st century lifestyles leading to poor mental health, short attention spans and flaws in critical thinking. Multigenerational miscommunication also adds to the mix.

Many leaders genuinely want to improve things, to find something that will help their people and thereby boost productivity. But too many organizations continue to deny the causes of fatigue in the first place. They refuse to talk about the origins of stress and speak of boosting resilience instead.

Refusing to look inwards, many businesses rely on superficial wellbeing perks – which in 2024 an Oxford academic found were nearly all pretty much useless.[3] Organizations who contribute to deep-seated fatigue and then look for an app to mend it are working in a way that is neither sensible nor sustainable.

Something else is needed: something that rethinks the way people are managed and that decisively benefits both employers and employees, something that leaders will be able to wholeheartedly embrace.

Organizations must accept responsibility for the impact of their working practices. This is the first step to tackling the issues they face. Secondly, organizations will benefit from a better approach to work. This can't be an optional extra for individuals; it must be the basis of a company culture that touches everyone and that recognizes the strengths and weaknesses of what it is to be human.

This desire among leaders to help their people brings us up to date in the dialogue between employer and employee. The relationship has brought us to within touching distance of a comprehensive rethink in culture, in engagement and in the fundamentals of the way we work together.

Who have we become? We have become a generation of leaders and employees who together can finally resolve the insidious challenges that have been undermining our relationship for decades.

Social wellbeing in practice

What sort of culture should organizations be aiming for in order to achieve sustainable engagement and productivity?

In Chapter 5, we recognized the need for a culture that would:

- **replace poor working practices** such as doing more with less, dismissing the need for human interaction, over-reliance on tech and a lack of employee autonomy
- **shore up organizational resilience** by giving leaders and employees the skills to find creative, resourceful solutions to disruptive global events
- **address some of the consequences of our use of social media**, particularly poor mental health, short attention spans and loss of skills in critical thinking
- **implement activities that recognize and support human nature** – for example, the need for authentic social connection and the need for personal development through learning

In developing a culture that would meet these objectives, we considered papers and analysis from a range of authors in academia and in business. From these, we noted the value of:

- belonging
- psychological safety
- autonomy
- collective intelligence
- group norms
- trust

We often found that these were each described in isolation, without reference to other values on this list. They were also described in a context of teamwork. By bringing them together in a single concept, we saw that this could benefit not just a team but an organization as a whole. This concept envisaged a cohesive approach to people, bringing them together in a workplace culture that we call social wellbeing.

Organizations can develop social wellbeing in four stages:

1 Move on from current ineffective wellbeing initiatives
Leaders can begin to address challenges to engagement by accepting that current wellbeing perks are ineffective. These can be replaced

with adjustments to company culture that will encourage the inclusive sense of belonging that improves engagement and productivity. This is the heart of social wellbeing and includes everyone from the C-suite down.

2 Develop future skills, such as agile thinking

Once social wellbeing is adopted as company culture, it becomes easier to help individuals break out of traditional mindsets and discover the future skills that companies are investing in as a priority – such as agile thinking, which leads to better problem solving and decision making.

3 Manage communication challenges

Human skills in communication cannot be easily replicated and give people an advantage over technology. By committing to future communication skills, organizations can bridge gaps in relationships, for example between people and tech and between younger generations and their older peers.

4 Learn to lead through change

Having developed social wellbeing for the workforce, and given future skills to key workers, employers can focus on acquiring the mindset to lead through the periods of change and complexity that will continue to disrupt organizations in the years to come.

Our four training modules, developed with these priorities in mind and detailed in Chapter 6, each contain a range of courses that can be selected in isolation or combined in tailor-made packages according to need. Together, they prepare organizations and their people for the challenges ahead.

These are the skills that will enable organizations to thrive in the turbulent 2020s. Economic uncertainty, geopolitical tensions, the threat of further pandemics and the rise of AI are likely to similarly overshadow the 2030s, a time when the climate emergency may lead to additional pressures relating to immigration, infrastructure and natural resources.

Organizations can prepare for the difficult years ahead by taking practical steps, such as:

- accepting that prevailing conditions demand a new approach to culture, leading to a thriving environment that is positive, creative and resilient

- encouraging managers to adopt the new thinking, for example by identifying 'culture champions' who can encourage trust, respect and safety

- developing inclusion and belonging so that all employees feel able to contribute their best, potentially leading to solutions from voices that might have previously gone unheard

- replacing annual appraisals with ongoing feedback that looks forward to future opportunities and commits to people's career development

When encouraged to do their best work, to commit to the team that trusts them and to follow their career aspirations, people feel motivated and engaged. This develops into a long-term sense of belonging. It regenerates motivation, replacing jaded feelings of fatigue with a reinvigorated sense of purpose. In short, it's a sustainable way of working.

Social wellbeing is the clearest signal we have of the shape of things to come. It offers a practical solution to productivity and retention challenges. It describes the direction of travel that organizations and their people are increasingly committing to and it opens the way to future skills.

'The secret behind successful teamwork lies in the ability to intentionally nurture and maintain healthy team dynamics', so says Microsoft in their 40-page handbook *The Art of Teamwork*.[4] Let's turn to some practical examples of how social wellbeing can support team dynamics. In each case, elements of social wellbeing are being successfully implemented to the benefit of all involved:

Developing a sense of belonging

As we saw in Chapter 5, Baumeister and Leary showed that the need to belong is a deeply rooted human motivation that can trigger a response as powerful as hunger.[5] Today, long after their influential paper was published in 1995, leading multinationals continue to be inspired by its conclusions. Belonging matters, isolation is hard to bear. When an anonymous writer wrote an article on feeling isolated at work for 45 hours a week, his experiences prompted 800 replies.[6]

Deloitte noticed that, in the past, organizations tried to develop a sense of belonging by – ironically – focusing on individuals.[7] Their analysis found that in the 2020s, 'leading organizations are forging a stronger link between belonging and organizational performance by strengthening workers' connections with their teams'.[8]

Belonging, along with wellbeing, featured at the top of Deloitte's *Global Human Capital Trends* survey (2020) as one of the most important issues facing HR departments. Deloitte found:

> Seventy-nine per cent of survey respondents said that fostering a sense of belonging in the workforce was important to their organization's success in the next 12–18 months, and 93 per cent agreed that a sense of belonging drives organizational performance – one of the highest rates of consensus on importance we have seen in a decade of *Global Human Capital Trends* reports.[9]

Deloitte's survey echoed findings from an earlier poll of 1,789 full-time US employees working in a range of industries.[10] This indicated that if people feel a sense of belonging, companies reap substantial bottom-line benefits. A high sense of belonging was linked to:

- a 56% increase in job performance
- a 50% drop in turnover risk
- a 75% reduction in sick days[11]

The survey found that, for a 10,000-person company, these numbers would result in annual savings of more than $52 million. Deloitte noted that a single incidence of 'micro-exclusion' can lead to an immediate 25 per cent decline in an individual's performance on a team project.[12]

At NASA, belonging is developed by fostering a strong sense of mission across the entire workforce, from federal employees to private contractors. 'From an astronaut to an accountant, we're all pulling on the same rope, in the same direction, trying to achieve the same thing', Robert Gibbs, associate administrator for NASA's Mission Support Directorate said. This approach might help to explain NASA's conspicuously low 3 per cent attrition rate.[13]

At Horizon Therapeutics, belonging is developed through a policy of 'allyship' in the workplace. This identifies and supports individuals who exemplify inclusive behaviours, people who go out of their way to look out for others, the kind of people we at Working Voices describe as 'culture champions'. Horizon looks for four characteristics in its allies:

- being good at learning and listening
- feeling comfortable with speaking up and speaking out
- owning and sharing their own story
- modelling positive, inclusive behaviours[14]

Through these efforts, Horizon is credited with creating a 'familial' environment. Employees feel connected to their work and their co-workers and believe they have a voice in decision making.[15]

Another approach to allyship focuses not on individuals but on support groups. Belonging can be enhanced through employee resource groups (ERGs) which create supportive communities within the workplace. ERGs at data management company Syniti include the Fitness Inspiration Team which actively supports all aspects of physical, mental and emotional wellbeing.[16]

Encouraging psychological safety

Like the work of Baumeister and Leary, Amy Edmondson's 1999 paper on psychological safety similarly continues to influence major companies.[17] Safety comes in various forms. It gives assurance to members of a team that they and their ideas will be given a fair hearing in meetings. It also offers reassurance to a team member who is struggling with a personal issue and needs a little extra space or understanding.

A middle manager from a global corporation summed up typical concerns by saying: 'I'm very careful when I stick my neck out and challenge the status quo. If I do and don't get my head chopped off, I'll do it again. If I get my head chopped off, you can rest assured I'll keep my ideas to myself.'[18]

For Microsoft: 'Team members who feel psychologically safe are able to take greater interpersonal risks, allowing them to bring their full selves to their work, which sets the stage for innovative ideas to flourish.'[19] The Microsoft handbook on teamwork offers the following definitions:[20]

> **Trust** is knowing you can be vulnerable with someone without being put down or hurt. For example, when a team shows unwavering support for a team member who is struggling with a personal trauma, that team member's trust in the team deepens.
>
> **Vulnerability** is entering into situations that involve risk and emotional exposure. For example, a team member may show vulnerability by confiding in their team about a personal trauma they are struggling with.
>
> **Psychological safety** is the brave space where an individual feels comfortable sharing their opinions and ideas without fear of recrimination, judgement or animosity. Psychological safety is created through the virtuous cycle of trust and vulnerability. For example, when the team member struggling with a personal trauma feels psychologically safe, they won't feel the need to hide their struggle, which allows them to show up fully.

At social media company Buffer, all new team members were originally required to go through a 45-day probationary period before being fully accepted into the company. This seemed to make good sense, allowing each side to see whether the other was working out for them.[21]

But Buffer later discovered that this policy was having a detrimental effect on psychological safety. Buffer's director of people Courtney Seiter explained: 'A 45-day probationary period is a big risk, especially for those who left other jobs to join Buffer. If teammates felt insecure and "on guard" for their first six weeks, we likely missed out on their candid thoughts and big, risky ideas.'[22]

Life sciences company Gilead Sciences wanted to support team members in Asia. It was hoped that skills in inclusive leadership would help people feel better able to speak up, make mistakes and be themselves without fear of judgement. Gilead instilled an atmosphere of psychological safety with the aim of encouraging individuals to feel they could challenge norms, break a culture of conformity and proactively rather than reactively identify issues and opportunities.[23]

Finding personal autonomy

No-one likes to be micromanaged. Without the energy-sapping impact of someone constantly gazing over their shoulder, individuals are better able to protect motivation and divert mental resources towards the task in hand. This is workplace autonomy.

Autonomy is not an expectation of radical freedom or entitlement. It's about employees participating in teamwork and collaboration through personal decisions and actions. Autonomy relies on allowing individuals to perform their job rather than treating them as if they're an extension of someone else's.

A survey on micromanagement showed that:[24]

- 79% of respondents had experienced micromanagement
- 69% said they had considered changing jobs because of micromanagement
- 36% actually changed jobs
- 71% said being micromanaged interfered with their job performance
- 85% said their morale was negatively impacted

Examining survey data from 20,000 employees, researchers at the University of Birmingham Business School assessed how the presence or lack of autonomy affected wellbeing. According to Dr Daniel Wheatley, the team found that greater levels of personal control over work tasks and schedule 'have the potential to generate significant benefits for the employee'.[25]

Organizations that are apprehensive about encouraging autonomy at work might simultaneously advocate an entrepreneurial spirit – which amounts to much the same thing. President and CEO of optical-fibre specialists Clearfield, Cheri Beranek, noted: 'Leaders who encourage team members to approach their jobs with an entre-preneurial spirit uncover more opportunities to do each job better'.[26]

Building collective intelligence

Ineffective meetings cost businesses $541 billion a year globally in lost productivity and employee time, according to Doodle's 2019

State of Meetings Report.[27] Meetings are ineffective when team members fail to work well together. Gallup found that as much as 85 per cent of employee time may be wasted on inefficient collaboration.[28]

The real impact of dysfunctional teamwork however runs deeper than money. Innovation grinds to a halt, agile thinking gets bogged down in internal competition, silo mentalities take hold and disengagement creeps up.

When Anita Woolley, Thomas Malone and others published their influential work on collective intelligence in 2010, for the first time companies were given a blueprint on how to get more from their teams.[29] Analysis by Woolley and Malone on collective intelligence called for stronger social sensitivity among team members and equality in 'turn-taking' during conversations. The stronger the sense of equality within the team, the more likely people would work better together.

Some organizations have taken these principles further, transforming teamwork by embedding openness and transparency into their company culture. At software company Buffer, openness is part of the core business model. Salaries are posted online, as are details about revenue and the number of customers. All company emails are accessible by everyone. 'Transparency breeds trust, and trust is the foundation of great teamwork', according to Buffer founder and CEO Joel Gascoigne.[30]

At Lenovo Group, the status bias that sometimes shapes teamwork in Asia was limiting plans to expand. Titles were paramount and people would only speak in hierarchical order. CEO Yang Yuanqing was called 'Chief Executive Officer Yang' by everyone.[31]

Seeking to change Lenovo's culture, Mr Yang put himself in the lobby of Lenovo's Beijing headquarters for more than a week. Wearing a 'Hello, my name is Yuanqing' sticker, and shaking hands with everyone who walked through the door, he asked employees to address him by his first name.[32]

Learning from Project Aristotle

Google's Project Aristotle (detailed in Chapter 5) brought together the work of Amy Edmondson and Anita Woolley in offering its own valuable insights on teamwork. Inspired by the findings of the Aristotle researchers, Google looked for ways of giving employees time and opportunity to express their creativity. This led to the practice of '20 per cent time' where employees are encouraged (but not required) to work on side projects that fall outside their job description.

Demonstrating commitment to psychological safety, 20 per cent time gave employees the confidence to try new things and take risks, knowing they could do so without being judged or punished. Innovations that came from this included developments in Gmail and Google Maps.

Other companies have shown similar commitment to their employees' psychological wellbeing. Microsoft offered in-person digital and telephone counselling, along with support groups and mental health workshops. Levi Strauss & Co, the iconic maker of jeans, have been described as 'setting the gold standard for taking responsibility for employee mental health'.[33] The company's chief HR officer Tracy Layney said: 'If we've learned anything from the last few years, it's that the old way of working just wasn't working.'[34]

Levi Strauss is building a holistic approach to mental health, including a culture rooted in empathy. For Layney: 'The "always-on" mentality contributes to burnout, no matter the level in your career.' Levi Strauss supports the mental health of employees through projects that include:[35]

- resources from coaching to virtual therapy
- robust employee assistance programmes, providing immediate support
- prioritizing paid leave policies to make sure no employee should have to choose between their job and taking care of themselves or their loved ones

Meanwhile, consumer goods giant Unilever has trained 4,000 of its global employees, so far, to be 'mental health champions', supporting their peers by looking for signs of people struggling with mental health, and then helping them reach services that can help.[36]

Unilever's Lamplighter programme assesses employees' physical and mental health and helps them develop work–life integration plans. Unilever's analysis showed that for every £1 spent on the programme, £3.73 was returned in higher productivity.[37]

In the UK, IT firms Cisco, Salesforce and Softcat took the top spots in a 2022 poll of the best workplaces for wellbeing, each of them being recognized for an integrated approach to wellbeing embedded across the organization.[38]

Developing trust

Dr Paul Zak, the neuro-economist who proved that trust was directly linked to the body's production of the neurotransmitter oxytocin, wrote in 2018: 'My research has shown that organizational culture makes a huge difference in how we feel about, and perform, at work.'[39]

Having spent a decade 'doing laboratory studies to understand the brain basis for effective teamwork', Zak tested his theories at a number of businesses including online retailer Zappos.com and office designer Herman Miller. In each case, he found: 'Teams that caused oxytocin release in each other were more productive and innovative, and enjoyed the tasks they were doing more, than those whose brains did not connect to their teammates.'[40]

Offering further evidence of the value of a trusting environment, Zak refers to examples of companies that have removed job titles, for example Morning Star Tomato which produces more than half of the US output of processed tomato products. 'Everyone is a colleague,' Zak found. 'Even owner and founder Chris Rufer's business card just has his name on it. Each colleague chooses which work group she or he will join based on a commitment to create value for the group.'[41]

Meanwhile, at SAS Institute, the world's largest privately owned software company, employee turnover is around 5 per cent, in an industry that averages around 15 per cent. 'Treat employees like they make a difference and they will make a difference,' SAS co-founder and CEO Jim Goodnight told Zak.[42]

'There are no human resources,' Zak wrote, 'just human beings. It's time to start treating those at work as the fallible, emotional, surprising and intrinsically wonderful human beings that they are.'[43]

Our own sentiments exactly.

Getting ready for bears

Organizations that are authentically committed to social wellbeing will be able to create a healthy workplace with a culture built on belonging and trust. This will support a motivated and engaged workforce who will be reliably creative and resilient and skilled in self-management and communication. People working for a forward-thinking employer bring their best self to work. In a safe environment, people feel 're-humanized', trusted and ready to fulfil their potential.

Naturally, some businesses are resistant to change. This is only to be expected in difficult and uncertain times. Nevertheless, in the long run a reluctance to join the direction of travel may prove costly. In short, organizations are advised to:

- upgrade culture by adopting social wellbeing, thus supporting retention and growth
- take a lead in 're-humanizing people', encouraging belonging and personal development
- give people an environment where they feel a sense of autonomy, authenticity and trust
- provide training in the future skills that support organizational resilience

These are not quick-fix recommendations. They are a plan for a steady, clear-sighted path forward, to be implemented by boardroom leaders, advocated by HR managers and championed by key employees.

Two hikers were lost in a forest, so the old story goes, when they were confronted by a bear. One yelled, 'Run!'

'What do you mean, "run"?', cried the other. 'How are you going to outrun a bear?'

'I don't have to,' said his friend. 'I just have to outrun you.'

At times, the future might feel like a fearsome prospect, all teeth and claws and approaching at pace. Weakness across mature economies is set to continue into the 2030s, according to global research organization The Conference Board, citing the rising cost of capital and ongoing economic and geopolitical uncertainty.[44] You won't be able to escape all the difficult moments ahead. By being prepared, however, you'll be able to outpace slower competitors. We hope this book gives you a helpful head start.

Notes

1 J Clifton et al (2022) Gallup State of the Global Workplace: 2022 Report, 2 May 2023, CCA Global, www.cca-global.com/content/latest/article/2023/05/state-of-the-global-workplace-2022-report-346/ (archived at https://perma.cc/L75Q-J632)

2 World Health Organization. Burn-out an "occupational phenomenon": International Classification of Diseases, 28 May 2019, www.who.int/news/item/28-05-2019-burn-out-an-occupational-phenomenon-international-classification-of-diseases (archived at https://perma.cc/B58A-VRLG)

3 W Fleming. Employee well-being outcomes from individual-level mental health interventions: Cross-sectional evidence from the United Kingdom, *Industrial Relations Journal*, 2024, 55 (2), pp. 162–82

4 J Fabiano. Microsoft researchers worked with designers to define the art of teamwork and they found this, 3 January 2020, Ladders, www.theladders.com/career-advice/successful-teamwork (archived at https://perma.cc/V9KC-6RZY)

5 R F Baumeister and M R Leary. The need to belong: Desire for interpersonal attachments as a fundamental human motivation, *Psychological Bulletin*, 1995, **117** (3), pp. 497–529

6 Anonymous. Workplace loneliness is a real problem. For 45 hours a week I feel isolated, 1 February 2016, The Guardian, www.theguardian.com/commentisfree/2016/feb/01/loneliness-at-work-introvert-sadness-bereft-in-bustling-office (archived at https://perma.cc/A6MU-UVKE)

7 J Schwartz, B Denny and D Mallon. Belonging: From comfort to connection to contribution, 15 May 2020, Deloitte Insights, www2.deloitte.com/us/en/insights/focus/human-capital-trends/2020/creating-a-culture-of-belonging.html (archived at https://perma.cc/5GU3-9BRE)

8 J Schwartz, B Denny and D Mallon. Belonging: From comfort to connection to contribution, 15 May 2020, Deloitte Insights, www2.deloitte.com/us/en/insights/focus/human-capital-trends/2020/creating-a-culture-of-belonging.html (archived at https://perma.cc/5GU3-9BRE)

9   J Schwartz, B Denny and D Mallon. Belonging: From comfort to connection to contribution, 15 May 2020, Deloitte Insights, www2.deloitte.com/us/en/ insights/focus/human-capital-trends/2020/creating-a-culture-of-belonging.html (archived at https://perma.cc/5GU3-9BRE)

10 E W Carr. The Value of Belonging at Work, 16 December 2019, *Harvard Business Review*, hbr.org/2019/12/the-value-of-belonging-at-work (archived at https://perma.cc/DHS5-JR64)

11 E W Carr. The Value of Belonging at Work, 16 December 2019, *Harvard Business Review*, hbr.org/2019/12/the-value-of-belonging-at-work (archived at https://perma.cc/DHS5-JR64)

12 J Schwartz, B Denny and D Mallon. Belonging: From comfort to connection to contribution, 15 May 2020, Deloitte Insights, www2.deloitte.com/us/en/ insights/focus/human-capital-trends/2020/creating-a-culture-of-belonging.html (archived at https://perma.cc/PT8Z-QV6F)

13 J Schwartz, B Denny and D Mallon. Belonging: From comfort to connection to contribution, 15 May 2020, Deloitte Insights, www2.deloitte.com/us/en/ insights/focus/human-capital-trends/2020/creating-a-culture-of-belonging.html (archived at https://perma.cc/PT8Z-QV6F)

14 J Schwartz, B Denny and D Mallon. Belonging: From comfort to connection to contribution, 15 May 2020, Deloitte Insights, www2.deloitte.com/us/en/ insights/focus/human-capital-trends/2020/creating-a-culture-of-belonging.html (archived at https://perma.cc/PT8Z-QV6F)

15 J Schwartz, B Denny and D Mallon. Belonging: From comfort to connection to contribution, 15 May 2020, Deloitte Insights, www2.deloitte.com/us/en/ insights/focus/human-capital-trends/2020/creating-a-culture-of-belonging.html (archived at https://perma.cc/PT8Z-QV6F)

16 C Reilly. Do You Have a Sense of Belonging at your Work, 19 August 2023, *Forbes*, www.forbes.com/sites/colleenreilly/2023/08/08/do-you-have-a-sense-of-belonging-at-your-work/?sh=2b84d59059df (archived at https://perma. cc/32DL-9DXA)

17 A Edmondson. Psychological Safety and Learning Behavior in Work Teams, *Administrative Science Quarterly*, 1999, **44** (2), pp. 350–38

18 SocapDigital. Why Google and Microsoft Obsess Over Psychological Safety, 28 April 2020, socapglobal.com/2020/04/why-google-and-microsoft-obsess-over-psychological-safety/ (archived at https://perma.cc/QQ4E-HBB7)

19 J Fabiano. Microsoft researchers worked with designers to define the art of teamwork and they found this, 3 January 2020, Ladders, www.theladders.com/ career-advice/successful-teamwork (archived at https://perma.cc/V9KC-6RZY)

20 J Fabiano. Microsoft researchers worked with designers to define the art of teamwork and they found this, 3 January 2020, Ladders, www.theladders.com/ career-advice/successful-teamwork (archived at https://perma.cc/V9KC-6RZY)

21 A Rigby. 6 real-life examples proving psychological safety is crucial, Marlee, www.fingerprintforsuccess.com/blog/psychological-safety (archived at https://perma.cc/76Z2-9ZMZ)

22 A Rigby. 6 real-life examples proving psychological safety is crucial, Marlee, www.fingerprintforsuccess.com/blog/psychological-safety (archived at https://perma.cc/76Z2-9ZMZ)

23 J Schwartz, B Denny and D Mallon. Belonging: From comfort to connection to contribution, 15 May 2020, Deloitte Insights, www2.deloitte.com/us/en/insights/focus/human-capital-trends/2020/creating-a-culture-of-belonging.html (archived at https://perma.cc/5H3K-SEJ4)

24 B Pterova. What Is Micromanagement and How to Deal With It? 24 October 2023, Slingshot, www.slingshotapp.io/blog/what-is-micromanagement (archived at https://perma.cc/LK9D-XJZ9)

25 R Hume. Autonomy in the workplace has positive effects on well-being and job satisfaction, study finds, 25 April 2017, University of Birmingham, www.birmingham.ac.uk/news-archive/2017/autonomy-in-the-workplace-has-positive-effects-on-well-being-and-job-satisfaction-study-finds (archived at https://perma.cc/F97N-CE9L)

26 C Beranek. How To Instill An Entrepreneurial Spirit And Empower Employees, 7 August 2023, *Forbes*, www.forbes.com/sites/forbestechcouncil/2023/08/07/how-to-instill-an-entrepreneurial-spirit-and-empower-employees/ (archived at https://perma.cc/7JHM-CRVK)

27 Doodle. The Doodle State of Meetings Report 2019, assets.ctfassets.net/p24lh3qexxeo/axrPjsBSD1bLp2HYEqoij/d2f08c2aaf5a6ed80ee53b5ad7631494/Meeting_Report_2019.pdf (archived at https://perma.cc/7LX6-PLGN)

28 J Harter. Dismal Employee Engagement Is a Sign of Global Mismanagement, 20 December 2017, Gallup, news.gallup.com/opinion/gallup/224012/dismal-employee-engagement-sign-global-mismanagement.aspx (archived at https://perma.cc/P5F9-ZMD9)

29 A Woolley et al. Evidence for a Collective Intelligence Factor in the Performance of Human Groups, *Science*, 2010, **330** (6004), pp. 686–88

30 P Zak. How Oxytocin Can Make Your Job More Meaningful, 6 June 2018, *Greater Good Magazine*, greatergood.berkeley.edu/article/item/how_oxytocin_can_make_your_job_more_meaningful (archived at https://perma.cc/7542-TUW9)

31 P Zak. How Oxytocin Can Make Your Job More Meaningful, 6 June 2018, *Greater Good Magazine*, greatergood.berkeley.edu/article/item/how_oxytocin_can_make_your_job_more_meaningful (archived at https://perma.cc/7542-TUW9)

32 P Zak. How Oxytocin Can Make Your Job More Meaningful, 6 June 2018, *Greater Good Magazine*, greatergood.berkeley.edu/article/item/how_oxytocin_can_make_your_job_more_meaningful (archived at https://perma.cc/7542-TUW9)

33 B Robinson. Levi Strauss & Company Raises The Bar For How Companies
        Can Support Employee Mental Health, 9 August 2022, *Forbes*, www.forbes.
        com/sites/bryanrobinson/2022/08/06/levi-strauss--company-raises-the-bar-for-
        how-companies-can-support-employee-mental-health/ (archived at https://
        perma.cc/SZ6P-72TV)

34 B Robinson. Levi Strauss & Company Raises The Bar For How Companies
        Can Support Employee Mental Health, 9 August 2022, *Forbes*, www.forbes.
        com/sites/bryanrobinson/2022/08/06/levi-strauss--company-raises-the-bar-for-
        how-companies-can-support-employee-mental-health/ (archived at https://
        perma.cc/SZ6P-72TV)

35 B Robinson. Levi Strauss & Company Raises The Bar For How Companies
        Can Support Employee Mental Health, 9 August 2022, *Forbes*, www.forbes.
        com/sites/bryanrobinson/2022/08/06/levi-strauss--company-raises-the-bar-for-
        how-companies-can-support-employee-mental-health/ (archived at https://
        perma.cc/SZ6P-72TV)

36 Great Place to Work. UK's Best Workplaces for Wellbeing 2022, www.
        greatplacetowork.co.uk/awards/uks-best-workplaces-for-wellbeing-2022/
        (archived at https://perma.cc/RM4M-J6J8)

37 P Zak. How Oxytocin Can Make Your Job More Meaningful, 6 June 2018,
        Greater Good Magazine, greatergood.berkeley.edu/article/item/how_oxytocin_
        can_make_your_job_more_meaningful (archived at https://perma.cc/
        7542-TUW9)

38 Great Place to Work. UK's Best Workplaces for Wellbeing 2022, www.
        greatplacetowork.co.uk/awards/uks-best-workplaces-for-wellbeing-2022/
        (archived at https://perma.cc/RM4M-J6J8)

39 P Zak. How Oxytocin Can Make Your Job More Meaningful, 6 June 2018,
        Greater Good Magazine, greatergood.berkeley.edu/article/item/how_oxytocin_
        can_make_your_job_more_meaningful (archived at https://perma.cc/
        7542-TUW9)

40 P Zak. How Oxytocin Can Make Your Job More Meaningful, 6 June 2018,
        Greater Good Magazine, greatergood.berkeley.edu/article/item/how_oxytocin_
        can_make_your_job_more_meaningful (archived at https://perma.cc/
        7542-TUW9)

41 P Zak. How Oxytocin Can Make Your Job More Meaningful, 6 June 2018,
        Greater Good Magazine, greatergood.berkeley.edu/article/item/how_oxytocin_
        can_make_your_job_more_meaningful (archived at https://perma.cc/
        7542-TUW9)

42 P Zak. How Oxytocin Can Make Your Job More Meaningful, 6 June 2018,
        Greater Good Magazine, greatergood.berkeley.edu/article/item/how_oxytocin_
        can_make_your_job_more_meaningful (archived at https://perma.
        cc/7542-TUW9)

43 P Zak. How Oxytocin Can Make Your Job More Meaningful, 6 June 2018, *Greater Good Magazine*, greatergood.berkeley.edu/article/item/how_oxytocin_can_make_your_job_more_meaningful (archived at https://perma.cc/7542-TUW9).

44 D Strauss. Generative AI's 'productivity revolution' will take time to pay off, 4 June 2023, *Financial Times*, www.ft.com/content/21384711-3506-4901-830c-7ecc3ae6b32a (archived at https://perma.cc/3LJA-3KY7)

INDEX

The index is filed in alphabetical, word-by-word order. Numbers within main headings are filed as spelt out; acronyms and 'Mc' are filed as presented.

Looking for another book?

Explore our award-winning
books from global business
experts in Human Resources,
Learning and Development

Scan the code to browse

www.koganpage.com/hr-learning-
development

More from Kogan Page

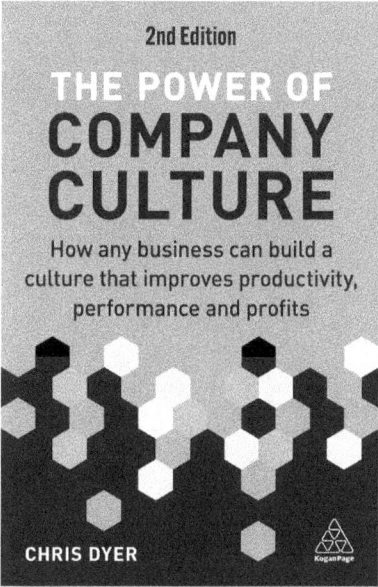

2nd Edition

THE POWER OF
COMPANY
CULTURE

How any business can build a
culture that improves productivity,
performance and profits

CHRIS DYER

ISBN: 9781398612594

TRANSFORMATIONAL
CULTURE

DEVELOP A PEOPLE-CENTRED
ORGANIZATION FOR IMPROVED
PERFORMANCE

DAVID LIDDLE

ISBN: 9781789661088

2nd Edition

EMPLOYEE
EXPERIENCE
BY DESIGN

**How to Create an
Effective EX for
Competitive Advantage**

Emma Bridger and Belinda Gannaway

ISBN: 9781398614369

Jessica Zwaan

BUILT
FOR
PEOPLE

Transform your employee
experience using product
management principles

ISBN: 9781398608023

www.koganpage.com

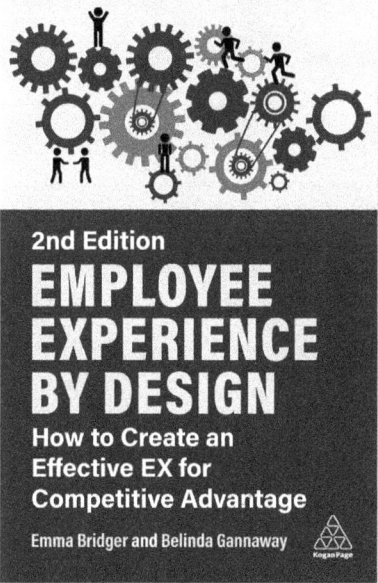

More from Kogan Page

www.koganpage.com

From 4 December 2025 the EU Responsible Person (GPSR) is:
eucomply oÜ, Pärnu mnt. 139b – 14, 11317 Tallinn, Estonia
www.eucompliancepartner.com

www.ingramcontent.com/pod-product-compliance
Lightning Source LLC
Chambersburg PA
CBHW071552210326
41597CB00019B/3211

9 781398 619722